1790

1695

1770

1775

1780

1645

H.C.P 1660

1770

Early American Dress

Early American Dress

The Colonial and Revolutionary Periods

Edward Warwick
Henry C. Pitz
Alexander Wyckoff

BONANZA BOOKS
NEW YORK

Copyright © MCMLXV by Edward Warwick, Henry Pitz, and Alexander Wyckoff
Library of Congress Catalog Card Number: 65-20869
All rights reserved.
This edition is published by Bonanza Books
a division of Crown Publishers, Inc.
by arrangement with Benjamin Blom, Inc.
a b c d e f g h
Manufactured in the United States of America

Contents

Americanorum Rex, Guisius

Introduction

Myths, legends, and conventions of decency and so-called good taste, often obscure the history of dress to the point where the whole truth is covered by a miasma of bias and half-truths. The codpiece, the tailored pouch covering the male genitals, has been expurgated from otherwise sound books because historians were embarrassed by the subject. The image of Puritan dress, as portrayed by Saint-Gaudens in his perfectly authentic sculpture, has become a popular super-image, obscuring all other characteristic dress of seventeenth-century New England.

At one time, clothing was considered of third-rate importance in the history of mankind. The subject was "useful" in designing costumes for plays or creating new fashions. It had a certain exotic attraction to the layman, and little else. Whereas scientific thinking was applied to fields from anthropology to zoology, almost anything written about dress was acceptable, except to the "inner core." Only of late has this attitude begun to change. Historians now realize that clothing is an integral part of life. What people wear, especially in their daily lives, reflects their own personality and the state of the nation: its economic fortunes, tastes, morals . . . in short, the entire gamut of life.

Once we accept this idea, the history of clothing becomes worthy of attention to other than those who "use" its findings for masquerades. And once clothing is removed from the sterile realm of the exotic, we must insist that the historiography of dress be grounded upon scientific principles. In the pursuit of the facts of dress, some of the past pitfalls must be avoided. And among these pitfalls, one of the most prevalent is the idea that we can find "the typical" dress of any period. How many times have we browsed through history books, read magazines, or even perused costume books which reproduce a few authentic sixteenth-century English paintings, and proceed to label these "the typical Elizabethan dress"?

II

The fallacy of labeling clothing "typical" becomes clear if we analyze the clothing of our own era. Would we try to select a few garments of clothing as typical of the entire twentieth century? Could we find the typical dress of even one year? Would such a "typical" garment encompass rich and poor? The reserved and the vain? North and South? Intellectual and Yahoo? The answer parades before our very eyes:

Stand at Hollywood and Vine to watch the eye-catching fashions swing by; on Washington Square to see its tensely relaxed, sweatered-and-panted inhabitants; on Ocean Boulevard of Miami Beach with its well-upholstered matrons in little-girl collars and flowered hats, and the men in flowered shirts and pastel Bermuda shorts; and at Fifty-Seventh and Fifth Avenue to wonder at the understated elegant ensembles of the sophisticates with hollow eyes. Or stand outside the Ford "Glass House" in Dearborn and see the endless stream of Organization Men in dark-gray suits and black ties (and then suddenly spot that heretic in the pale-pink shirt, and speculate how long that miscreant will last within the swarm of conformity).

Are any of these *the* typical American daytime dress of 1965?

If we were asked to select the typical swimming suit worn by women in the twentieth century, which would we choose: Mack Sennett's bathing beauties in ruffles, skirts, bloomers, mobcaps and stockings . . . the covered-up form-fits of Annette Kellerman . . . the itsy-bitsy bikini of Marilyn Monroe . . . the "topless" of the Sixties . . . or (perhaps) the "bottomless" of the Seventies?

Despite mass manufacturing methods, we rarely see two people identically dressed, even in huge groups. There are always subtle but discernible, and frequently significant differences, both in the clothes themselves and the manner in which they are worn. The amazingly infinite variety with which people clothe themselves is merely a reflection of the amazingly infinite variety of people.

What holds true for our own age, also is true for the past. Throughout the ages, individuals have displayed differences due to rank, occupation, family traditions, geographic location, and other factors. These differences have always been reflected in dress, but they are all too often ignored in books on dress. Fortunately, we do have today books by such scholars as Laver, the Cunningtons, Leloir, Hansen, Broby-Johansen and Sronkova, to name a few, who have avoided this type of faulty thinking and picture labeling. The pursuit of the typical can only lead to the ludicrous. The most we can hope to discern is a representative or prevailing *style* of dress, a basic style which encompasses myriads of variants.

If we found ourselves in Philadelphia, 1750, we would have considerable difficulty finding people dressed like those in the paintings of the period. Probably few would be clothed in the exact garments described in this or any other book. If we keep in mind the durability and cost of clothing, we realize that the Philadelphian of 1750 probably thought little of seeing his fellow citizens dressed à la 1740, or even 1730. Even the more affluent citizens in the course of their daily occupations would not be likely to discard their older style apparel merely because a new fashion had been introduced.

No book can give a full picture of all the variations of dress seen in one city during the course of even one day. We can determine the newness of a particular fashion, and see this "new fashion" accepted by so large a group that it becomes the "characteristic style" of that period. That characteristic style, as discussed in the text and seen in the illustrations, is all this book can give to the reader. Once this has been determined, the dress historian may concentrate on the psychological, sociological, or other aspects of clothing: that is purely a matter of individual choice and philosophy. There are many paths open to those doing research in this field but, no matter what the approach, there are problems common to all, including the reliability and proper use of contemporary pictorial evidence.

III

Contemporary pictorial evidence, in the form of paintings, drawings, and other illustrated source material, is of paramount importance to the historian. An authentic American portrait whose dating is beyond dispute can be the basis for drawing sound conclusions on the nature of clothing during that era. Unfortunately, however, "indisputable" evidence can mislead. So-called objective facts may be bound by myths and legends which have obscured reality. Take, for example, a hypothetical painting hanging on a museum wall. Its label reads, "—early eighteenth-century American." For the casual viewer, this may suffice. But before we proceed to build a series of premises based upon this work of art, certain questions must be asked: is the dating accurate; the clothes portrayed American; is the style of dress depicted in the painting the same as the date it was painted; is the rendition of the clothes faithful, or a figment of the artist's imagination? Indeed, we may have to ask: "Is this portrait American in any shape or manner?" To answer this last question, let us survey certain facts concerning art in Colonial America.

In a very real sense, most American colonists were self-made. As they rose in affluence, they felt the need to display, preferably by means of portraits, their roots in the mother country. In this quest for tradition and family roots, genealogical accuracy was sometimes secondary. Perhaps by written purchase to the mother country, or by commission to a friend travelling there, or even in their own travels abroad the colonists obtained portraits from England or the Continent. The fact that the subject was in no way related to them did not stop them from proudly hanging the painting over the mantel. In most cases no act of deception was intended, and it is safe to assume that in almost all cases the original owners made no claims that these were either "American" paintings, or paintings of Americans, a then demonstrably impossible claim. But with the passage of time (aided by firewood), the painting gathered credibility, smoke, and prestige in equal amounts. By family possession and legend, the portrait now became "our" ancestor.

Generations passed, and the portrait became a distant echo of an almost lost past. Except for family gatherings, at which time the new generation would be reminded of their glorious ancestor, now in a new frame, the world at large paid little attention to such a seemingly minor work of art. But in the later nineteenth century, with a revival in taste for things Colonial, the portrait took on an unexpected attraction: monetary value. The painting is sold to a respectable dealer who dutifully demands its pedigree. The family states, in perfectly good faith, and with some justification, that the painting has been in their possession since their ancestors came to these shores. Obviously, the dealer reasons (also in perfectly good faith), this is a genuine portrait of an early American: family tradition and myths provide the "proof."

The dealer finds an eager buyer who realizes how tight the field of genuine early American art has become. After a number of years, the buyer decides to share this rare example with the public. First it is "loaned" to a number of museums and is exhibited widely as early American art (a process which by catalogs and labels codifies its claims to authenticity). Finally it is presented to a museum.

Now, up to very recent times, American museums relied very heavily upon European, or European-trained experts. Many of these experts were remarkably fine scholars and critics of European art, and in that capacity they made valuable contributions to the American cultural scene. These men may have been quite adept at identifying and dating the more obvious, indisputably "American" canvases. But when it came to the less well known works of American art, they were misled time and time again on dating, attribution, subject, and even national origin. A museum, no matter how imposing its structure in the area of scholarship, is only equal to the knowledge of its staff. If that staff has the same background as do the dealers and their experts, the same standards will prevail. Confronted with our hypothetical painting (its pedigrees, documents, exhibition labels, date and sometimes the artist's signature) they will confirm it to be a genuine early American painting. (There is a persuasive weight to a museum's statements which deters many an individual from pitting his judgment against the official *terminus post* and *ante quem's*.)

And so the "genuine early American" painting is hung for public viewing, more genuine than ever before. The formidable gentleman of the portrait looks down from the austere museum walls at the passing streams of his newly certified "fellow countrymen."

There is however, a slight problem. Not a single shred of evidence, pictorial or written, substantiates any claim that the dress in the portrait is American. No such fashion ever reached these shores, except possibly on the back of a visitor whose style of dress left no impact upon our colonial ancestors. Even if we assume that the sitter was an American who had his portrait done during a trip abroad and in his newly acquired and decidedly European suit, we may wonder how long he would wear such garb in the colonies where it would be completely out of style. Therefore, as far as the dress historian is concerned, the question of whether or not a single suit of this sort ever reached these shores becomes a moot issue. If the dress is that unique, it loses all significance.

This hypothetical example of a so-called "early eighteenth-century American" portrait has been included to make vivid the problems inherent in picture accreditation. It serves to emphasize the point that no matter how imposing the array of official evidence may be, the dress historian must cherish his doubts until every question can be resolved.

Despite tremendous advances in research over the course of the past decade or two, and despite the work of an outstanding new group of experts learned in American art, we are still saddled with many of the false attributions and dating which at the turn of the century created near chaos. This is a problem which is by far more serious in American than in European art. Brush techniques, composition, subject treatment and other factors would have to be considered before we can accept the "American" label as the "unvarnished truth." The phrase illustrates the point.

IV

Relatively speaking, the problem of authenticity is almost minor compared with what the notions of decorum and decency can do to obscure and distort the primary sources of dress history. Take, for example, underclothing. Today the subject is widely discussed and advertised. An historian, working on the subject in the twenty-first century, would have no difficulty gathering textual and pictorial matter on the most intimate of undergarments worn today. But during the early part of the nineteenth century, today's advertisements would have sent the publisher, copywriter, illustrator, distributor and seller to the gallows. Some advocate this today, although not necessarily for the same reasons. (We will ignore these extremists.) In that now distant nineteenth century the concepts of decency and so-called good taste suppressed mention of undergarments to the point where little or no evidence indicates their existence. The Cunningtons have recorded what evidence there is.

Once such censorship suppresses the facts of its own age, it tends to impose its standards upon historical events—retroactively. Many a historian, certain the views of his age are beyond question, proceeds to ignore that which offends the sensibilities of his readers. And if he can't ignore it, he will attempt to reconstruct it to fit the taste of the times. Consider the case of the missing codpiece.

The codpiece was a very necessary and practical small garment. Introduced during the fifteenth century, it continued in vogue for almost two hundred years. It was a tailored pouch covering the male genitals, and it masked the division between the then two separate parts (legs) of the breeches. (The word "breeches" is, after all, always rendered in the plural.) The codpiece was originally instituted as a gesture toward modesty. Male nether garments, then called *chausses*, were rather like two waist-length stockings, open in the center, fore and aft. This was a handy, if drafty arrangement. As men's upper garments grew shorter, during the early Renaissance the structural problem, so to speak, became obvious. The codpiece was introduced as a very practical covering. Never content to let well enough alone, man did what he always does: he embellished and decorated that not yet offending codpiece, which continued in fashion even after breeches were worn over the *chausses*. Pictorial representations of the codpiece in all of its various and burgeoning stages are not at all difficult to discover (see the works of Brueghel the Elder for instance).

Yet generations of historians have carefully studied thousands of European representations showing male fashions of fifteenth, sixteenth and seventeenth centuries—trunk hose, round hose, pumpkin breeches, slops, and even armor—all of which include the codpiece, and have just as carefully ignored it. (This is an achievement in its own right.) Some of the codpieces, puffed and padded by the peasant, and bombasted, beribboned and bejeweled by the monarch, are really quite difficult to ignore. Redrawings of such breeches quite commonly disregard, or minimize almost to extinction, this most necessary garment. The word "codpiece" apparently does not appear in any English costume history index of the nineteenth century. As late as 1958, a book of general information for the young reader expurgates the codpiece from the uniforms of sixteenth century Swiss soldiers. In the redrawn illustrations, other accessories or sections of garments are frankly invented to conceal the lack of codpieces.

The insistence of the nineteenth and early twentieth centuries, particularly in English-speaking countries, that men, clothed, have no genitals at all has only begun to relax in the last decades. Quite probably this occurred because the use of knitted stretch fabrics in our contemporary skin-tight trousers makes such insistence observably untenable. Could it be mere coincidence that, during the past decade, codpieces have begun to resume their historically accurate life in theatrical costume productions and designers have used the codpiece with a deliberately stunning effect? The films, presumably, will follow suit with a more devious emphasis.

The problem is not limited only to blatant suppression and expurgation of facts, but also to the interpretation of authentic source material. For example, can a statement always be taken at face value? When in 1639 the General Court in Massachusetts issued an edict that women must not appear in public "with naked breasts and arms," did they mean "not to the navel" (a seventeenth-century version of the "strapless-topless")?

In ancient Crete, they might have meant literally that. But the fashion historian must know the social background of 1639, and thus he must seek to discover where from the point of view of the General Court (and not that of the historian no matter how bemused) a low décolletage became "naked breasts." But distortions do not occur only because of expurgation or the uncritical acceptance of statements made in past centuries: the attempt to describe colors and their hues can be misleading.

V

Time after time, nineteenth-century comment refers to the taste of the previous century as "gaudy," certain that the gamut of brownish tones used during its own period was "good taste." In the twentieth century, we would hardly describe the colors of Watteau, Lancret and Gainsborough as being "gaudy"; if anything, we would dub them "pastel."

Color has been a problem all through painting and fashion history. There is invariably a discrepancy between the pigments shown by the painter and the dyes used for clothes. In spite of many an artist's claim, there has never been a precise meeting of the two. The trained artist will render the color, if he aims at verisimilitude at all, as it appears to him in the actual light of the moment. Henry Reuterdahl, a Naval artist during the First World War, rendered the blue of the sailor's uniform in full sunlight as emerald green. This entailed endless arguments with Navy "brass," for when a swatch of actual navy-blue cloth was placed next to the painted uniform on the mural, there was a marked discrepancy. Reuterdahl was painting in an era when the momentary effect of a particular light on a given surface at a precise moment of time was of acute interest to artists. But the point still holds: the hue of a dress in a portrait may or may not have little to do with the actual hue of the original material.

The historian of dress must knife through opinions, biases, and interpretations of color to a firmer ground. In a surviving eighteenth-century dress or coat, often the true color is retained in the turnover of a hem, or on the edge of the material under a bound or felled seam. The historian need not like that color and may also think it "gaudy," but he must report its existence. He may often find his clue in an advertisement for stolen clothing, where the object is to get the articles back, not to comment on their appearance or propriety. Such an advertisement, in 1758, listed:

> . . . a scarlet tabby negligee, trimmed with gold; a green tabby petticoat trimmed also with gold; a white damask trimmed with a blue snail blond lace . . . a scarlet flowered damask mantua petticoat with gold; one of red-flowered velvet with silver; a blue and silver one; a brown sattin sack; a white sattin gown embroidered in yellow; a scarlet unwatered tabby sack; a brown sattin sack brocaded with silver; a red sattin fly petticoat; a blue and gold tabby silk sack and petticoat. . . .

Scarlet, red-flowered, blue and gold, silver-brocaded brown—the sense of color is positive, and certainly does not suggest a pale quality. However, our contemporary "image" of eighteenth century color as pastel is conditioned, not only by an unconscious comparison of our contemporary color with that of the eighteenth-century but also by the opinion and comment of an era other than our own.

Caricatures and cartoons cannot be indiscriminately used as source material because they are essentially satiric comments. Look at caricatures and cartoons of a specific time. Where do facts stop and exaggeration begin? Was a wig ever three feet tall? Did it carry a ship in full sail, or only a dinghy? But at the same time, caricature is of incalculable value because it can, and frequently does, point to the essence of a style in the fashion of a very specific period.

Even the actual, preserved garments of another day might lie in the realm of half-truth. How could one possibly be misled by an actual surviving garment? What could be more real? However, that garment is more likely to be a "special" one made for a particular occasion and then carefully saved, because it was too important to be worn at casual events. It might be a wedding gown, more apt to have been sentimental or nostalgic than chic in style. (Today's woman wears her bridal gown one day in her life; yet, it is this "least typical" garment that she is most likely to preserve for posterity.) Or, that real garment might be one which was ordered and tailored, but was never worn because it did not "feel" right or seem to suit any occasion. The owner probably saved it because it was too expensive to give away or destroy. The situation is not peculiar to any century, and a "real" garment of Colonial times may have been preserved precisely because it was not, and never had been, in good style or truly fashionable. All this does not mean that a preserved garment used in its proper terms and in relation to other evidence and artifacts cannot play a significant role for the dress historian. It is the misuse of such evidence to which the historian must object.

VI

We use portraits as evidence for the history of dress. Frequently, the portraits are authentic and dated correctly. But any painting is subject to the original knowledge and intent of the artist. Did he know and want to report the "unvarnished truth"? Or, did he intend to deceive, flatter, or change the status of the sitter?

The portrait painter rarely felt any duty to posterity in his rendering of clothing. He may well have invented the clothes in his portrait to satisfy a current fashion in portraiture itself. Greenough's portrait statue of George

Washington shows him wearing an eighteenth-century wig and draped in a Greek himation, with his bare arm uplifted, and finger pointing. Without other corroborative evidence, the Greek himation can only be listed as a unique exemplar. (As for Washington's gesture, the dress historian may conclude that the General was gesturing for his proper clothes to be sent down from the regions to which he was pointing.)

It becomes almost axiomatic that the greater the artist, the more likely he is to alter the actual fashions of his day. The magnificence of Rembrandt's art needs no comment. However, from the point of view of the dress historian, Rembrandt's *Oeuvre* can drive one to drink. He obviously was concerned only with the dramatic and pictorial effect of a garment, and not its authenticity. It must also be kept in mind that an artist may use perfectly authentic clothing which was no longer in fashion. A good example is Gainsborough who, in 1782, was still painting his sitters wearing lace-edged "falling bands" which had gone out of fashion a century before.

In his concept of fashion the portrait artist may have even been satisfying his own aesthetic vanity. One artist thinks he paints silk better than cotton, blue better than brown; another artist believes he paints brocades better than plain surfaces. It would be an interesting study to determine whether it was a matter of fashion which dictated Reynolds' clinging draperies, or whether it was because of his belief that he painted soft material better than he did satin. At any rate he left satins to Gainsborough. In this case fashion may have been derived from the painting, not the painting from the fashion.

When we consider the manner in which portraits were created by some itinerant painters in early Colonial times, we find even more reason for proceeding with utmost caution in our evaluation of pictorial evidence. It is known today that many of the Early American painters rendered during the long winter a goodly number of stock portraits, minus faces, and sometimes hands. When the weather permitted the artist to take to the road and he found a buyer for the unfinished portrait, he would add the final touch—the client's face, comfortably placed above the fine suit of clothing the artist had so carefully painted the winter before. Did this situation apply to the portraitist Robert Feke? In 1748 he painted separate portraits of Mrs. James Bowdoin and of Mrs. William Bowdoin, showing each of the ladies in handsome satin gowns, identical to the smallest tuck and ruffle. Many such instances can be seen among Early American portraitists: John Wollaston and Jeremiah Theüs similarly were "gown repeaters." The problem for the historian of dress is apparent: did that handsome gown belong to both ladies—or to neither? What were the origins of the fashion—a creation of the artist, or that of the ladies?

And what a technically awkward painter could make of the most graceful of sitters and the richest of dresses! A portrait of Lucy Windsor painted by Dr. Rufus Hathaway in 1790 is an example of inept brush work transforming a lady of high fashion into a woman observing the customs of modesty by keeping herself decently covered. The dress, the hairdo and the hat were the height of style in Paris in January of 1787. Mrs. Windsor, undoubtedly fashion conscious, had this wardrobe in her possession as fast as the style could reach these shores and travel inland to her. Unfortunately, the effort this entailed was wasted. Mrs. Windsor might just as well have settled for any little old American dress. It all meant the same to Dr. Hathaway who failed to render nuances of style even if he did observe them.

Then too, almost always the nationality of the painter influences his work. Certain Dutch painters in early New York gave a Low Country air to all of their portraits regardless of the sitters' ancestry. Many English artists, defying Nature, converted some typical Dutchmen into Englishmen on their canvases. With this transfer of nationality went an accompanying change in the character of the sitters' dress. The changes were slight, but nonetheless real. They involved no actual alteration in the garments worn, only a difference in the way they were handled and draped to the figure.

In the main the painters in the colonies worked in the then prevailing English tradition, and this was reflected in their canvases. This was as it should have been; for always the dress of colonial days was predominantly English. Even in the communities not settled by the English, such as among the Dutch in New York, the Germans in Pennsylvania and the Swiss of New Bern, the tendency was to discard the habits and habiliments of the home country and to acquire the English ways of the new land.

Genre painting—pictures that depict everyday life in action—is one of the oldest forms of painting and has served as an important source of information for the dress of all classes of society. But the only truly colonial genre painting of note until the Revolutionary years is John Greenwood's "Sea Captains Carousing at Surinam." The servants shown of course, are not American.

The more affluent persons were depicted in portraits, and their value, to the dress historian, is always sharply scrutinized. But when we come to the dress of the "common man" our difficulties are compounded by the fact that little or no early American pictorial material of any kind exists, and the existing record is frequently unreliable. Minor tradesmen, serving girls and others in a service position, including indentured persons, must have worn a characteristic dress. These "working clothes" were probably modified by the necessities of the work they were doing and in accord with the traditional dress of their station in the home country.

Just what the results of these modifications were, however, remain a matter of conjecture. For today's practical purposes, such as the "costumes" of the working class on the stage, adaptations of the recorded dress of English servants may be used. But for the dress historian, concerned with historical accuracy, the actual mode of "working clothes" presents great difficulty. There is almost no record of the dress worn by American servants and tradesmen. Throughout the eighteenth century a few servants appear in portraits, but they are almost always "body servants" who appear to be uniformed for the occasion. The only clue to a servant's everyday wear is in the printed advertisements asking for the return of runaway indentured servingmen. On occasion these notices mention the clothes worn. The garment most frequently mentioned is a "frock," a coat which will be discussed in some detail later. Because the frock is frequently referred to as the "master's," it is perhaps safe to assume that it was an old one, made for the master and now used by the servant. Belonging to the house, as does many a doorman's uniform today, it would have been worn by the servant only for such formal occasions as "serving table," equerrying the mistress when she "drove abroad" and opening the door to "callers." There were advertisements too for runaway serving maids or wenches, but nothing to indicate that the clothes they wore had any distinguishing mark of color or cut. We can only assume that this was the case, for it was commonly the pattern in Europe.

Thus far we have discussed conditions in art which limit the value of a painting as a factual record of clothing. On the other side of the coin is the fact that we today take an artist's rendition and use its quite authentic data to create a fashion "super-image." This image so dominates our view that it excludes all the other styles and fashions existing in that given area. Thus, it is nearly impossible for us today to visualize Henry VIII clothed in anything but the skirted doublet as rendered by Holbein, or Philip IV of Spain in any garments other than those depicted by Velasquez. On this side of the ocean the super-image of Puritan dress was created by the sculptor Saint-Gaudens in his statue "The Puritan." That statue of Deacon Samuel Chapin is a remarkably careful reconstruction of the dress of a small group of seventeenth-century New England Puritans. The general public today has come to believe that *all* Puritans dressed like Deacon Chapin and, indeed, that all New Englanders dressed in this manner, regardless of their religion or social function. During Thanksgiving little boys and men dress in gray paper-cambric copies of the garments worn by the Deacon. It is ironic because undoubtedly the Deacon's very least desire would have been to be immortalized as a fashion model.

The problem of the historian of dress is doubly difficult in such a situation, for his rôle assumes an iconoclastic fervor in his attempt to limit the scope of this compelling super-image. He must emphasize—with what might seem undue force—that these garments are accurate but actually were limited to a rather small group.

VII

Yet another problem peculiar to the historian of dress is the proper dating of pictorial material by the appearance or disappearance of a style or a fashion detail—the familiar *terminus post quem* and *terminus ante quem*. This is particularly true of dress in Colonial America where the beginning of a style might be recorded only in a single painting. (Here a single piece of evidence becomes significant because it is the forerunner of a fashion later seen or recorded by many sources.) If that painting is dated by documentary evidence, the established date is taken as the beginning of the style or style detail. Actually, the style may have begun earlier than the date of the painting, but it was not recorded. In effect, did anyone wear the Van Dyck beard or the Van Dyck collar before that artist painted them so vividly? There is sufficient evidence in other portions of early seventeenth-century European art to prove that that beard and that collar were indeed pre-Van Dyck fashions. But the researcher is not always fortunate enough to discover a plethora of corroborative material.

If the painting has been dated by museum authorities on internal evidence alone without corroborative documents, and other evidence, the situation becomes doubly precarious. The researcher must embark upon a journey of investigation to track that style or fashion detail to its source, with no guide but a fervent prayer to St. Jude.

It is even more difficult to tell when a particular style is no longer worn. After high fashion has become everyday dress, how long does the style endure? Although a fashion might be absolutely out of date according to the high fashion press, somewhere, someone continues to wear it with complete ease and assurance. And, those garments will continue to haunt the researcher, appearing in illustrations or written records long after it has been declared officially "dead" and superseded by yet another high fashion.

The dress historian must never give the impression that styles in any period change overnight or erupt fully formed like Athena from the head of Zeus. Many a style starts in the streets, worn quite unwittingly by some artisan's wife; then it is seen and, under the magic hands of a designer, becomes high fashion. Fashion deaths are rapid; style deaths, however, always linger and like the old soldier they just fade away.

VIII

With all of these problems of mythical, legendary, exaggerated, interpreted and biased "facts," how shall the dress historian proceed? How will he tell the "unvarnished truth"? For almost four centuries, historians of dress and its fashions have attempted this feat with varying degrees of veracity and varying degrees of success. As a profession, we are not young—"costume" books have a rather long history. Before Gutenberg most of the world had its information through pictures—either actual images or the image created in one's mind by travelers, myths and the like. After the invention of movable type, the printed description was added. As the world grew and horizons extended beyond the range of the established man, his curiosity about people and animals, plants and resources was insatiable. This was true not only for those who could read, but for those who could not. Therefore, the picture book filled an important need. One of the earliest of these "picture books" contained a series of ninety-nine drawings, "representing scenes and personages of ancient history, sacred and profane" and entitled (in translation) *A Florentine Picture Chronicle* which appeared in 1460. Its exact purpose is not really known, but the intent to represent costume is very apparent. Another pictorial volume, Baïf's *De Res Vestiaria Libellus*, published in 1526, contained thirty-seven wood-cuts, supposedly from personal observation. But it was a geographer, Nicholas de Nicolay, in the service of the king of France, Charles IX, who had the most stunning impact on costume books in the second half of the sixteenth century. In 1567 he published a record of his series of long and arduous trips to Turkey and points along the Mediterranean. His account was copiously illustrated with his own clear and detailed drawings of the clothing worn by the inhabitants of various villages, towns and provinces. The drawings have the ring of spontaneous authenticity, and de Nicolay's comments concerning the customs as well as the dress of the regions visited are sometimes delightful, as well as astute. In describing the women of Algiers he says:

> The female Moorish slaves of the city of Algiers are nude except for a piece of cotton cloth of diverse colors around their waists (which cloths they voluntarily open with little provocation); they wear bracelets, collars and anklets for decoration, made of brass and set with imitation jewels. But the ladies, Turkish or Moorish, seldom go on the streets uncovered; because they wear a great "Barnuca" made of cotton cloth—white, black or violet, which covers their whole persons and their heads

Surely this must have been written with a desire to tell the (semi-) "naked truth" regarding fashions, although his prime purpose was to survey these lands in terms of geography and natural resources. Nicolas de Nicolay's publication was an early "best seller." It was widely disseminated and translated from the original French into Italian, German and English. Whether or not his publication enhanced or augmented the vogue for actual books about dress is beside the point. The degree of its popularity can be noted by the fact that his compatriots pounced upon his clear drawings with all the glee of the successful plagiarist. They interpreted, redrew, borrowed from, embellished and changed his original drawings. The semi-nude figures were expurgated from later editions and translations of his own work. The offending drawings were torn from his volume. Then, as now, publishers inevitably bowed to the weight of majority opinion in matters of decorum or good taste.

Nicolas de Nicolay's plagiarists had a far reaching influence and an extended life. Some of de Nicolay's original illustrations are clearly traceable through three centuries of "costume book" illustrations, although they are embellished, altered, added to and subtracted from. The recurring figure" with updated dress is also familiar to works of art, but this is a different matter because in art the figure retains its original title and dating in the successive versions. But in costume histories de Nicolay's engravings are so inaccurately copied that it is difficult to recognize their original source. But the alterations are clearly interdependent, and when one places the original de Nicolay engraving next to all of its "descendants," the direct line of inheritance is unmistakable—in pose, silhouette, features, garment pattern and stylistic rendering.

Consider the case of a persistent "Lady of Macedonia." De Nicolay originally presented her in garments Turkish in total effect. She wears a long sleeved robe of mid-ankle length, cloth-girded at the waist and embellished with a moderately high, standing collar. Her accessories include a double strand necklace, a hat with a feather and a chin-strap of pearls. Her hair is braided and brushed behind her ears. She carries a loaf of bread.

In 1577, Abraham de Bruyn published his volume entitled *Omnium Poene Gentium Imagines*. His "Woman of Macedonia," obviously derived from de Nicolay's book is reversed. She now faces left. Her robe is less circular in cut and is gathered at the waist. De Bruyn has shortened her robe and compensated by adding two decorative bands on its hem. The loaf of bread carried by de Nicolay's lady has become a melon.

Next Jean-Jacques Boissard joined the procession of borrowers in 1581 with his *Habitus Variarum Orbis Gentium*. In his plate entitled *Virgo Macedonia* the lady was again turned about, this time back to her original position—facing right. However, her robe shortened like de Bruyn's, has become an overdress, with a full length underskirt below. The crease-like fold in the sleeve of the de Nicolay drawing had been interpreted as an oversleeve with a scalloped edge. Boissard has added a long scarf which encircles the lady's neck, and continues in length to the bottom of the (new) overskirt. He has changed her hairdo from braids to ringlets, one before each ear, one on the shoulder, the rest drawn back. Her hat has lost both its feathers as well as its chinstrap. She carries no lunch at all.

The best known of this group of sixteenth century costume historians, Cesare Vecellio, published his *Habite antiche et moderni di tutto il Mondo in 1590*. He included the same Macedonian, except that he has conferred nobility as well as maidenhood upon her. His illustration is entitled *Nobile Donzella Macedonica*. Her garments are copied from Boissard. Vecellio has further shortened her overskirt and added squared interstices between the scallops on her sleeves. He has removed her collar, rounded the neckline and dropped it considerably lower. He has added a strong, barred pattern to the scarf—the Boissard innovation. All her ringlets are lost, save two.

Just short of a century later, in 1757, the weary Macedonian makes another appearance, this time in England. She now appears in Thomas Jefferys' *A Collection of the Dresses of the Different Nations, Ancient and Modern*. His plate "Habit of a Lady of Macedonia in 1568" credits de Nicolay as the source, but Jefferys has redrawn that "Habit" to conform to eighteenth-century tailoring. The top of the original robe has become a front-closing bodice with a high neck and small collar. Jefferys keeps Boissard's oversleeve, but removes its scalloped edge. The skirt is full and tubular and ends well above the ankle. The chin-strap has been returned to her hat, but the feather has gone with the wind. She finally delivered the loaf of bread and the melon—her hands are now quite empty.

Finally, we come to 1891, to find our by now exhausted Macedonian lady in Friedrich Hottenroth's *Trachten der Völker*. In the established tradition, Hottenroth has changed Vecellio's overdress to a long sleeved coat and added an abbreviated bodice over it. The underskirt is long enough to trail on the ground (it is 1891, isn't it?). Her figure and garments are obviously based on Vecellio who, you will remember, borrowed them from Boissard who, in turn, had borrowed them from de Bruyn who had borrowed them from Nicolas de Nicolay.

It is not our intention to minimize the works of Boissard, Vecellio, et al., but rather to insist upon the necessity of returning to original sources in research for the history of dress. The interpretations of the seventeenth and eighteenth century historians, commenting on another time and area, can be instructive as a clue to the thinking of that time. However, it must be remembered that these deviations are second-hand sources.

IX

The more aware dress historians of the nineteenth century realized the necessity of returning to the original source for their material. Their archeologic approach was serious and thorough. Not only were the art objects then available carefully studied, but documentary evidence was introduced to support their conclusions. From Planché to Racinet, from Von Heyden and Hefner-Alterneck to Häberlen, the interest in careful reconstruction of archeologically accurate dress was intense. Several scholars overrode the bias of their generation. One further difficulty remained: they were handicapped by a technical problem—the original source material could not yet be photographed and reproduced. It had to be redrawn, and any artist rendering a clothed figure inevitably selects, interprets, and changes that figure and its garments. The change can be ever so slight and even done subconsciously. No art historian is in the least surprised to find that Flaxman's redrawings of figures of Greek and Roman times have as much of the late eighteenth century as they do of classic times.

Another group of dress historians developed the draping method as a means to reconstruct actual garments, partly to remedy the problem of inaccurate redrawings, and also with the firm conviction that clothes were worn by three dimensional people, not bas-reliefs. Heuzy, Kohler and Wilson, among others, reconstructed garments on living, fully rounded models. They believed that this method would clear away a good deal of confusion regarding classic dress and that of the Near East. The "drapers" also made it abundantly evident that a dress historian, in order to understand style, must have a working knowledge of tailoring and draping. Otherwise, he will be misled, particularly when the sources are based upon formalized art. As progress was made in photographic reproduction, the early twentieth century dress historians gratefully utilized this more direct method of presenting authentic period dress. Other commentators used exclusively contemporary portraits, reproduced as half-tone illustrations and then reinforced the illustration by documentation and glossaries. This approach has obvious advantages. The visual source material stands only one step removed from its pristine physical state. And that one step— the artist's interpretation—can be ascertained by the knowledgeable reader.

The disadvantages of these methods, however, are also apparent. Can the reader recognize the garments being delineated in a badly deteriorated fresco, or a "crazed" portrait—sometimes the only available source material for a garment? Another problem is how does one present source material from those many periods in art history where formalistic rendering makes the material very difficult to decipher? And what of those gaps in art history where there is no visual evidence for the existence of a given fashion, but a great deal of convincing documentary evidence (letters, diaries, etc.)?

In order to present a comprehensive fashion history, it seems clear that actual photographs used as source material must be augmented by analytical line drawings. This is particularly true for those periods of art history when painting or sculpture was neither realistic nor representational, or when actual techniques used by the artist were illusionistic and details were intentionally not clearly rendered. A line drawing of a given garment or part of a garment immediately clarifies the statement the historian is making. Inevitably these line drawings will take on a character of their own, although that will be apparent only in retrospect. But the inclusion of reproductions of the original, or parallel source material, such as photographs, serves as a stabilizing point of reference.

Because works of art, no matter how well reproduced—and I will *not* go into that!—cannot be taken at face value, text must be added. The addition of a detailed and perceptive text "rounds out the picture," giving the reader the full image of a given period of history. A textual presentation can also give the reader the historical background, the social customs, mores and conventions.

With this type of presentation, the reader is freed from the "typical" image. Consider for a moment a phrase used in the early part of this Introduction, "the well-upholstered matrons in little-girl collars and flowered hats. . . ." No one assumed we were indicating that those two items were the only garment the ladies were wearing—even after one of those Miami hurricanes. It was the reader's total knowledge of our own contemporary social customs and of the limitations of our own contemporary moral codes which made it possible for him to sketch in unerringly as much or as little of the remainder of those ladies' garments as he desired. This same total comprehension of a previous era must be acquired by the student of fashion history. Only then can he interpret an era other than his own with similar clarity.

It is the obligation of the dress historian to present so complete a picture of any given period that the limitations of that period are clearly defined. But within that framework, and given a clear presentation of the units of style with which to realize the garments, the infinite number of variations within that period may be genuinely adduced

Part of the "adducing" process emanates from one of the most important tools at the disposal of the historian: intuition. Bernard Berenson tells us that historians can never hope to record all that has happened. They can only try to guess, and the best guesses rely upon intuition. May I add that the best guesses are born of experience. Intuition, I like to think, is a trained guess based on experience. All of us do it in our everyday life. We see thousands of garments, each different. But if we spot one suit which is not only different, but ever-so-slightly "foreign," we immediately, and "intuitively" take note. That sense of recognition comes from observation "in quantity," plus our individual sensitivity and powers of observation. But the process is not quite as mysterious as it may have appeared at first.

X

Notes and comments above by no means exhaust the subject. I have, however, tried to emphasize that a basic philosophy of utilizing pictorial evidence must be established, and that we must not discard material which may appear suspect (caricature, redrawings, and so forth), or accept primary sources (works of art, artifacts, etc.) without realizing their limitations. A sound general history of dress must utilize all forms of pictorial matter and add to that, in equal weight, a descriptive and analytical text. The myths and legends, conventions of decency and good taste, biases and half-truths may then be overcome, and the history of dress be viewed by the intuitive—if slightly jaundiced—eye of the historian.

A.W.
Spring, 1965

To The Reader

The terms "costume," "dress," "fashion," and "style" have been interchanged, both in daily usage and even by historians, to the point of total confusion. In this series "costume" will refer to that area of clothing which is created for theatrical presentation (and similar public displays) and certain aspects of ceremonial and cult garb. "Fashion" concerns itself with the time and place in which clothing of a certain style is worn, and "style" refers to the "cut and fit" of garments and the manner in which they are assembled and worn.

"Dress," within the context of this series, will mean the sum total of all garments people wear as clothing, be it as part of their daily garb, or "Sunday best," and this definition excludes "costumes." However, the demarcation line between "costume" and "dress" cannot always be clearly defined. For example, when Richard Brinsley Sheridan mounted his production of *The School For Scandal* in the clothing of his day the actresses appearing in that production wore dresses. Today, replicas of these same dresses would be costumes. Another example is the area of folk clothing: folk dress may become folk costume if worn primarily for the entertainment of tourists.

"Costume" will not be discussed in this volume, although in subsequent volumes in the HISTORY OF AMERICAN DRESS this area will be discussed. Our concern will also not be limited to "fashion," although its vicissitudes, permutations, and adaptations will be discussed at some length. In *Early American Dress* our main concern will be all the articles of clothing, of any function, which people have worn in America in all the manifold activities of their existence—dress from head to heel, and skin-deep. This, and the subsequent volumes, will be a chronicle of American clothing in which contemporary iconography, modern drawings, and textual analyses are combined in order to present an accurate guide to the subject.

Glossaries and lists which record each known garment, when it appeared and disappeared, have been omitted. We feel a general history of dress should be mainly concerned with those who do the dressing. If "clothes do not make the man," man has indeed made the clothes. And why he made that specific garment, in that cloth, in that color—all these and related questions can only be understood by removing him from the glossaries and catalogs of clothing, and placing him within the background of the era which produced him.

II

Picture book after picture book appears on the way of life in Colonial America, but only when one considers them together does the repetition of material reveal how little has been newly researched. Even in many of the better books inaccurate nineteenth century redrawings of Colonial events can be found. These drawings are represented as being made either in Colonial times, or as a true pictorial representation of that era. Still other illustrations, based on uninformed sources, are still in use. For the historian (of art, dress, or any facet of Colonial life), this is regrettable because the use of such illustrations tends to mislead. Their repetition in reputable journals and otherwise worthy books lends credence to their claim of authenticity.

Forty, or even thirty years ago, when the serious study of early American art was still in its infancy, this situation was inevitable. The major source of data, portrait painting in Colonial America, was in complete disarray. The late years of the nineteenth and early years of the twentieth centuries had been a field day for dealers in American paintings, and their policy was markedly *caveat emptor*. They almost completely ignored the so-called crude American canvases which we today call "primitives." Few, if any, of these genuinely American paintings—in style, subject, and technique—found their way into our museums, which in the earlier years of our century were furnished largely by gifts of individual donors. Added to this neglect was a near chaos of misdating and erroneous attributions, for many paintings were dubbed "American" which had no claim to the name. Only of late, and perhaps greatly stimulated by the W.P.A. artists' compilations of American art, has there been any extensive collecting and study of all the forms of painting native to this soil. Although critics and historians have utilized these new sources in their writings on early American art and life, the field of early American dress is still in dire need of thorough review.

When Benjamin Blom asked me to undertake a history of American dress, I was only too acutely aware that the period from about 1790 to the present has never been properly treated. There are admirable, pioneering efforts by Mrs. Alice Earle (whose book does not discuss the subject beyond 1820) and Elizabeth McClellan (with 1870 as the termination date of her book). Although historians are forever indebted to these pioneering scholars, their findings must be re-examined in the light of a vast body of material which is now available to us. As a result of scientific and historical investigations made since that time many of their statements must be challenged.

In documenting dress before 1790 a volume of real merit does exist entitled EARLY AMERICAN COSTUME by Henry Pitz and Edward Warwick. Warwick and Pitz approached the study of dress not as masquerade, but as the means of determining the "what-how-and-why" of people choosing and wearing clothing. This meant a study not only of portraits and artifacts but also of dress in relation to cultural, historical, and other "non-dress" factors. This approach is one to which I fully subscribe, and it made me decide to use their book as the basis of volume two of the HISTORY OF AMERICAN DRESS. The other four volumes will be entirely new.

Most of these scholars' original research and writings have been retained, especially their excellent descriptions of specific garments. Nearly forty years after publication, these descriptions remain, in light of modern scholarship, the most accurate observations on the characteristic style of Colonial dress. But much of the background comment has been changed throughout this book, and entirely new sections have been added. For these excisions, additions, and revisions, I must assume full responsibility, for it would be unfair to saddle others with opinions and observations which, to borrow the well worn phrase may not necessarily be theirs.

The need for extensive revisions of and additions to the original Warwick and Pitz text was apparent not only to me, but to these authors, and they have given me every imaginable encouragement and cooperation in the compilation of this new book. All of us were also acutely aware of the need to remove from this volume some of the portraits in the 1929 edition which, on later investigation, proved to have been other than American.

The Introduction and the To The Reader sections in this volume incorporate the cautions expressed by Warwick & Pitz in the 1929 edition of EARLY AMERICAN COSTUME. They cautioned against mis-dating, false attributions, and other pitfalls related to early American art. This is a tribute to these authors' keen critical judgments during a period when a great deal of confusion in the field of American art scholarship was rampant.

The plates now used have been selected with the best knowledge presently available. When no American painting has come to my attention that could give an example of colonial dress or ways of wearing it I have substituted foreign material to illustrate the point. In order to provide a ready visual division between foreign material and American portraits, all non-American reproductions are from engravings, drawings or means other than oil painting. This does not mean that all the portraits used are by "American" artists. Many have been done by artists temporarily resident in America. To the best of my knowledge all these works of art represent American subjects in American clothes.

III

The portraits are presented with only dates accompanying each plate. No other identification except the plate number is provided. The date is one that I have assigned to the *garb* shown in the portrait and therefore does not necessarily correspond to the date the painting was executed. My dating may or may not agree with the date assigned to the portrait by its owner. If such a discrepancy exists, I must take the sole responsibility for the new date.

In the list of illustrations on page 281, I have given pertinent data about the artist, the subject, the date assigned to or shown on the painting, the name of the owner and/or the place of repository. Many of the paintings introduced have been retouched, restored, or even repainted in the nineteenth century or today. Such "fresh" works usually reproduce quite well. Those that were in their original state at the time the photograph was taken reproduce poorly for they have darkened, "crazed," or chipped because of their age. I have not used any portrait in which the repainting was not, in my judgment, a faithful rendering of the original. However, if a point of information could be made only by using a much restored painting, I have noted it in the text.

The matter of chronology in a region so large and diverse as the Colonies also presents some problems. The arrangement used in this volume seems most workable. Each region is treated separately and in accordance with its term of importance in the development of the Atlantic seaboard; for clarity, men and women are described separately; there is a separate chapter on children's clothing. The line drawings throughout the text have been placed as near as possible to the pertinent text.

The reproductions of the portraits (half-tones) are placed together in this edition. Many of the plates were not in the old edition. In fact some were specifically photographed for this work, and these works of art are thus reproduced for the first time. The illustrations have been arranged in the order in which the subject is mentioned in the text. For those desiring a purely chronological pageant of American dress, I have added a table which lists all the half-tone plates by the date of the dress of style.

Preceding the specifically regional chapters and the one on children, Henry Pitz has drawn, for this new work, double-spread illustrations explicative of the life and dress of the time. This is of major importance: instead of the usual Colonial half-portraits, we see here the entire figure from head to toe. Instead of the formal poses of early portraits, Pitz's drawings show several of the figures in motion We also see the people in relation to each other, with a clear indication of their social station, and set against the background of the period. Following many of these new double-spread drawings is a sketch of a building representative of the area. An entirely new bibliography has been prepared, taking note of the standard reference material and of the more significant books that have been published lately.

The present volume discusses clothing in the American Colonies and in the early Republic, up to 1790. Subsequent volumes in the HISTORY OF AMERICAN DRESS will deal with the periods from 1790 to 1866 (volume three); 1866 to 1917 (volume four); American Military and Civil Uniforms as they were worn for parade and in the field, to World War I (volume five). The dress of the American Indian will be volume one.

ACKNOWLEDGEMENTS

In the writing of the new material for this volume, the revisions of the old text, and the compilations of the new illustrations I am indebted to a legion of learned workers in portraiture and related fields whose help was invaluable. In trying to mention all these persons, inadvertently, I may have forgotten some names. I hope they will forgive me—one grows rapacious in the face of exciting material. Also, in the rush to find a new portrait my single-track mind may have forgotten to record who led me to it.

Above all I want to thank Edward Warwick and Henry Pitz, for theirs was the initial inspiration and platform upon which this new book is founded. Without their research and authorship of the original edition, I would not have ventured upon this undertaking. In the writing of this book, theirs served as the essential foundation, and I hope that my changes and additions have retained both the spirit of the original, and added to an already sound work of scholarship.

I am deeply indebted to Benjamin Blom for his work on the entire manuscript, and to Dr. Emma Mellencamp for her work on the Introduction. Their contributions go well beyond the confines of style and phrase. Benjamin Blom, by prodding, encouragement and challenge, aided in reshaping much of the old, and introducing much of the new material in this volume.

Much gratitude goes to Miss Louisa Dresser for her counsel, direction, advice and criticism. I wish to thank William P. Campbell who even anticipated my cry for help and at the first hint of a problem prepared material voluntarily. He has given unstintingly of his crowded time throughout the preparation of this book. John Sweeney and Jonathan Fairbanks of Winterthur have been most cooperative, as have Helen McCormack of the Gibbes Art Gallery, Bessom Harris of the Essex Institute, Dorothy Merrick of Pilgrim Hall, Marguerite Gignilliat of Colonial Williamsburg and James Servies of the College of William and Mary. I must also thank Clifford Shipton, Gudmund Vigtel, Paula Hancock, Margaret Toole, Kathryn Rumsey, Elizabeth Riegel, Malcolm Freiberg, Carolyn Scoon, Elsie McGarvey, Hobart Williams Jr., Harriett Seabrook, Marjorie Colt, Donald Reichert, Joseph Butler, Milo Naeve, A. M. Schlatter, Charles Montgomery Jr., Thomas Thorn, Margaret Scott and for their great patience Hannah J. Howell of the Frick Art Reference Library and her staff. Without that amazing institution our work would be most difficult. The historical societies and the art galleries and museums have been, as is their wont, most helpful. A wealth of material and knowledge has been made available to me by the Albright-Knox Art Gallery, Amherst College Art Collection, the Brooklyn Museum, the Carolina Art Association-Gibbes Art Gallery, the Art Institute of Chicago, The National Gallery of Art, The Museum of the City of New York, the New York Public Library, Mr. Henry L. Shattuck, the City Art Museum of St. Louis, The Telfair Academy of Arts and Sciences, the Virginia Museum of Fine Arts, the College of William and Mary, Colonial Williamsburg and the Henry Francis DuPont Winterhur Museum. I am particularly grateful for their patience in meeting my demands.

Mrs. Yolanda Melniker, among those who assisted in the difficult task of unifying the styles, idiosyncrasies of phrasing, punctuation and spelling of three authors, carried her work to its conclusion with her sense of humor intact. She also, together with Robert Du Beer, managed to decipher the manuscript and produce the neat typewritten pages without which no compositor could have set these words in print.

My staff has been equally patient and on occasion understanding; Carl Hauptmann, artist and draughtsman; George Bretherton, historian; Lister Shaw, librarian; Monica Peyton, index. For their aid, I thank them.

A.W.

Spring, 1965

[*It is appropriate that I add to the list of acknowledgments for this new work, the original list compiled by Warwick and Pitz. This is far from a historic exercise, because several of the scholars and institutions mentioned by Warwick & Pitz have contributed advice, criticism, or special knowledge for this new work. But whether new or old, all have made it possible to write this volume, and I join the original authors in extending thanks and appreciation to: Dr. Fiske Kimball, Dr. Arthur Bye, Thomas B. Clarke, Arthur F. Street, Richard C. Greenleaf, Mrs. Charles H. Russell, John C. Livingston, Henry W. Kent, Clarence S. Brigham, Walter H. Siple, Anna E. Smith, Ethel L. Schofield, Alexander J. Wall, Miriam A. Banks, Mrs. William B. Schofield, Benjamin H. Stone, Daniel Beard, Alexander Weddell, F. W. Bayley, Mrs. Lockwood, Ernest Spofford, and Dr. Samuel Woodhouse, Jr.*

The authors would further register their acknowledgment to: the Pennsylvania Museum of Art, the Metropolitan Museum of Art, the Essex Institute, the New York Historical Society, the American Antiquarian Society, Boston Museum of Fine Arts, the Bowdoin Museum of Fine Arts, Pilgrim Hall, the New Haven Historical Society, the Rhode Island School of Design, the Wadsworth Athenaeum and Morgan Memorial, the Worcester Art Museum, the Fogg Museum, Yale University, the Massachusetts Historical Society and the Historical Society of Philadelphia.]

European Background

ELISABETH
1603

Queen Elizabeth in 1603. Engraving with elements of Nicholas Hilliard's drawing of about 1595 and the engraving by William Rogers of about 1601.

CHAPTER I

European Background

The American continent has its roots in the Old World. Spanish, Italians, Portuguese, French, English, and other Europeans charted its coasts, explored its interiors, and brought back to their homelands accounts which enticed thousands to emigrate to the new found lands. In the Northern Hemisphere, the earliest immigrants (settlers, pioneers, call them what you will), were mainly of British, French, Dutch, and Swedish descent as well as slaves of African descent. Each group brought its own customs and culture. In the subsequent amalgamation and mutation of these customs, influenced in turn by the indigenous Indian cultures, lies the history of early North American civilization.

In a sense, we may look upon the movement of European peoples across a still strange ocean as the culmination of the Renaissance which first flowered in what was much later to become Italy. The Italian peninsula was a region rich in treasures of classic and Byzantine art, dotted with trading cities in touch with the advanced communities of northern Africa and Asia Minor. These regions, in turn, had been influenced by the art, science and philosophy of the great Indian and Chinese civilizations. These and other factors had produced in the Italianate states and cities, by the middle of the fifteenth century, a force of such power and magnitude that it re-fashioned the entire life of Western Europe and, in turn, determined the course of the sixteenth-century civilization, including the exploration and the settlement of the North American continent.

The force of the European Renaissance flowed in a thousand channels. It transformed art, science, religion, government, the social order and, in short, every field of human endeavor. It filled men with an inexhaustible fund of energy. It impelled them to delve into the storehouses of classic art and learning and to venture into unknown fields of thought and practice. Italy became the fountainhead of art for Western Europe. Great palaces and churches built in new styles arose in her cities. Her nobles and merchant princes surrounded themselves with the glitter and luxury that the new art produced. The wealth and talent of the land created a magnificent background for one of the most brilliant, beautiful and perhaps dissolute societies ever known.

Modern science was dawning. Copernicus and his followers were plotting the system of the heavens and were demonstrating to an astonished world that man's earth was not the core of the universe, but a subordinate part in a great scheme of things. Inventions were playing their part in the upheaval. Printing made knowledge accessible to all. Gunpowder had destroyed the power of the mounted knight. The compass had given navigators confidence to venture uncharted seas. Travelers were bringing back tales of remote lands. Mental and physical horizons were widening. The half-remembered images of classic Rome were revitalized. The almost forgotten knowledge of classic Greece was re-introduced. With the revival of learning, Aristarchus of Samos' belief that the earth is round and revolves around a larger sun again took hold of the minds of learned men and appeared in scientific writings. It was a study of such writings that gave Columbus impetus to sail westward until he had reached the shores of North America.

In 1495 Charles VIII, king of France, led his army in the first of the French invasions of Italy. Accustomed to the comparatively restrained and bleak life of the French court, he was dazzled and captivated by the splendor of the Italian cities. When, after an almost bloodless conquest, he returned to France, Charles and his courtiers brought back with them paintings, tapestries, gold and silver work, brocades, and other rare objects of the new art, as well as tales of Italian magnificence. Charles' successors, Louis XII and Francis I, in 1501 and 1515 respectively, followed the same paths of conquest into Italy, and were also carried away by its wonders. The Italian Renaissance had a profound influence upon France, and this in turn played a major role in shaping the life of the Northern countries.

Europe found that the world had grown vastly larger. Limitless treasure and strange overseas kingdoms seemed to be hers for the taking. Soon her square-sailed ships were plowing the secret seas of the new hemisphere. Spain and Portugal seized the greater portion of the New World. When the more northern nations had summoned sufficient interest and strength to enter the new arena, they found South and Central America, Mexico, the West Indies, and large portions of the Orient under the banners of these Iberian countries. Only North America lay open. Spain had found rich but unwary civilizations awaiting her plundering soldiers. The first explorers of the northern continent hoped to find equal opportunity for spoil and conquest. They were slow to realize the stark and prosaic facts of the new land. Their fancy pictured it with all possible delights and marvels—fabulous cities roofed with gold, mountains of precious stones, and miraculous fountains that would restore youth to aged frames.

The extravagant fancies that possessed the minds of the early explorers were also believed in all ranks and orders of European society. It was an age of credulity. It is not difficult to understand how, in the first flush and wonder of finding their minds stimulated by the new concepts, men found it impossible to set bounds to their imaginations. They were too restless for cool analysis. They were stirred to vehement effort, to an almost frenzied lust for fuller life and more complete knowledge This desperate release of energy penetrated every field of human endeavor. Before this ardor cooled, it had changed the complexion of Europe and had planted a young civilization in the Western Hemisphere.

North of the Alps the new spirit awakened questions of religious authority. An impetus for this challenge was undoubtedly the invention of printing in the years soon after 1450 (1454 is the generally accepted date) which had brought the Bible to the masses. Its interpretation became a matter for even the common people. Growing religious doubts among the populace found ready sympathy among the nobles and princes who were weary and jealous of the power of the church. For political and material reasons, they were ripe for revolt. Supported by the desire of the lower ranks for a church free from abuses and corruption, and for a faith more nearly approaching the primitive teachings of Jesus, they cast off the authority of Rome in a revolt inspired by Luther in 1517. It was a revolt that involved Europe in years of bloodshed. In the end, neither Rome nor the new Protestant faith was wholly triumphant. England, Sweden, Norway, Denmark, Holland, Bohemia, and most of Germany established national churches under the control of their princes; Europe was half Protestant, half Catholic.

The Reformation, however, did not stop there. Despite the fact that the Northern princes and nobles were now content with the new churches under their authority, many of the common people sought further reforms, insisting upon their own interpretation of the Bible as an inspired guide. Harassed and persecuted by the authority from which they had revolted, they looked toward the new lands across the sea, which offered them freedom and release from persecution at home. From their ranks came thousands of the early settlers of the North American colonies.

There were now six strong states in Europe—England, Spain, France, Portugal, Holland, and Sweden. All of these were powerful enough to enter the struggle for new territory. Five of them contributed something toward building the American colonies. Spain, France, Holland, and Sweden planted settlements within the limits of what is today the United States. Some of these settlements have vanished utterly leaving no trace; others have left their mark upon the history of the nation; but England absorbed the efforts of the other countries and molded the character and future of the New World.

It was England, alone among the nations of Europe, that possessed all the elements necessary for the giant task of colonizing a distant continent. Due to the fortunes of war and to the triumphs of diplomacy, in the early years of the seventeenth century she was the equal, if not the superior, of any European state in human and material resources. Spain's greatness was passing. She was showing evidence of internal decay, and the destruction of the Armada had robbed her of her sea power. Portugal had lapsed into apathy. Sweden was only able to make half-hearted attempts at colonization, because King Gustavus Adolphus wasted her wealth and manhood on the battlefields of central Europe. Holland, although enterprising and possessing a strong navy, was small and had only a limited population to draw upon. Moreover, the ambitious French under Richelieu and Louis XIV pressed close upon her frontiers.

France alone was a serious menace to England's colonial ambitions, but she suffered from the foolish policies of her monarchs. These monarchs had spent her strength in futile wars and empty conquests on the Continent and had driven beyond her borders the bulk of her artisan population, the Huguenots.

One tremendously important source of England's colonial success was an abundant population anxious to solve their economic ills by emigration—or forced to do so by bonds of indenture. It has been estimated that these indentured servants, as well as men, women and children forcibly sent to these shores, constituted 20 to 30 per cent of the population of the New World in the latter part of the seventeenth century. England also possessed a supply of agricultural laborers freed from feudal obligations and accustomed to a life of toil and hard living. In the process of winning their freedom, they had developed qualities of independence, determination, and industry, all essential to the life of the colonist. Finally, the rise of the English woolen industry had changed large areas of cultivated land into pasturage for sheep-raising. The farm laborers thus dispossessed were ripe for any adventure that promised wage and opportunity.

A step higher in the social scale were the yeomanry and small farmers, all landowners in a modest way. They understood the business of raising crops, the care of animals, and the management of laborers. A practical-minded class, they were self-sufficient, competent, and not without education. Great numbers of them, for religious or political reasons, or because of the lure of vast acreage, migrated to the colonies.

Finally, there were the landed gentry, owners of large estates, men of substance and standing. They too understood the soil, were accustomed to the supervision of labor, the handling of accounts, and the administration of local justice. They came to America in smaller numbers, but they furnished many leaders of colonial thought and action.

The position of the Englishwoman was of equal importance. She was acquainted not only with the household arts and the hard labor of the fields but had entered the larger spheres of trade and the industrial arts. According to her station, she knew something of the handling of people and property, possessing likewise no small influence in religious and political matters. The leaders of colonial policy recognized very early the important role family life plays in permanent colonization, and they did everything possible to encourage the migration of women and of entire families.

English sea power played no inconsiderable part in England's colonial success. She had, of necessity, taken early to the sea, but she was only beginning to perceive that her future as an empire lay in a command of the broad oceans of the world. Coincident with her growth in sea power, and largely responsible for it, was England's expansion in trade. This expansion was followed by the consequent rise of a large and influential merchant class. Successful trade and commerce demands stability of government and freedom from oppression. Thus, the great power and wealth of the new classes were brought to bear to secure these ends. It was a test of strength between the old and the new order. In a struggle lasting many decades, clergy, aristocracy, and royalty were gradually stripped of most of their political power. This step in the direction of democracy influenced the thought and action of the colonists.

In addition to becoming more interested in the affairs of state, members of the new merchant class gained experience in the handling of large commercial ventures. They learned the value of collective action and they acquired the capital, the machinery, and the organization necessary for transporting and maintaining distant outposts. Their great trading companies, like the East India and the Muscovy, kept in constant communication with the Far East and with the interior of Russia. Now, with a new continent open for exploitation, a group of new companies was formed to link it with the mother country.

From England's social and political background came the elements that were to become the foundations of the new structure. Her law and system of justice, her manners and social customs, her domestic life, and her intellectual interests all made the journey across the sea. Her religious differences, her political upheavals, and her economic changes a so found their way across three thousand miles of water.

The Hoe, Plymouth, whence the "Mayflower" sailed, the 6th of September, 1620.

Captain John Smith. From the map of New England by Simon Van de Passe, 1616.

CHAPTER II

Virginia

1607-1675

Pocahontas or Matoaka. "Rebecka Rolff, Daughter to the Mighty Prince Powhatan"—
An engraving of 1616 by Simon Van Der Passe.

CHAPTER II

Virginia

1607-1675

A little company of one hundred and five men sailed from the England of James I and established the first of the permanent English colonies in America. In the bright spring weather of 1607, three ships entered the Chesapeake, finally coming to anchor in a river they called the James. On its banks they built a few rude shelters and named the settlement Jamestown.

They were an oddly assorted company by training and temperament, ill-fitted for the desperate business of maintaining themselves, and for wresting a living from this new land. More than half of them were gentlemen, real or self-styled, who had embarked upon this adventure stirred by rumors of fabulous riches easily attainable in the New World. They had not reckoned with the hard manual labor attendant upon the founding of a colony. Some were tradesmen, some servants, and among their number were listed "jewellers, gold refiners" and even "a perfumer." Twelve laborers, a few carpenters, a blacksmith, a mason, a barber, a tailor, were also part of this band of adventurers and were probably the most prepared of this group for the difficulties at hand. The few leaders of proved courage and capability were Wingfield, the first president; the mariners Gosnold and Newport; and most notable of all was Captain John Smith.

Old engravings and the drawings give a good idea of how these gentlemen adventurers appeared when they first set foot on Virginian soil. Their dress represents the current English mode. It can be noted that the influence of the Spanish bombast style was waning. (See page 60 *et seq.*)

The doublet, made of stiffened materials, tapered to the waist, was worn over a white linen shirt. Close-fitting sleeves were sometimes attached at the shoulder, covered by a wing or padded roll fastened to the doublet. Lace cuffs adorned the wrists. Pleated ruffs (or, even more commonly, wide upstanding collars) adorned the neck. The padded trunk hose were of varying lengths and were sometimes worn with the tailored stockings attached or in conjunction with canions reaching to the knees.

The needlessly heavy and clumsy English trunk hose must have been a hot and burdensome garment in the warmer climate of Virginia. One wonders whether the immigrants looked upon the relatively easier garb (or lack of it) of the natives as a wiser way to dress. However, some of the English dress was appropriate. Boots, for example, were characteristic footgear of the period and must have been particularly suitable for the marshes and the tangled underbrush of the Virginia coast. Another article of attire suited to the rough life was the buff jerkin made of leather and worn over the doublet. Sometimes it was of sufficient thickness to repulse an arrow. The wide-brimmed hats of felt and beaver were excellent protection against the hot southern sun; although the close-fitting Monmouth cap was probably more suited to the narrow forestways. Add a cloak for cold or inclement weather, short hair, and a pointed beard and mustache, and one has a fairly complete picture of the Jamestown settler.

Courtesy of the New York Public Library.

Captain John Smith and Pocahontas—From Pieter Van Der Aa's *Voyagien* (Edition of 1727). Material probably copied from Smith's 1624 account, the first to mention Pocahontas.

Living as they did under constant dread of Indian assault, there were certain accessories that must have formed an indispensable part of their clothing—weapons and armor. Pistols were often thrust into a broad sash or a leathern belt around the waist. The long, straight, rapier-like sword was suspended at the left side from the older-fashioned sword belt, or from a broad shoulder belt or decorated baldric. The half-armor of the time consisted mainly of the breastplate and backplate buckled together at the sides, and of a steel hat or morion.

Courtesy of the New York Public Library.

Captain Smith Taketh the King of Pamaunkee prisoner, 1608. From a broadside of 1624 (The Generall Historie).

The materials of the gentlemen's dress were usually rich and expensive—silks and satins, elaborately patterned brocades and velvets, gold and silver braid, lace and fine linen. Their dress was as rich in color as it was lavish in material. Picture them, scarlet and gold and multi-colored against a setting of dark forest, flowered clearing, and sluggish tidal rivers. They must have seemed strange, exotic figures as they moved about in their Old World finery, under the blazing Virginia sun, among the log and reed-thatched huts of Jamestown, in the rude wooden church or storehouse, upon the dusty drill ground, or by the stout log stockade that surrounded the entire settlement. Even in the heat of midsummer, when comfort demanded the doffing of doublet and jerkin, doubtless some in that motley company, jealous of their station and its proprieties, still clung to the stifling doublet to the limit of endurance. As a good example of the useless additions used as adornment which seem to be instinctive to man is the shoulder knot of the seventeenth century. It consists of a bunch of ribbons, usually dangling from the right shoulder, but on occasion from the left, and must have served as a "status symbol" for the merchant adventurer. As do many such symbols, its meaning changed. In later periods it became the mark of livery worn by a servant.

Powhatan receives Ralphe Hamer. From the *Voyagien*.

During the next three years the little colony struggled painfully for life. Men bickered and fought among themselves. The swamplands about the settlement spread pestilence in the torrid summer weather. Indians hovered in the shadow of the great trees, ready to attack the unwary. The food supply was exhausted, resulting in famine. Occasional ships from England brought men and supplies, keeping up a spark of life in the stricken colony, but by the spring of 1610, of a company of five hundred, less than sixty remained alive.

There are no pictorial and few written records of this terrible time. However, it is certain that the original clothing brought from England by the settlers, now badly worn and soiled, was patched and supplemented with fur and leather obtained from animals they had killed or had bartered for with the Indians. These makeshift garments probably were made with little regard for cut or for fit. They were presumably the first crude beginnings of essentially American dress.

June of 1610 brought three heavily laden ships under Lord de la Warr, and the colony took on new life. The Virginia Company in England learned from experience. The vessels it sent now carried settlers of the proper temper, "honest and industrious men, carpenters, smiths, coopers, fishermen, tanners, shoemakers, shipwrights, brickmen, gardeners, husbandmen and laboring men of all sorts." The colony grew more rapidly than heretofore and prospered. Cattle, horses, sheep, and livestock of all sorts were brought in. A variety of crops were planted, and the banks of the James and even parts of the Eastern Shore became dotted with tiny settlements and lonely cabins. The new colonists turned to the resources at hand. Soon lumber, sassafras root, bayberries, fish, skins and furs, tar, pitch and turpentine was being prepared for export.

For a time it seemed that Virginia might develop into a province of small holdings, diversified pursuits, and a democratic social structure. A new product of undreamed of commercial importance, however, changed the entire course of the colony's growth. Tobacco, first planted in John Rolfe's garden in 1612, became, in a short time, the article upon which the economic fabric and prosperity of the colony was to depend. England and the Continent were already importing large quantities from the Dutch and Spanish who had obtained the leaf in the Indies. It was fast becoming a necessity rather than a novel luxury. When it was discovered that the black forest mold of the Virginia clearings would yield surpassing crops of the weed, the entire energy of the colony turned toward raising tobacco. In five years it became the most important article of export.

Virginia became a tobacco province, its entire life revolving around the yellow leaf. Tobacco even displaced currency, and the success or failure of the crop affected all her inhabitants alike. Slowly it shaped her society into well-defined classes, building up an economic foundation differing markedly from that of her northern sisters.

Tobacco planters amassed wealth rapidly. They pushed farther up the shores of the bay and its tributary streams, clearing the forest and constantly adding to their acreage. As they grew richer and more powerful, the gulf widened between themselves and their poorer neighbors. New fields demanded more laborers, and the planters sought for available sources of supply. Highly colored descriptions of the country were published in England in an effort to stimulate immigration.

In another effort to obtain laborers, white servants, or redemptioners, were brought over and bound to their employers for a term of years (an average of five, but not infrequently ten or even fifteen). During this term they received no wages, and their masters set the hours and conditions under which they must labor. After serving their term of indenture, they were sometimes furnished with clothing, equipment, and a small parcel of land. In the pressing need for more and more labor, however, less legitimate schemes of recruiting were resorted to. Men were kidnapped in the streets and lanes of the English seaports; convicts were shipped from the London jails; and many boatloads of the rebel followers of the Duke of Monmouth were sentenced to virtual slavery in the tobacco fields.

The labor supply was still inadequate. When, in 1619, a Dutch ship arrived bringing with it twenty black slaves, another element was added to strengthen the ascendancy of the planter class. The use of African slaves, now called Negroes, spread gradually. They were cheaper than white laborers. Blacks began to displace white men in the fields and, in fact, became the mainspring of that society. But in the 1680's, indentured servants still outnumbered Negro slaves four to one.

The African slave arrived in this country naked, although he did of course have a rich tradition of dress and ornamentation in his indigenous habitat. Upon his arrival in the Western Hemisphere he was generally given the cast-off clothing of his masters. To the best of our knowledge, not until the late 18th, early 19th century does the Negro begin to develop a characteristic garb of his own.

The history of Negro clothes has never received proper attention—at least not in published form, despite the fact that Negroes constituted 20 per cent of the entire population by the time of the Revolution. The problems are manifold. Few, if any, authentic seventeenth-century portraits exist, and only a handful of indisputably eighteenth-century American paintings portray the Negro in any capacity. In the most important exhibit of the Negro in art of our time—"The Portrayal Of The Negro In American Painting," Bowdoin College, Maine, 1964—diligent search failed to alter this gap. Of the five early American paintings, one is reproduced in this volume (Plate 93 B); of the others, two show slave boys from the waist up, while the others are so pictorially poor as to be of questionable documentary value.

Unless new illustrative material is discovered, our only reliable sources are textual. Most, if not all, of these were written by white men and women, and their objectivity is questionable. Nonetheless, in the forthcoming volumes in this history of American dress, an attempt will be made to convey a fairly accurate account of Negro dress. Unlike the seventeenth and eighteenth centuries, in the nineteenth century, a vast amount of reliable textual and illustrative material can be tapped. The subject of the dress of servants and other menial workers will also be more fully explored.

A shipload of ninety women arrived the same year as the first Negro slaves. All of these white women were prospective wives for the colonists. Each woman's passage, one hundred and twenty pounds of tobacco, was to be paid by the man whose wife she became. [Until this time Virginia had been almost entirely a colony of men; although two women, Mistress Forest and her maid, Anne Burras, had landed in 1609.] These ninety women were not, of course, ladies of quality. They were poor maidens and widows, "young, handsome and chaste." Their gowns were probably neither of the richest materials, nor of the finest cut. But, considering the nature of their quest, it is certain they lavished upon their persons as much as their means permitted, following as closely as possible the latest London mode.

They doubtless wore some form of the farthingale, a wide voluminous skirt distended by means of hoops or a bolster (also known as a bum-roll, although not in "polite" terminology). Or, they may have worn a simpler kind of skirt, made very full, but not built out in any manner. This skirt, originally called a "kirtle," was now called a "petticoat." By 1650 the old name of kirtle was no longer in use. Usually, in either type of skirt, the material was cut away in front, showing an underskirt of different material. The bodice was stiff and straight in outline and was laced in at the waist, where it descended to a point. Ruffs, bands, and collars were much like those of the men, as were also the various cloaks and the high-crowned hats. In fact, with the exception of the skirts, the other articles of feminine attire closely followed the masculine mode. The dress in the portrait of Pocahontas, painted in England about 1616, was doubtless similar to that worn by the ninety women. (See page 67 *et seq.*)

At this same time, and continuing through the second quarter of the century, the dress of the men was undergoing a steady change and modification. The tendency in general was toward greater length and fullness of the principal garments. The doublet was gradually losing its stiffness, and the tabs at the waist were lengthening. By the middle of the century the doublet had become loose fitting and longer. Sleeves were getting wider, and were often puffed and slashed. The broad collar now fell upon the shoulders, and with the passing of the short trunk hose in the early twenties came a type of full knickerbockers gathered at the knee with ribbons. Long hair was again the fashion. The long curls and lovelocks, together with the wide-brimmed sombrero hat, were two marked characteristics of the time of Charles I. This period was usually termed "Cavalier." (See page 70 *et seq.*)

It must be remembered, the constantly changing English fashions were not always followed immediately in the colonies. Possibly the royal governor and his little retinue adopted the latest mode as quickly as the means of communication of that time permitted; but in the remote plantations news of London was very slow in arriving. Then, too, many of the older men of the colony resented the intrusion of new styles, and clung jealously to the fashions of their youth. It would not have been unusual in any large gathering to find the mingled fashions of several generations.

Meanwhile, to the north, Maryland had been settled by a mixed band of Catholics and Protestants under Leonard Calvert in 1634. They built the little town of St. Mary's on a tributary of the Potomac. Farms and plantations soon sprang up around it. Tobacco became a principal crop; slaves were brought in, and social life very much akin to that of Virginia developed. Dress did not differ essentially from that worn in Virginia except, perhaps, for the black habits of the Jesuits, who were not found in the older colony.

With the middle of the seventeenth century came the first of a flood of royalist fugitives from England. Charles I was beheaded in 1649, and his followers fled to the Continent and to the New World. They found a haven in Virginia, Governor Berkeley having sent an invitation to all Cavaliers to make his province their home. They came in large numbers until the Restoration in 1660, giving a markedly Cavalier caste to Virginian society. Many were "nobility, clergy and gentry, men of the first rate"; but the term Cavalier included people of all classes and kinds. It denoted political leanings rather than either station or lineage.

No matter what their rank, they must have come in their best ribbons and laces, flaunting their Cavalier fashions as a badge of allegiance to their cause and to their departed king. The dress, of course, was not new to Virginia. In fact, it had gradually become the mode in upper circles. The arrival, however, of great numbers of elegant and beribboned men and women placed a definite complexion upon the Virginian dress and manners. Moreover, it was a type of dress that fitted into the light-hearted and rich living plantation life that was fast becoming the tradition of the Old Dominion. Virginia now became not only the Tobacco Province but the Cavalier Colony.

The newcomers dressed in a doublet that hung loose and straight from the shoulders to a little below the waist. The bottoms were square-cut or tapered to the front. An older type of doublet that was still worn sloped in from the shoulders to a high waistline, often decorated with points or ties. These points were cords with tips (frequently metal) used to join garments together, i.e., the breeches to the doublet. Even after their use was discontinued, the points remained as decoration. Sleeves were wider and looser, and frequently were slashed or paned. Much display was made of the fine linen shirt, through the opening of slashes, the unbuttoned doublet, and the rolled-back cuff. Knee-breeches were less full than in the previous quarter of the century, and sometimes sloped from the hips to the ribbon-garters just below the knees. The broad linen collars followed the line of the shoulder. Cuffs were turned back at the wrists. Among

the upper classes these collars and cuffs were of the richest and most
expensive lace. They were carefully stiffened with the best Dutch starch.
Although one finds mention of colored starches such as red, blue, yellow,
and "goose-green," they must have been used either infrequently or have
been of very delicate and scarcely perceptible tints. An examination of
hundreds of old portraits discloses no evidence of any decided color in
ruffs, collars, bands, or cuffs.

The Cavalier often wore boots of soft leather with wide mouths
pulled above the knee, or turned down in a flapping collar below the
knee. His stockings were of silk, his shoes square-toed and tied with
ribbons, or adorned with rosettes. He was fond of capes and cloaks thrown
back over the shoulders, and his wide-brimmed hat usually contained a
feather. His locks were long and curled, and hung in careful disorder. The
Cavalier liked black velvet contrasted with pale blue, yellow, or cream-
colored satins. The materials were of the finest—plush, silk, satin, fine
linen, and lace. He wore them with studied ease, being fond of little
touches that would give him an air of careful negligence. He was a figure
of elegance and distinction, of nonchalance and sophistication.

The Cavalier's lady would also appear in looser and less formal dress.
The skirt was full and wide, and sometimes gathered back to disclose
the satin petticoat. The bodice was high waisted and at times almost
covered by the great falling collar of linen edged with lace. The sleeves
were loose and ample, commonly ending part way down the forearm in
a turned-back cuff, or by a falling wristlet of lace. Her hair fell in curls
about her shoulders, often with a fringe of them across the forehead.
Occasionally the hair was brushed back from the brow. No lady of fashion,
in those days, considered herself ready for the compliments of polite society
until she had carefully gummed at least one black silk patch on her face.
These patches had fetching shapes—circles, stars, and crescent moons were
common. However, ladies of enterprise and an original turn of mind
would venture forth with silhouettes of full-rigged ships or of a coach-
and-four spotting their cheeks and foreheads.

The dress of humbler folk, in a simpler and less extravagant way,
copied that of the upper circles. The body garments were shorn of much
or all of their ornament, and they were made of cheaper and ruder materials—broadcloth, kersey, leather, and homespun. Leather breeches, jerkins,
and stockings were generally used by those engaged in rough labor. These
leather garments possessed remarkable wearing qualities. It was not unusual to find such articles serving for two or even three generations. In the
outlying districts where game was plentiful, the poorer families used
leather almost entirely for outer garments.

In the years of comparative quiet that followed under the Commonwealth, the Roundhead government interfered to a surprisingly slight
extent with Virginian affairs. In fact, the colony enjoyed virtual independence from a remote mother country. The ideals of Cromwell were
not those of Virginia, and the sober dress of the Roundheads found small

welcome there. Instead, Virginia kept her Cavalier ways and dress, so that, with the coming of the Restoration in 1660, the feverish and hysterical reaction that upset the thought and fashion of England was not duplicated in Virginia. Virginia dress had always been essentially Cavalier.

The extravagances and extremes of the clothes worn during the reign of Charles II were a natural continuation of the dress of his father's reign. Ribbons and knots, frills and laces, multitudes of buttons, bows and ornaments, all the excesses and absurdities marking the dress of the English court were worn at the governor's court in Jamestown and among the more modish planters. Yet its fripperies were too extreme for a colony in the making. Only in a much simpler form was it used by the people of lesser rank: the lengthened doublet was now beginning to resemble a coat, and the shoulder collar was developing into two falling bands at the throat.

By the beginning of the last quarter of the century the wilderness south of Virginia was being penetrated and settled. In 1653 a band of Virginians established the first permanent settlement in the Carolinas on the banks of the Chowan and the Roanoke. Later a handful of New Englanders built some huts on—or near—Cape Fear. The country was settled slowly, largely with outcast or restless persons from Virginia. Virginian life was reproduced on a much ruder scale. The settlements were isolated, life was rough and hazardous, and the settlers hardy and independent. Their dress was simple and practical, consisting for the most part of leather and homespun, such as those described in a later chapter on frontier dress. Of all the colonies, North Carolina was the least responsive to European influence. It was frontier land until late in the next century.

Its twin province, South Carolina, was included in the same charter of 1663, but the first successful expedition did not land until 1670 when three English ships arrived from Barbados. Charles Town [later called Charleston] was founded in 1672. Later the center of a polished and sophisticated society, during the remaining years of the century it was still a new and raw settlement, struggling to lay the foundations of its future greatness. There was nothing particularly distinctive or individual in the dress or life of the province in these early years. That came later when Charleston had grown into a city of fashion and culture.

By 1675 Virginia's fertile tidewater country was well covered with plantations. The Indian had been conquered within the colony, and in the foothills a thin fringe of cabins and blockhouses stood between the aboriginal inhabitants and the tobacco-raising territory of the coast. The social order was gradually forming into four fairly defined classes. First, the planters and high government officials; second, the middle class of tradesmen, artisans, and owners of small holdings; third, the white indentured servants or redemptioners; lastly, at the bottom of the scale, the slaves.

The planters were growing into a strong and controlling aristocracy, ruling their miniature states in something approximating the old feudal manner. They built their houses as large and pretentious as their wealth and conditions permitted. Wood was the most common material used; but some houses were constructed of bricks made on the estate or nearby. Not many of these seventeenth-century manor houses possessed the architectural interest and beauty of those built in the next century, but inside these houses was revealed an almost medieval picturesqueness.

The furniture, brought from England in the tobacco ships, was rather massive and richly carved, such as court cupboards, long refectory tables of oak, lighter tables, and chairs of walnut. The chairs were high-backed and carved in the Flemish manner with cupids, crestings, and heavy scroll-work. There was spiral turning on the legs, and the seats were of rush or cane, although some of the newer and more unusual forms were uphol-stered in cut velvet or Russia leather. The walls of the great room, or dining hall, were often paneled in wood. On these walls, suspended from pegs, were saddles and harnesses, guns, swords, powder-horns, and trophies of the chase. Sometimes above these hung family portraits brought from home. Crockery cupboards and linen chests stood about. On the holland or damask cloth of the great dining-table were silver or pewter tankards and plates of earthenware, small pieces of Bristol glass, knives, spoons and, in a few instances, that implement new even to cultured circles, the fork. At meal time it would not be unusual for the favorite hounds to lie beside the master's seat and be fed scraps from his plate.

Around the plantation house were clustered the servants' quarters and slave huts, tobacco barns, granaries, smoke-houses, stables, and cow pens. An orchard would be near the house, as well as a garden hedged in and filled with shade trees and bright English flowers. Beyond were the broad tobacco fields, and the smaller ones for grain, hay, and vegetables.

These plantations were almost always on or near some navigable body of water. Once a year the tobacco ships nosed up to the planter's landing stage, and through the late spring and early summer months they lay moored, the center of bustling activity and interest. Negro slaves and white redemptioners unloaded bales of stuffs and chests of fine clothing from the London tailors and drapers, crates of furniture and barrels of canary, port, claret, and fine French wines, casks of sugar and hampers of crockery. The ships refitted and took on water and supplies; for cargo they emptied the bulging warehouses of their ripened tobacco leaf. From the inland plantations the tobacco was rolled down in great casks fitted with axles and drawn by yokes of oxen, by teams of horses, or even by gangs of sweating slaves. It was the gayest and most colorful event in the year for the wealthy Virginians. People thronged to the wooden wharves and warehouses, or were entertained in the hospitable manor-house. English and New England mariners and dark-skinned sailors from the Mediterranean regions mingled with the bare-bodied slaves. It was a time when leather-breeched and canvas-doubleted craftsmen, elegant ladies and gentlemen from the great house, and buckskin-clad hunters from the back country would all be seen watching the climax of the year's labor.

Lavish with the money received from the new crop, the planter held open house for all. Like his English cousin, the country squire, he rode hard, gambled, and drank with his friends. He and his lady danced and dined with their neighbors, dressed in the latest London fineries unloaded from the ship. He was eager to display the latest wrinkle of fashion, as ordained by the select circles of London. He spared neither expense nor trouble to have himself and his household garbed in rare and unusual materials. In fact, he must often have overstepped the bounds of good taste in his anxiety to dazzle and astound; for many of these early planters were not fit by birth or training to transplant the sophistication of London society into the primitive setting of the Virginia of 1675. Many of them had climbed to their present position from the ranks of merchant adventurer. Several generations would pass before their manners matched their station. The first families of Virginia were still in the making.

The planter of 1675, playing host to a houseful of guests, was a replica of a London figure of fashion of the previous year. He would be a more familiar figure to us than would his ancestor of early Jamestown. His principal garment would be the coat. This article of attire, displacing the doublet, was a garment which is still worn in different adaptations to the present time. The coat might be of dull red or green velvet, falling from the shoulders to mid-thigh, or even lower. It would be slit to the hips on either side and in the back. The sleeves would be turned back at the elbow in a broad cuff, showing the silk lining and exposing the full ruffled shirt sleeve of linen. The unbuttoned coat commonly showed the short, straight-cut vest of silk or satin, figured, perhaps, or embroidered.

A planter probably wore the latest thing in neckwear, the cravat or neckcloth—a spreading fall of fine lace tied at the throat with a bow of ribbon. His breeches, of the same material as the coat, were of moderate width and gartered with ribbons at the knee. Ribbons were likely to appear on his garments in almost any place, for they were the mark of the age.

Boots were no longer the mode. It was now fashionable to wear light-hued silk stockings and square-toed shoes fastened with long, bright-colored ribbons or, perhaps, in the newer manner with small silver buckles. Lastly, the planter would wear upon his head the latest encumbrance dictated by a tyrant fashion, a heavy periwig of long, thick curls which fell over the shoulders. This early Virginia planter was an important figure, not only in his own eyes, but in ours, for he represents an important turning point in the history of clothes. Behind him lies the fancy and color and peacock raiment of the Renaissance. Before him stretches a century of wig-wearing, and two centuries of gradually increasing sobriety in the dress of the male.

His lady was not unaffected by the fashions emanating from the court of Charles II. (See page 86 *et seq.*) Her bodice was now longer in the waist and descended to a point in front. Her neck and much of her shoulders were left bare, or were perhaps draped with a scarf of lace or gauze. The sleeves were sometimes puffed, sometimes wide and straight.

They reached to about the elbow, where they terminated in a fall of lace or a fringe or ribbons. Sometimes the full sleeve of the chemise was allowed to show.

The skirt was still full, gathered snugly to the waist in pleats and looped back in front to display the satin petticoat. As in the case of the attire worn by men, ribbons were apt to appear almost anywhere on the women's attire. They were often worn in the hair, which was brushed back and allowed to fall in curls to the shoulders. Headgear was out of fashion for women, save for light scarfs or, in bad weather, a hood of heavy material. Shoes were becoming more pointed, and heels were high in the French fashion. The planter's lady, when she went abroad, often wore a mantua, that is, a loose gown of the open robe type. It had no boning and, although worn as an informal dress, had a train. (A "mantua-maker" was in fact the common name for a dressmaker.) Or the lady might wear a long traveling coat cut in much the same fashion as her husband's coat. Like him, she would wear leather or woolen stockings over her fine silk ones. He would probably favor long riding boots of soft leather, and in winter a match-coat of sewn skins with the fur inside.

Very little of the apparel of the wealthy classes was of native cut or manufacture. The homespun linens and woolens were too coarse, and the local tailors too inexpert for an exacting taste. Homespun and home tailored articles were worn by servants and the poor. The slaves probably were given the homespun garments once these were completely worn out by the original owners. The social pressures upon the planter were such that he had to have new clothes from London every year, regardless of his financial state. Robert Beverley, in his "History and Present State of Virginia," published in 1705 a quarter of a century later, says of them:

> They have their Cloathing of all sorts from England, as Linnen, Woollen, Silk, Hats, and Leather. Yet Flax, and Hemp grow no where in the World, better than there; their Sheep yield a mighty Increase, and bear good Fleeces; but they shear them only to cool them. The Mulberry-Tree, whose Leaf is the proper Food of the Silk-Worm, grows there like a Weed, and Silk-Worms have been observ'd to thrive extreamly, and without any hazard. The very Furrs that their Hats are made of, perhaps go first from thence; and most of their Hides lie and rot, or are made use of, only for covering dry Goods, in a leaky House. Indeed some few Hides with much adoe are tann'd, and made into Servants Shoes; but at so careless a rate, that the Planters don't care to buy them, if they can get others; and sometimes perhaps a better manager than ordinary, will vouchsafe to make a pair of Breeches of a Deer-Skin.

The fact of the matter is that there were such huge profits in a successful crop of tobacco that neither thought nor energy could be spared for pursuits less lucrative. Many were cognizant of the one-sided development of the colony, and of its dangers, but efforts to institute spinning-schools and to encourage local industries usually had but indifferent success.

Such materials as were spun and woven at home and fashioned into garments fell, of course, to the lot of the poorer classes. No man wore homespun if he could afford London clothes. However, as much as the small planters, farmers, and tradesmen might wish to imitate the dress of their wealthy neighbors, their imported wardrobes often had to be supplemented by the cheaper and less skilfully woven linens, broadcloths, kerseys, linsey-woolseys, and friezes of the province. In cut they would follow the best fashion as well as they could. Their dress was essentially the same as that of the wealthy, save that it was simpler and stripped of much of its braid, embroidery, and ribbons. The artisans were content with fustian, canvas coats, and leather breeches, with a suit of broadcloth for Sundays.

Thus poor as well as wealthy followed as best they could the dress and manners of the homeland, and, in spite of the distance and slow sailing ships of the day the contact was remarkably close. The Virginia of 1675 was still a river province in which the planter from his own wharf, and often in his own ships, kept up an almost uninterrupted communication with England.

I. MEN'S DRESS
1607–1620

The dress worn by the earliest Virginian settlers was in the English style associated with the reigns of Queen Elizabeth and James I. This style appeared in England and western Europe about the middle of the sixteenth century and can be traced directly back to Spain. It is, in fact, usually referred to as the "Spanish bombast" style, and lasted until the end of the first quarter of the seventeenth century.

The chief characteristics of this style in men's garments were a rather uncompromising rigid outline, brought about by tight-fitting or corseted doublets, with collars rising high about the neck, and topped with ruffs, bands, and whisks. The trunk hose was greatly distended with buckram and bombast, while the men's legs were incased in tight, close-fitting stockings or tights (Fig. 1 A c).

THE DOUBLET.—The long-tight-waisted, stiffened doublet underwent many minor changes from the time of its introduction in England to 1625. During its period of greatest exaggeration, from 1580 to 1600, it became exceedingly fantastic in form, especially in the peascod-belly type, where it was stuffed out in a ridge down the front and overhung the girdle. It was not seen in America in this exaggerated form. However, there is a trace of this peascod-form in the long ridge down the center

of the doublet, ending in a pointed waistline. (Fig. 1 c). This shaping
lasted until the end of the period.

The use of buckram and padding made the doublet rigid in outline. Corsets, termed busks, were generally worn under the doublet, and
laced in tightly at the waist (Fig. 1 A C. Fig. 2 B C). The doublet might
be provided with skirts below the waistline (Fig. 1 A. Fig. 2 B C) or simply
end at the waist (Fig. 1 c).

As a rule, tight sleeves were worn with the doublet (Fig. 2), although
a full sleeve tapering from the shoulder to a tight band at the wrist was
often preferred (Fig. 1 A C). The sleeves were usually separate and tied
to the armholes of the doublet by means of points. ("Points" take the
name from metal ends, or points of laces similar to todays shoelaces.)
Where the sleeve met the doublet the joining point as a rule, was hidden
by a roll of material crescent in form (Fig. 1 A. Fig. 2 A), or by a jutting
piece of material called a "wing" (Fig. 1 B., 2 B C). Slits and cloth strips,
known as panes, often decorated the front and back of the doublet (Fig.
1 A. Fig. 2 B).

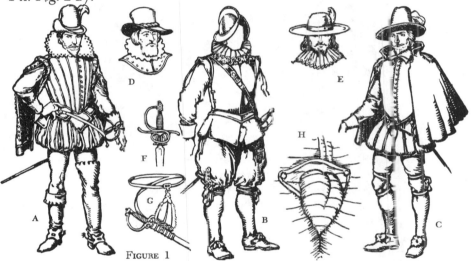

FIGURE 1

RUFFS, COLLARS, CUFFS.—The high tight collar of the doublet
might be surmounted by a stiff linen collar or band (Fig. 1 c), which
was a continuation of the fine linen shirt worn under the doublet. This
stiff collar, or falling band, never seems to have gone out of style during the entire period and was in great favor in the colonies.

For dress occasions the ruff was worn in various degrees of size and
richness. It was starched, and the sets, held together by wires, took the
place of bands (Plate 1 A B. Fig. 1 B. Fig. 2 A).

About the time of the first settlement of Jamestown, the fan-shaped
whisk, encircling the head and ending in a square line under the chin,
was seen (Fig. 1 A. Fig. 2 c). It was also about this time that the upstand-

ing ruff descended over the shoulders, developing into the type known as the falling ruff (Plate 2. Fig. 1 E. Fig. 2 B). During the Cavalier period this falling ruff further developed into the lace collar that fell over the shoulders. (Plate 18). At the wrists were turned-back cuffs (Fig. 1 A B C. Fig. 2 A B) or ruffles (Fig. 2 C), which were usually in harmony with the neckpiece.

THE JERKIN.—The jerkin was cut on the same lines as the doublet and was made to fit smoothly over it. In the drawings and paintings of the period, it is very difficult to distinguish the jerkin from the doublet. Leather jerkins were especially a favorite with soldiers, and must have been extremely serviceable in the colonies. The jerkin, however, was out of style in England by 1630. In Figure 1 B a leather jerkin worn under a breastplate is shown.

FIGURE 2

BREECHES.— [also see page 74] In breeches there was quite a selection, the most popular being the "pumpkin-shaped" trunk hose, with long, tailored stockings attached (Fig. 1 A C). Trunk hose were of every variety and size, from small rolls around the hips to the trunk hose which were cut full and descended to within a few inches of the knees (Fig. 3 A). Sometimes the trunk hose spread out from the waist, ending in a square base, as in Figure 1 C.

Trunk hose were made of vertical strips attached at the top and bottom, allowing the lining, usually of a contrasting color, to show through.

By the time the colonists came to America the fuller knee breeches, termed venetians, were in wide use (Plates 2 D, 15, Fig. 1 B. Fig. 3 B. Fig. 4 A B). They had become popular in England as early as 1575. They fitted tight around the waist and were very full over the hips, tapering to below the knees, where they were either tied or buttoned. Open breeches of knee length cut very full, cylindrical in shape, and trimmed at the side of the knees with a fall of lace, were also in vogue.

It is common to find breeches with what are called "canions." The nether hose or stocks (stockings) were usually sewn to the trunk hose, thus making a garment. When cut short, the upper part of the stocks, or a similar piece of material, attached to the leg opening of the breeches, were referred to as "canions." Attached as the stocks had been they were close-fitting, descending either to above or below the knees (Fig. 1 c). Often they were made of richly figured material. Knitted stockings generally accompanied canions. If the canions were tight at the knee, the stockings were pulled up over them and confined by garters placed below the knees. These garters were crossed in back and carried to the front above the knee, where they were tied in a bow at the side (Fig. 1 c). If, however, the canions were loose, the stockings were worn under them.

FIGURE 4   FIGURE 3

CLOAKS.—Cloaks formed an important part of clothing and were of great variety in cut and length. In Figure 1 c is seen the short Spanish cloak reaching to the hips, and with a high-stepped upstanding collar. According to the taste of the wearer, it might be considerably longer or shorter than this. Cloaks reaching to the ankles must have been conducive to warmth and comfort in the Virginia winters, which Captain John Smith notes were cold and damp. From time to time these English made cloaks were copied in furs for which the settlers had bartered with the Indians. Cloaks were worn in many ways: suspended in the usual manner, thrown over the shoulder, or worn diagonally across the back.

FOOTGEAR.—Tight-fitting boots of soft leather were generally worn. They could be pulled up over the knees, where they extended to about mid-thigh; or they could be rolled down below the knee (Fig. 1 A. Fig. 5). It was not an unusual thing to see a man of this period wearing one boot pulled up and the other turned down.

When boots were worn, they were usually accompanied by boot hose. Boot hose were strongly made stockings worn to protect the regular stockings from the wear of the boot.

By the time Jamestown was settled, shoes with heels were in quite general use. The shoes had a moderate round point or a slightly square ending. They were held in place by a band over the instep. Slippers were pulled on over the shoes as a protection for out-of-door wear.

FIGURE 5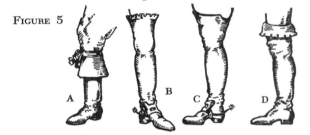

HEADGEAR.—The Monmouth cap (Fig. 30 B) which had once been a sort of beret with a brim was now made of knitted wool fitting firmly to the head. It had a brim as before and a long peaked top that hung over one side and ended in a tassel. It must have been a fairly common sight in Virginia during the cooler seasons of the year.

Besides this cap, there was great variety in hats. Hats with either tall, short, round, peaked, or truncated crowns were all in vogue. The brims could be narrow (Fig. 1 A) or wide (Fig. 1 C D E. Fig. 2 B C), decorated with feathers or left plain. Probably the hats with the wide brims were the most popular as they gave better protection from the sun during the hot summer months.

HAIR AND BEARD.—The hair was a matter of considerable attention and could be worn in many different ways. However, the hair cut close to the head was the most popular style (Fig. 1 A. Fig. 2). Occasionally one finds hair worn long enough to hang upon the shoulders (Plate 18 Fig. 1 C D E).

The pointed beard was the most common form of beard (Fig. 1 A C. Fig. 2); only the younger men have their faces clean-shaven. However, one does find (Plate 1 A Fig. 1 D) square and spreading beards and, in rare instances, forked ones. (Fig. 1 E).

GLOVES.—Men's gloves were, as a rule, richly embroidered, provided with gauntlets, and often fringed. They became a very fashionable part of his dress (Plate 1 B).

SWORDS.—The sword and dagger were now generally worn with civilian dress. The sword was the long, thin, tapering, rapier-like blade used for thrusting (Fig. 1 A). The grip, pommel, and quillon were further provided with a complicated guard (Fig. 1 F G). The dagger was long, straight, and tapering, with an ornamental hilt. It was carried in a sheath and hung from the sword-belt on the right side.

The sword-belt was a narrow strip of leather encircling the waist, and from which the sword sheath was usually suspended by a hanger (Fig. 1 A G. Fig. 2 A).

ARMOR.—In Europe there was a noticeable deterioration in the art of making armor a considerable time before the year 1600. The encouragement formerly given to the art of the armorer was now centered in the productions of the swordsmith, the gunsmith and the cannon founder. The use of armor had lost its importance. This was due to the improvement in guns and ammunition, and the development in new military tactics, which demanded the more rapid movement of troops all of which gave new importance to the infantry.

During the reign of James I the cavalry likewise showed a general tendency to discard heavy, cumbersome armor as being no longer effective. This was especially true among the officers, who now appeared at the head of their troops protected only by a cuirass. In a short time this fashion spread to the troops, so that in the reign of Charles I whole regiments were thus accoutered. Later, under Cromwell, the cavalry was usually armed in three-quarter suits. After the Restoration, in the time of Charles II, James II, and William and Mary, while officers still wore the breastplate over their buff coats, armor for the common soldier was practically abandoned.

Therefore, by the time of the first Virginia settlement, full armor had gradually given place to half and three-quarter suits, and later to the simple cuirass worn over the buff coat. While whole suits of armor may have been worn from time to time during the early years of the colonization of America, it is difficult to conceive of this as being a general practice. If this was so, these complete suits were probably only worn by the officers and soldiers guarding the fortified towns. As has been seen, armor was heavy and cumbersome. When one remembers the poor roads which were mere rutted tracks, the endless miles of wilderness to travel, and the nature of Indian warfare, it is easily comprehended how the wearing of much armor was soon discouraged. So, from the beginnings of colonization armor was gradually being discarded until, with the coming of the Cavalier period, the breastplate, the backplate, and the helmet alone were retained.

A half suit of armor (Fig. 6 B), dating from the end of the sixteenth century and worn all through the first quarter of the seventeenth century, consisted of a breast and backplate in the form of a cuirass, the waistline descending to a slight point in front. The breastplate had a slight tapul. The armholes were edged with a rope border from under which protruded the goussets. A tace of one plate was attached to the lower part of the breastplate, and from the tace hung three tassets, protecting the upper part of the thigh. Upon the head was worn the morion, or perhaps the burgonet, or even a broad-brimmed hat.

The sword was the long, thin, tapering blade with an ornamental guard, and it was held in a scabbard suspended from hangers attached to a narrow strip of leather encircling the waist and serving as a sword belt.

Heavy gloves protected the hands, and boots of the same material pulled up over the knee or rolled down were invariably worn.

A three-quarter suit of armor of a later date is shown in Figure 6 A. It dates from about the end of the first quarter of the seventeenth century, and is a good example of the type of armor worn until armor was discarded by both Cavaliers and Roundheads. The suit consisted of a back- and breastplate and a gorget of several lames protecting the neck. The shoulders were protected by laminated pauldrons. Brassarts, vambraces, coudières, and gauntlets protected the arms and hands. From the tace depended the tassets, covering the front of the legs. Genouillières guarded the knees and were attached to the bottom lame of the tassets. A small helmet (Fig. 6 A), a burgonet (Fig. 6 C E), a morion (Fig. 6 B D), or, later, the triple-barred helmet were the various types of protective covering for the head.

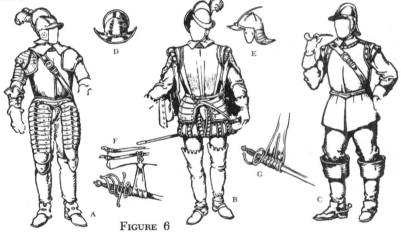

FIGURE 6

It was customary, from the early years of the seventeenth century, for officers and soldiers to put aside most of the armor, retaining merely the cuirass and helmet. A man of the Cavalier period so armed is shown in Figure 6 C. Here the body armor and helmet alone are retained. The backplate and breastplate, buckled over the shoulders and down the sides, were usually worn over the buff coat, the skirts of which extended below the cuirass. His head was protected by a burgonet, having a laminated neck guard, cheek pieces, buckled under the chin, and a visor. A shoulder strap crossing the body from the right shoulder supported the sword that hung from hangers on the left side. Stout leather breeches and boots formed part of the general scheme.

II. WOMEN'S DRESS
1609–1620

The year 1619 is a memorable one in the history of Virginia and has a direct bearing upon the clothing of the colonies, for it was in this year that ninety young women came to the New World to be wives of the settlers. Unfortunately, there is no contemporary description of the garments they wore, nor of the wardrobe they brought with them. Conclusions of necessity, must be largely a matter of conjecture, based upon knowledge of dress as worn by Englishwomen in the last years of the reign of James I and upon the position these young women held in society before they were recruited. The problem is made more difficult because clothes in the year 1619 were in the last stage of the Elizabethan style, which had extended from about the middle of the sixteenth century until the seventeenth year of the reign of James I. During the next ten years, 1620 to 1630, dress was to undergo a complete transformation. Farthingales, ruffs, tightly laced and long-waisted bodices were soon to go out of fashion, making way for the simpler and more "easy-fitting" clothing of the Cavalier period.

If the young women who had elected to throw in their lot with the colonists of the New World had been of the wealthy upper classes instead of women of the middle class, generally lacking in funds, they might have appeared in large cartwheel or Spanish farthingales with elaborate lace collars and ruffs and long, tightly laced bodices. Some of the ladies may have had just such a garment in a rather crude style among their belongings, to be worn at the opportune moment to dazzle the eyes of their prospective husbands. (Fig. 7 A). On the whole, however, their wardrobe must have been selected with a view to the sterner necessities of life they would have to face in Virginia. In those early years colonial life was not one of ease and pleasure. This phase was to come later when the colonies began to prosper and grow rich.

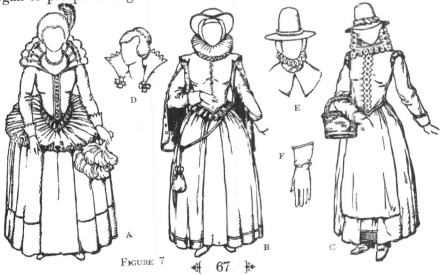

FIGURE 7

THE BODICE.—The bodice was generally long-waisted. It was tightly laced and descended into a decided point in the front (Fig. 7 A B C. Fig. 8 B). The style for low-neck gowns, edged with an upstanding collar of lace, was very fashionable among ladies of wealth and position, and in a modified way was worn by women of the middle classes (Fig. 7 A. Fig. 8 A). In the middle classes the high-neck gown, the collar surmounted by a medium-sized starched ruff, was more usual (Fig. 7 B. Fig. 8 B). With but a few additions of their own, all the different forms of ruffs, bands, and collars worn by the men were also worn by the women.

An even plainer bodice might be one that was not as stiff or tightly laced, but made to fit closely to the figure (Fig. 7 C. Fig. 8 A). A wired out whisk of linen that spread from a square base was worn around the neck (Fig. 7 C). For those who dressed in the simplest manner, a broad, falling collar of white linen was worn (Fig. 7 E). The sleeves would have been tight, finished at the wrist with linen cuffs, turned back and matching the collar.

Close-fitting sleeves with cuffs of pointed lace at the wrists were generally worn. (Fig. 7 A. Fig. 8 B). These tight sleeves could be varied by fairly full sleeves (Fig. 7 B. Fig. 8 A). Often a hanging sleeve was found falling from the elbow or shoulder (Fig. 7 B). Crescents (Fig. 7 C. Fig. 8 B) or more usually wings (Fig. 7 B) were worn at the shoulders, where the sleeve met the bodice.

FIGURE 8

A   B

Robings, an edging to the bodice, can be seen in an early stage of development (Fig. 8 B). Running straight across the back of the shoulders, the edging came down over the breasts, converging at the waist. It was sometimes carried to the hem of the overskirt. The robing was often of "self-material." Later versions show some contrast and in the last stages they had embroidery.

SKIRTS.—As the ninety young women came to Virginia at the time the farthingale skirt was still in fashion, it might be of interest to briefly describe its makeup. It is closely associated with Elizabethan styles, and first made its appearance from Spain to England and western Europe, in about the middle of the sixteenth century. At this time it was cone-shaped, formed by graduating hoops of bone, fastened to a skirt. It was large at the bottom, gradually lessening in size as it reached the waist. Over this the skirt was worn. About the end of the third quarter of the century, a new form appeared, known as the French farthingale. It consisted of a bolster tied around the hips, over which the skirt was draped, causing it to extend to its fullest at the hips, and from there falling straight to the ground. Toward the end of the sixteenth century this style was further accentuated by a wheel of pleated material that was worn like a great ruff around the waist and resting upon the bolster tied around the hips. This cartwheel farthingale was the most popular form during the first quarter of the seventeenth century; but the original Spanish type was worn at the same time, and was never completely ousted from favor by its rival.

The simplest type of skirt was one having no farthingale under it, but was cut full and hung in rich folds to within a few inches of the ground (Fig. 7 A B). Most of the skirts had an opening in front, exposing an underskirt of a different material (Fig. 7 A B C). Usually, if the outer skirt was plain, the underskirt was of a figured material. The opening often took an inverted V-shape form (Fig. 7 B).

COIFFURES.—There was a growing tendency to leave off hoods and caps in order to show the hair. A fashion of dressing the hair quite high over the forehead and decorating it with feathers was much in vogue (Fig. 7 A). A great deal of false hair was used in creating these high coiffures. When the openwork bonnet of lace, linen, or cambric was worn (Fig. 7 B), the hair was dressed low, with a roll placed under the hair in front. This bonnet was made on a wire frame bent to the shape desired.

Even at this time the hair was occasionally dressed in the manner usually associated with the reign of Charles I. The curls hung in clusters on each side of the head, and the front hair was worn in a bang or fringe over the forehead.

HEADGEAR.—As can be seen in the familiar portrait of Pocahontas and Figure 7 C E, women had adopted a masculine style of hat, in form a high-peaked or truncated crown and a wide brim. A rolled band of some rich material was placed around the crown, a feather usually ornamenting the side. Other forms of masculine hats were worn, particularly for riding and traveling. These, because of the long sea voyage, were undoubtedly the headdress chosen by the group of women who came to the colonies.

CLOAKS, ETC.—For warmth during the ocean voyage, and for the winter months, women wore shawls crossed over the shoulders which descended to points in front; or an oblong piece of material was worn over the head and shoulders. Capes, long and short, similar to those worn by men, were also part of these women's attire.

ACCESSORIES.—Gloves with long gauntlets that came up over the wrist, and decorated with needlework, were quite common and very fashionable (Fig. 7 F). Small muffs (Fig. 8 B), feathered fans (Fig. 7 A), paint, powder and patches, and small mirrors hanging from the waist, made up the accessories to the costume.

FOOTGEAR.—Shoes were usually hidden by the long skirts. But when skirts of ankle length were worn, one could see that the shoes were quite similar to those worn by men. They fitted the foot closely, ending in a square toe and decorated at the instep with a ribbon rose. As a protection in wet weather, pattens with thick cork or wooden soles were worn over the shoes.

III. CAVALIER DRESS: MEN
1620–1675

By 1625 the Virginia colonies had begun to sense the coming of that prosperity which was soon to give them the opportunity of turning their attention to other things in life besides the laborious work of home building. In fact, even at this date, 1625, men and women eagerly watched the changing styles of dress as they occurred in England. They followed each new fashion as closely as it was possible, considering the distance and the time it took to get new ideas from the mother country.

The stiff Jacobean style was gradually giving way before the simpler and more elegant clothing of the reign of Charles I. It took a decade, however, to bring this about, and the years between 1620 and 1630 were the years of transition, during which the Cavalier dress underwent many changes and finally emerged in its full development.

DOUBLETS.—During the years 1620 to 1630 the doublet lost much of the rigidity of outline that had characterized it up to this time. Whalebones were gradually discarded, although the waistline in the more fashionable types of dress still retained its pointed form with a skirt of overlapping tabs decorated with bow-knots or points (Fig. 9 A). In the everyday doublet the freedom from stiffening and busks was still more evident. The waistline was beginning to straighten; but, the skirts still kept their pointed form (Fig. 9 B). A doublet made of leather, canvas, fustian, or linsey-woolsey, shaped to the body without any clearly marked waistline but having full skirts, was the type adopted by people of moderate means for general wear (Fig. 10 A).

The body and sleeves were often slashed or paned, allowing the linen shirt, worn underneath, to show through (Fig. 9 A B). Wings at the shoulders were common and the sleeves usually full (Fig. 9 B) or full and paned from the shoulder to the elbow, and from the elbow to the wrist, fitting quite close (Fig. 9 A).

By 1630 the Cavalier dress was established in England. However, the great exodus of Cavaliers to Virginia from England did not begin until

1649, when Charles I was beheaded at Whitehall, and it is reasonably sure that it was some years after 1630 that the new style was adopted by the rich planters and Cavaliers in the colonies.

Gradually the waistline was carried higher up, the corset shape done away with, and the skirts increased in length (Fig. 10 B. Fig. 11 A). From 1630 on, the fashionable way of wearing the doublet was to leave it unbuttoned from below the breast, so that a glimpse of the linen shirt would be exposed to view (Fig. 10 B). The sleeves were usually cut quite full, tapering to the wrist. They were open down the front seam, and through the opening could be seen the voluminous sleeves of the linen shirt. Points were not always worn at the waist, but often done away with entirely, especially in the doublets of the lower classes, as will be seen also in the Puritan New England dress.

FIGURE 9

A

B

A

FIGURE 10

B

Shortly after 1640 the doublet became quite changed in appearance. The waistline with its accompanying points and skirt practically disappeared, resulting in a much shorter doublet built upon fairly straight lines. It was buttoned part of the way down to about the breast, from which point it was allowed to remain open (Fig. 11 A B). The sleeves were generally cut full and were open down the seam. They could also be closed by buttoning (Fig. 12). Although one still saw the earlier type of sleeve cut full and paned on the upper arm, the close-fitting sleeve from the elbow to the wrist was also seen.

FIGURE 11

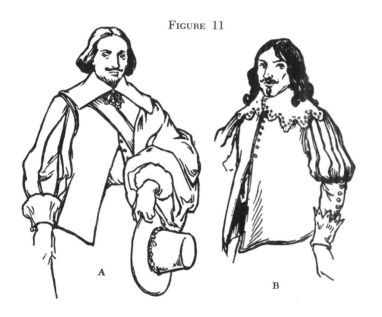

A

B

FIGURE 12

The last phase of the doublet was ushered in about 1660. While it remained in fashion for some time after the introduction of the coat and vest, during the last quarter of the seventeenth century it gradually gave place to those newer and more fashionable garments, the coat and vest. The doublet was still further shortened, and opened in the front, until it was a mere abbreviation of its former self and resembled a small jacket (Fig. 13 A B). This gave a better opportunity to show off the shirt in front and all around under the doublet, where it fell in full pleats over the waistband of the breeches (Fig. 13 A B).

Sleeves varied in character. One style reached to the elbow, fit fairly close, and possessed a small cuff turned back. From under this cuff the full sleeve of the shirt spread out to be confined at the wrist in a band edged with a ruffle (Fig. 13 C). This sleeve was in style from about 1660 until the doublet went out of fashion.

Still another variety of sleeve can be seen in Figure 13 B. Here, the sleeve of the doublet reaches to a little above the elbow. Instead of the turned-back cuff, the sleeve is bell-shaped. The sleeves might be closed or slit down the front, either buttoned up or left open. A very fashionable sleeve is shown in Figure 13 A, where the rather full sleeve is turned back in a broad cuff ending a little below the elbow. At the shoulder there might be a cluster of ribbons. Beneath the cuff is seen the very full sleeve of the linen shirt tied in several places with ribbons.

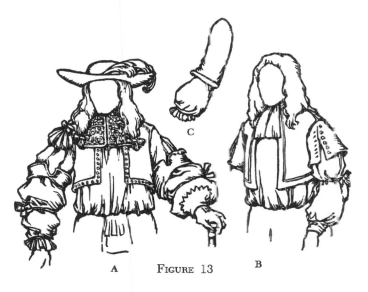

C

A   FIGURE 13   B

The leather jerkin, or buff coat, must have been worn a great deal, because it not only offered good protection from knife thrusts, but also a fair protection from Indian arrows. It was especially serviceable for rough out-of-door wear. It was really the military garment of the seventeenth century, and Planché says it was "formed of the hide of a buffalo, whence its name." It was made very strong, and the leather from which it was constructed was often as much as an eighth of an inch in thickness. The buff coat was probably first worn under armor. Although armor gradually fell into disuse, the buff coat was retained. It was worn either as the sole protective garment (Fig. 12), with the breast–and backplate over it (Fig. 6 c. Fig. 2 A), or with the neck alone guarded by the metal gorget (Fig. 1 D).

The buff coat was usually provided with quite long skirts reaching to the hips, or even to mid-thigh (Plate 3; Fig. 6 c, 35 B). It was generally laced up the front with points. The sleeves could be made of either leather or some strong material. The buff coat, however, seems usually to have been made without sleeves, in which case it would be worn over a doublet to which sleeves were attached.

Occasionally a sash was worn around the waist and tied with a bow-knot on the left side (Fig. 2 A) Page 62. The sword hung on the left side, being attached to a baldric, or shoulder strap, crossing the body from the right shoulder (Fig. 12). A bandolier in the form of a shoulder belt hung across the body from the left shoulder. From it hung a "bullet-bag, priming box and a row of little cylindrical boxes or cases, each containing a single musket charge of powder." A small falling band, a linen or a lace collar was worn at the neck (Fig. 25)

In place of a hat, a helmet might be worn. It would be either the triple-barred helmet of the burgonet type, often called lobster-tailed because of the joined flaps covering the back of the neck (Fig. 6 E), a small helmet (Fig. 6 A), or even a morion (Fig. 6 D)

BREECHES.—Just as the doublet lost its rigid and bombasted outline, so the breeches followed the same general tendency. Trunk hose were probably worn for some time after 1620, but toward 1625 full knee-breeches cut on the pattern of the old venetians, but no longer padded and stuffed, were worn. (Fig. 14 A). These breeches usually reached to about the knee, or a little below it, and they were either fringed with points, loops or ribbon, or tied with ribbon garters.

FIGURE 14

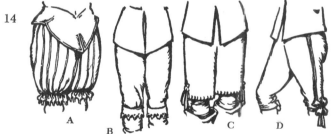

Two other styles of knee breeches came into fashion by 1630. The first shown in Figure 14 D were shaped like bellows. The waistband was high and tight, the breeches being full over the hips and tapering to below the knees. There they were fastened by ribbon garters tied in a bow on the outside of the knee, the end of the ribbons hanging in points. In place of the ribbon bow, a ribbon rosette might be used. The other variety of breeches (Fig. 14 B) was cut the same width all the way down and brought over the knee, but they were not fastened. Sometimes, as in Figure 14 C, they just reached the knee and loops of ribbon also hung free, forming a stripe on the outside of the leg as well as ornamenting the hem with loops. Most of the breeches of the period were decorated with braid or loops of ribbon running down the sides as well as with points or bunches of ribbon knots and rosettes. The styles just described were worn well into the sixteen sixties.

The petticoat, or Rhinegrave breeches, were the favorite style in England during the greater part of the reign of Charles II. As early as 1658 they came into use in England, coming from western Europe where they had been in fashion since 1655. These breeches were called "pantaloons" at the time, a name applied to close-fitting trousers a century later. Shortly after their introduction into London fashion they found their way into the court circles of the colonial governors, and were also included in the wardrobes of the rich planters of Virginia and the South. It has been noted that the planters kept in close touch with the latest fashions of the mother country.

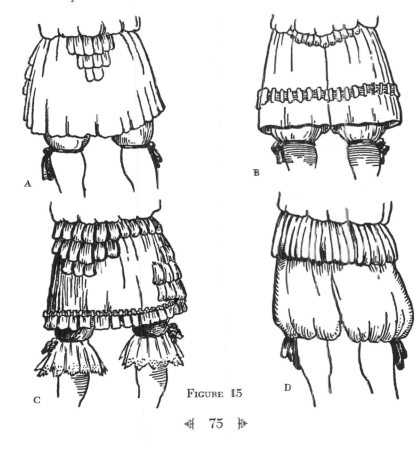

FIGURE 15

The petticoat-breeches consisted of a wide skirt or kilt (Fig. 15 A C), usually made in the form of a divided skirt (Fig. 15 B). The lining of the breeches was very full and hung lower than the skirt. It was gathered and tied above the knee, thus forming the breeches. The breeches were adorned with bunches and loops of ribbons and edgings of lace (Fig. 15 A B C). Very often they had a fall of ribbons descending over the waistband (Fig. 15 A B C). Although with the advent of the long tailored coat they began to lose favor about 1670, these breeches persisted as a fashion until about 1680.

Contemporaneously with these petticoat-breeches, many planters still wore the fully cut breeches that were "fulled at the waist and the knee," after the Dutch fashion, and similar to our modern knickers, with ribbon loops falling over the waistband (Fig. 15 D).

STOCKINGS.—As the manner of wearing hose with the petticoat-breeches is so characteristic of this type of dress, it might be well to treat of them here. The usual type of stocking, gartered above the knee, was worn by many. But among men of fashion the "long stirrup hose" was used. These had previously been worn between the silk stockings and the boots to protect the stockings when boots were so generally the fashion. These boot hose (made of some stout material) were very wide at the top, where they were fitted with eyelets and points with which they were made fast to the breeches (Fig. 15 A B). Often a second pair was worn over the first, these being gathered below the knee with a garter and turned down (Fig. 15 C). It is reasonable to suppose that this drooping top might have been simply a piece of lace, silk, or linen worn in the same manner (Fig. 17 D E).

Canons or Port-canons, as these drooping frills were called, were of course not connected with the breeches and, therefore, should not be confused with canions. (See p. 62.) Later, as has been seen, they were worn in conjunction with the petticoat-breeches.

Silk stockings were the fashion for those who could afford such luxuries. The humbler people wore knitted stockings of wool or of some coarser material.

William of Nassau, Prince of Orange; style of George Glover, or the style copied by him. Holland, or England, about 1645.

CLOAKS.—In the early years of this period the short cloaks and capes of the Jacobean fashion were worn, but these soon gave way to cloaks of greater length. These cloaks were worn either slung over both shoulders in the conventional way (Fig. 16 B), diagonally across the back, or simply draped over one shoulder (Fig. 16 A). By the time the Cavalier dress was developed, however, large silk or cloth cloaks took their place. These cloaks were used as wraps, and were often thrown over one shoulder and arm (Fig. 16 C) and wrapped around the waist.

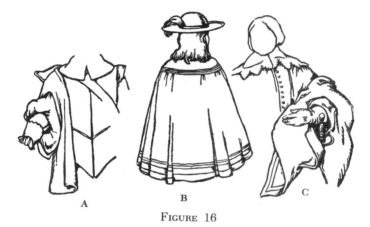

A   B   C

FIGURE 16

FOOTGEAR.—It is a matter of conjecture as to whether or not the fine, handsome, swagger boots of the Cavaliers were worn to the same extent by the colonists as they were in England and France, where a gentleman was seldom seen without them. The hot climate of Virginia and the South, together with the rural life on the plantations, must have made boots rather unpopular for everyday wear. There is no doubt, however, they did wear them for traveling, hunting, riding, and for dress occasions.

Tall, square-toed, close-fitting boots with a shaped spur leather protecting the instep were much in favor (Fig. 17 A). Square-toed boots were well in style by 1635 and remained in vogue for a bit over a century. They were pulled up over the knees and thighs for riding and hunting; or, they were turned down below the knees (Fig. 17 C) for walking or dress wear. The tops became more and more enlarged, so that a little before the middle of the century they were exceedingly exaggerated, being pulled down below the knees in a wide cup (Fig. 17 D). The part of the boot over the ankle and calf was very much creased and wrinkled. This gave an opportunity to show the boot hose with its decorated top, or the rich lining of silk or lace that was sometimes used instead (Fig. 17 D E). Note the boots and canions in the figure on page 77.

Contemporary with the boot just described was a short boot of stiffer leather that reached to about the knee. The swelling shape from the ankle to the knee gave it the name of bucket-top boot (Fig. 17 B).

Until the middle of the century, there was very little change in the shape of the shoes. Heels were low, and the shoes were cut out at the sides and fastened over the instep with "side latches." The general tendency was for a rounded or square toe. A large bow, rosette, or "shoe rose" was placed on the shoe over the instep (Fig. 18 D E G.) About the middle of the century the shoe had a tendency to lengthen, and to end in a square toe (Fig. 18 C D E etc.) It could be open at the side and fastened with ankle straps (Fig. 18 B D G), or it could be closed (Fig. 18 A C E). The shoe roses were gradually replaced by bow-knots of ribbon or by "ribbon ties" (Fig. 18 A B). Heels gradually became higher, and the heels and soles were often of red leather. As a protection for out-of-door wear, clogs of wood (Fig. 18 F) were worn over the shoes.

HEADGEAR.—Broad-brimmed hats of the sombrero type, that had been introduced about 1620 to 1625, were universally worn until they were supplanted by hats of the Restoration period in 1660 (Fig. 9 B, 10 B, 19 A), when the brim might be caught up on one side, the crown being only moderately high. For those who could afford it, ostrich plumes decorated the crown and hung over the brim. Others wore them with only a band around the crown. A very fashionable hat worn at the same time as the sombrero is seen in Figure 19 B. The crown is high and tapering to a flat top, the brim only moderately wide. Plumes could be worn on the sides, or dispensed with in favor of a ribbon band.

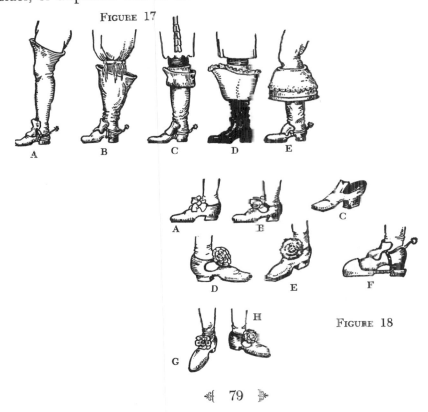

FIGURE 17

A   B   C   D   E

A   B   C

D   E   F

G   H

FIGURE 18

Another form of less pretentious fashion is shown in Figure 19 C. The chief characteristic of the "copotain" is the sugar-loaf shape of its tall crown, usually worn with a band or occasionally with a feather. It follows the same general type worn by the Puritans in New England. A late form of a low-crown hat with a wide brim, richly ornamented with plumes, is seen in Figure 19 D.

FIGURE 19

Mr. Alderman Abel—1641.

LINEN.—The linen shirt was worn under the doublet. As the doublet lost its rigidity and tight fit, the shirt was made more and more full in the body and the sleeves. The extreme exaggeration in the ample cut of the linen shirt came with the short and abbreviated doublet during the time of Charles II when the shirt was seen in the opening in the front as well as all the way round the waist from under the doublet, the folds of the shirt often falling over the waistband of the breeches (Fig. 13 A B). The sleeves of the shirt were also full at this time, their fullness exposed from under the short elbow sleeves of the doublet. They were tightened at the wrists with ribbons, and often tied around the elbow in the same manner (Fig. 13 A B C). At the wrist, deep ruffles of lawn or lace were worn.

Gradually the stiff, upstanding ruff gave way to the falling ruffs (Plate 2. Fig. 9 A Page 71) and the small wired-out whisk (Fig. 1 A). Note the smartness of the effect on Captain Smith, page 42. In the portrait of an ancestor of the Bowdoin family, signed in 1647, the upstanding ruff is still seen, although this member of the Bowdoin family must have been one of the last persons to wear it (Plate 1 A). Among the younger men the whisk and falling ruff soon gave place to the falling band which, as early as 1627, was worn on the Continent. It may be seen in many Dutch portraits of about this date. John Evelyn, writing in his diary in

1633, mentions a recently struck medal of Charles I, and says: "The King wears a falling band, a new mode which has succeeded the cumbersome ruff." Evidently it may be judged from this that the falling band, plain or edged with lace, was a new fashion in England in 1633.

Among the Puritans of New England the falling bands were plainer and supposedly not so large. However, in the South, for dress occasions, the Cavaliers followed the fashions of England, the falling bands of fine linen or lace, or linen edged with lace, that spread well over the shoulders (Fig. 9 B. Fig. 10 B. Fig. 11 B) Pages 71, 72. These falling collars were often called simply a "fall." Plain linen bands without the lace edge were more usual for everyday wear (Plates 4, 5, 6. Fig 10 A. Fig. 11 A. Fig. 12) Page 72; but they might be edged or scalloped. From a little after 1640 to the middle of the century the band often decreased in size and was worn without the pointed lace edging (Fig. 19 A C). About 1660 it further narrowed into a very deep and oblong collar of lace or lawn, falling over the breast (Fig. 13 A. Fig. 19 D. Fig. 20 A) Pages 73, 80, 83, continuing in this form until it was almost hidden by the great curled wigs. It finally went out of fashion at the end of the third quarter of the seventeenth century.

The cravat, or neck-cloth, was worn contemporaneously with the falling band, and in time was to supplant it. It was introduced into England from France somewhere around 1664. Shortly after this date one finds it mentioned in American invoices. It consisted of short spreading ends, usually caught with a bow of ribbons at the throat (Plate 7, 8) or with full rich ends of lace falling in broad folds over the chest (Plates 9, 10, 11, 12).

Until 1660 to 1665 the cuffs were turned back over the sleeves of the doublet. From then on they were composed of full ruffles of linen or lace.

° Sir Nathaniel Bacon, engraved in 1632—

probably by Thomas Cross.

° Note: There is a confusion between Nathaniel Bacon, the author and Puritan, and Sir Nathaniel Bacon, the painter who apparently dropped his title. Sir Nathaniel Bacon died before the date of this engraving. Cross did the frontispiece for [author] Nathaniel Bacon's "St. Anasthasius," printed in 1644.

HAIR, BEARDS.—At the beginning of this period, 1620, a beard in some form was worn by most men (Fig. 9 A B etc.) Page 71. During the time of Charles I the pointed chin beard and mustache, both carefully trimmed, were universal (Fig. 11 B) Page 72. See also a portrait engraving of Sir Nathaniel Bacon, probably the grandfather of Nathaniel Bacon of "Bacon's Rebellion," on Page 81. After 1660 only the small mustache was worn. With the advent of the great periwigs, however, the mustache and beard went out of fashion and every man was smooth-shaven.

The Cavaliers wore their hair long, and the tendency was toward ever-lengthening locks (Fig. 10 B. Fig. 11 B), until finally they fell down the back and over the shoulders. The hair was either parted in the middle and brushed back on either side of the forehead, or bangs were worn. This was also the day of the love-lock, and some men wore a lock of hair on either side of the face and tied at the end with a bow of ribbon (Fig. 13 A). The period of natural hair was soon to end, and great wigs worn over the shaven head were to be the fashion.

The wig as an important and indispensable part of a fashionable attire worn by men appeared first in France during the reign of Louis XIV. At that time it was known as the periwig, and was richly curled and formal in its makeup. It is now generally accepted that it came into fashion about the year 1660. In spite of the absurdity of this extraordinary fashion, where a man shaved off his own hair in order to wear a wig of false hair that was heavy, expensive, and difficult to keep in order, the style spread rapidly over western Europe. During the opening years of the Restoration, it was worn in England. From England it almost immediately came into fashion in the colonies.

James II of England c 1660.
From the portrait by Nicolas de Largillière.

The periwig, however, was not introduced into England by royal favor. In fact, Charles II seems to have been opposed to it at first. It is not until 1663, according to Mr. Pepys, that the king, following the lead of his courtiers, conformed to the new style. In the State Library at Hartford, Connecticut, is a painting by "Reilly" of Charles II, whose head is adorned by a periwig of black hair falling over his shoulders in luxuriant curls. Many loyal followers in the colonies conformed to the fashion endorsed by the king. (Plates 8, 10).

When the great periwigs came into fashion, hair powder with which to sprinkle them came more and more into general use. The powder used was costly, increased the untidiness of wig-wearing, and added to the weight of these monstrous periwigs. Often as much as two pounds was used at a time. The early form of the periwig (Fig. 20 A) was introduced a little after 1660. At this time it was parted in the center and brushed out smoothly over the sides of the head, and hung over the shoulders in a free, naturalistic wave or in curls. By 1670 the periwig had assumed large proportions (Plate 10. Fig. 20 B) and had become more and more artificial in appearance. It consisted of an arrangement of formal curls that hung down over the breast and back.

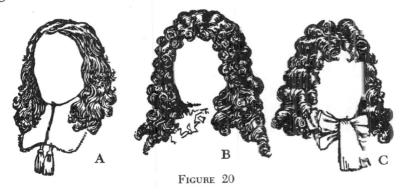

FIGURE 20

In the colonies the demand for wigs steadily increased, and by 1715 wig-wearing was common. In a subsequent chapter the periwig, as it appeared then and later, will be discussed at length.

ACCESSORIES.—Canes of convenient walking length were generally carried. At times they were provided with an ornamental head (Plates 10, 12), or simply with a loop of ribbons or a tassel cord. Gloves were also extensively worn, and they can be found in many portraits of the time (Plate 1 B,) The gloves of these early years were of various materials, "cordevant, buckskin, shammy, sattin, Irish lamb and glazed lamb's wool." The more expensive gloves were richly made, being provided with deep gauntlet cuffs, that were often embroidered as well as edged with a fringe. After the middle of the century, however, the gauntlet cuffs, while long, were not so stiffened, nor do they appear to have been so richly embroidered.

Snuff-boxes of metal, horn, wood, or porcelain were carried. Often they were handsomely decorated.

The sword was the long, rapier-like blade, with an ornamental hilt, which was worn suspended either from a belt around the waist, provided with hangers (Fig. 6 F G) Page 66, or from a shoulder-strap. This was either a simple leather strap, buckled over the front of the body, or a wide and richly decorated band, once known as a "baldric." See the portrait of Sir George Downing, Plate 10. The dagger was no longer generally worn.

Handkerchiefs of rich materials, silk or linen edged with lace or with a gold edging, were carried as part of the effect of the costume. Cotton handkerchiefs were soon to be used everyday.

IV. CAVALIER DRESS: WOMEN
1620–1675

Women's dress followed the same general tendency exhibited in men's attire. After 1625, dress gradually lost much of its severe and exaggerated outline and tended increasingly toward an easier fitting and more beautiful style. Of course, the old styles lasted for some time, especially among the older women, those of simple tastes, and those who could not afford the latest fashions from England.

The farthingale, after being much reduced in size, was the first of the old fashions to be discarded. Bit by bit the bodice lost its stiff-boned, long-waisted character. Finally, the ruff, the whisk, and the wired out lace collar gave way to the lace or linen collar that fell over the shoulders.

The years from 1620 to 1630 were transitional years and therefore difficult for the study of clothing. Unfortunately, during those years little contemporary American portraiture of women from which to draw a knowledge of their dress is available. But, as everything tends to show the close relation existing in fashion between England and the colonies, many deductions may be made from material obtained from English sources. As the planters were mainly Cavaliers, they had none of the severe outlook upon life and dress so often associated with New England. As a matter of fact, theirs was a natural flair for rich clothing, with the result that very little effort, if any, was directed toward its curtailment either in richness or extravagance. Indeed, many letters and diaries have been preserved, leaving no doubt that women gave a great deal of thought and attention to dress. They soon gave up the pioneer simplicity that went with the early years of home and plantation building, and followed the latest modes from London.

In Charleston and Annapolis, as in all the large towns, there was great rivalry in rich and fashionable dressing. The plantations, on the contrary, were widely separated and often isolated. Consequently, the women did not see each other for days at a time. Thus, rivalry in dress was not an everyday occurrence but reserved for special occasions. The parish church, the center of social life at that time, seems to have afforded this opportunity. Here the planters and their wives came from great distances to attend the Sunday services; here was the moment so eagerly awaited—to display their latest acquisition. Fairs, tobacco markets, the racetrack, weddings, and holiday celebrations were other occasions for parading their most fashionable attires. The incongruity of rich clothes imported from England to be worn in the crude surroundings of the early settlements seemed in no way to have bothered them. By the survival of lists sent to London, ordering the latest fashions, it is known that their gowns were as handsomely made and from as fine materials as those worn by the women of England.

BODICE.—The low-cut, long-waisted bodice finished with tabs around the waist, the *décolletage* edged with an upstanding collar of linen or lace, was to persist, especially among the wives of the rich planters, during the years 1620–1630 (Fig. 21 A). The sleeves were full and tied around the elbow with a ribbon knot. Linen cuffs, plain or edged with lace, were turned back from the wrists. Occasionally, one finds a more unusual bodice shaped very much like the doublet of the men. It was worn until about 1635 (Fig. 21 B), was cut to a sloping waistline, coming to a point in front. The tabs forming the skirt of the bodice were similar to those worn by the men. Shoulder wings were attached to the armholes, and from under these wings appeared the full paned sleeves coming to a close band at the wrist. Over the wrist, turned back linen cuffs were worn. At the neck was the falling ruff.

FIGURE 21

By 1630 or 1635 the stiff-boned bodice gave way to a low-neck, high-waisted bodice of much easier fit. From the high waistline depended small tabs, forming the skirt. They extended around the waist and centered in a round tab in front (Fig. 22 B). The *décolletage* was either square, round, or V-shaped. The sleeves might be very full and paned and made into a puff above and below the elbow by a narrow ribbon tied with a bow or a rosette (Fig. 22 A). A later fashion, *circa* 1635, was a full puffed sleeve of about elbow length that was no longer paned but edged with lace (Fig. 22 B). Around the waist a ribbon sash was secured by a bowknot tied at the front or a little to one side.

By 1645 a bodice that fitted fairly close, either ending in a straight waistline or descending to a point in front, again became popular (Fig. 22 C). It followed the fashion by being high waisted. Pending from the waistline, one finds the tabs. The sleeves, while full, were not nearly so voluminous as they were originally and did not extend much below the elbow.

FIGURE 22

After 1660 the tabs forming the short skirt to the bodice are seldom found. The bodice again assumed its long-waisted, tightly laced form (Fig. 23 A), usually descending to quite a long point in the front and rounded at the back (Fig. 23 B). The neck and shoulders were left bare (Fig. 22 A B). Above the bodice the line of the *décolletage* was softened by an edging of the fine chemise (Fig. 23 A B). The bodice might be laced down the back, the slight opening in the front being then brought together with jeweled clasps or with bow-knots of ribbon (Fig. 23 B). If the opening was down the front of the bodice, it was brought together and decorated down the front with ribbon knots (Fig. 23 A). The bodice sleeve was usually of elbow length, quite full, and looped or gathered with a clasp on the upper side. From under it to a little below the elbow was the full sleeve of the fine linen chemise (Fig. 23 E). The sleeve could also be slashed along the outer seam and brought together with lacings (Fig. 23 A). One finds sleeves of very full dimensions made into two puffs by tying ribbons around the arm above the elbow and half-way between the elbow and the shoulder (Fig. 23 C).

FIGURE 23

SKIRT.—Gradually the farthingale disappeared and in its place there came an extremely full skirt, hanging quite free from under the bodice and reaching to the ground (Fig. 22 A B). Until the middle of the century, many skirts were cut in an inverted V in the front, disclosing the petticoat (Fig. 22 C). After the middle of the century the skirt was more frequently worn closed. Instead of being worn in the previous free loose manner, it was gathered into small pleats over the hips where it met the waistline of the bodice (Fig. 23 A B). It seemed to have been quite common to gather up the skirt on the left side, allowing it to hang diagonally across the body in a studied, careless manner (Fig. 23 B). The inverted V-shaped skirt never quite went out of favor. It was often worn looped up over the hips, and fastened in the back, thus revealing the petticoat all the way round (Fig. 23 C).

GOWN.—As has been seen, the farthingale was the first garment of the old style to go. This left a skirt cut very full to accommodate the farthingale. To make use of this excess material, the skirt was fashioned into a full, loose gown fitting over the shoulders. It was open all the way down the front and confined at the waist with a ribbon. The opening in front exposed the long pointed stomacher and the straight tabs of the boned bodice, as well as the decorated skirt of a contrasting color (Fig. 22 A).

LINEN.—The standing, wired-out lace collar (Fig. 21 A. Fig. 22 A), the ruff (Fig. 7 B) Page 67, and the falling ruff (Fig. 21 B) remained in fashion for some time, but gradually went out of favor in the forties. Their place was taken by a lace collar or falling band, worn over the shoulders (Fig. 22 B C E). It was often edged with rich point lace or decorated with embroidery. The falling band and lace collar were worn in many different ways. Where it was fastened to the edge of the *décolletage*, it fell over the shoulders (Fig. 22 B C). Where it encircled the neck, it fell over the shoulders and hung down in front in two points over the breast (Fig. 22 E). In the portrait of Mrs. John Freake (Plate 13) there is not only the collar, but a lace tippet under it.

A small shawl, or kerchief, commonly made of linen or some soft material, was often worn around the neck and over the shoulders. It was folded in such a manner that the two ends fell over the breast in front (Fig. 23 D).

After the middle of the century the more fashionably dressed ladies bared their shoulders more and more, edging the horizontal *décolletage* with small collars of lace. After 1665 to 1670 the lace and linen collars gradually went out of style, and one finds the low-cut bodice merely edged with the softening line of the fine chemise (Fig. 23 A B).

When sleeves were long, the cuffs of linen to match the collar were turned back from the wrist in a funnel shape (Fig. 21 A B), but as the sleeves shortened to elbow length the funnel-shaped cuffs were discarded. Descending from under the sleeve of the bodice was the full sleeve of the fine linen chemise (Fig. 22 B C. Fig. 23 A, etc.).

HAIR.—Early in the period the hair was brought back from the front and sides of the head and dressed in a high roll (Fig. 21 A. Fig. 22 A). Soon, however, the new manner of dressing the hair was introduced from London, the hair being pulled back tight over the top of the head and confined in a small coil at the back. At the sides the hair was bunched out in curls that framed the face. A bang or fringe of straight hair hung down over the forehead (Fig. 22 B C). This close fringe gave way to a fashion of small separate curls edging the brow and the cheeks and gradually merging into the cluster of curls hanging on either side of the face (Fig. 23 A). Pearls or ribbons could be intertwined and dressed into the coil at the back of the head. In time the curls along the brow were dispensed with and the hair was brushed straight back (Fig. 22 E). At the same time the curls at the side, carried out in clusters, and supported by wires are seen (Fig. 23 B).

HEAD-COVERINGS.—For out-of-door wear, hoods and veils were generally worn. Unless the weather was severe, however, the women were apt to go bareheaded. The most common hood seems to have been in the form of a scarf or kerchief folded and placed over the head and tied loosely under the chin (Plate 13. Fig. 22 D). Hoods were more often worn, and were of greater variety in New England and the central colonies, where the winters were more severe, than in the southern colonies. The portrait of Mrs. Wensley, which was probably painted earlier, shows a 'cornet' under the hood (Plate 14).

CLOAKS.—Cloaks that hung over the shoulders and enveloped the figure were much worn. They were usually lined with fur or some warm material, and probably cut on the same general lines as the "cloak of raccoon skins" given to Captain John Smith by King Powhatan.

SHOES AND HOSE.—Shoes, hidden by the skirts, followed the same general shape as those worn by the men. They could be protected by clogs and pattens for out-of-door wear. The hose were woven and varied considerably in color, the most popular being "white, scarlet or black."

ACCESSORIES.—There was a great deal of gay and elaborate finery accompanying the dress of the time. Jewelry in the form of clasps, pins, pearl earrings, and necklaces was much used. Strings of pearls and beads were wound in the hair. With the shortening of the sleeves, long gloves reaching to the elbow came into fashion (Fig. 22 c). These were the fashionable gloves, and were made to fit tight to the arms. They were, as a rule, imported. Gloves of local manufacture were made of yarn, buckskin, or sheepskin. Those who could not afford gloves wore mittens.

The wearing of "gum patches" on the face was exceedingly fashionable. The ladies in the South, particularly, indulged in this form of adornment.

Muffs were generally carried and often suspended from a ribbon worn around the neck.

Fans made of plumes and feathers, with richly ornamented handles, were either carried in the hand or attached to a girdle at the waist.

Aprons worn over the skirt, and made of "muslin, silk, serge and blue duffel," formed part of the dress for special occasions as well as for everyday wear.

St. John's Church, Hampton, Virginia, 1660-67.

The Countrey wee now call Virginia beginneth at Cape Henry distant
from Roanoack 60 miles, where was Sr Walter Raleigh's plantation
and because the people differ very little from them of Powhatan in any
thing, I have inserted those figures in this place because of the conveniency

OULD

VIR GI NIA

Mountaynes forest
Waldens Oake
Masons bushe   LD: Lenox rock
Mangoack Richmonds   steps   Ramushonoq
Cawwuock   Howards Mountaynes   L: Salvage Rocke
Pananaioc   Stuards reach   Bedfords valley   Ohanoack   Beaushamps playne
Nusioc   Secota   Woratuck flu: Chawanok flu:
Anadates chase   Alice
Setuoc   Metoccum   Catoking   Smith
Pue chace Ile   field
Mecopen   Moraton   Segars grove
Cotan   Cecils Harbor   Mascoming   Chisapeack
Tamasqueack   Chepanu
Abigails Ile   Paquinip   Heriots Ile   Townsrows end
feare   Laya flu   Pasquenock   Ildmaids roade
Salvage Ile   Pomeiock   P. Corbett   P Bacon   C Henry
Gordens Ile   P. Box   Dasamonpoock   Roanot   P Gonne
Abbots Ile   P. Vaughan   Trundells Ile
Greenevills rode   Pox Ile   Crester inlet
Hertfords Ile
Bermidas

Accordamus

A Scale of 10 Leaues.
1 2 3 4 5 6 7 8 9 10

Vincere et Viuere

Graven and extracted out of ye generall history of Virginia, New England, and Somer Iles, by Robert Vaughan.

CHAPTER III

The New England Background

1620-1675

Henry C. Pitz

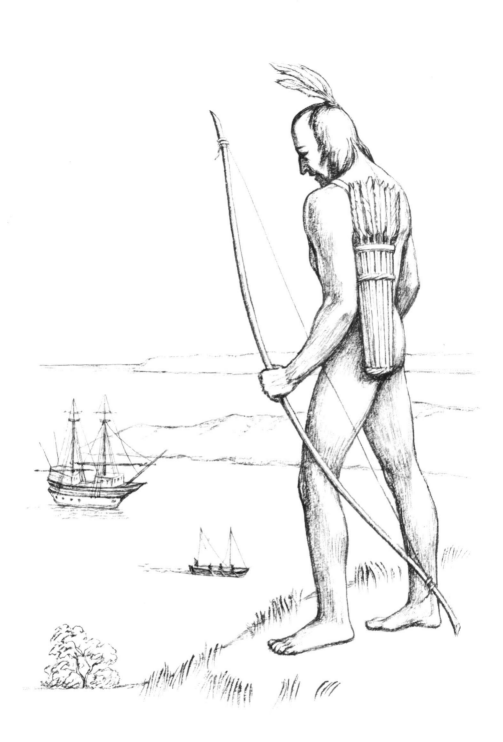

CHAPTER III

The New England Background
1620-1675

The early seventeenth century New England settlers offer an interesting contrast to the colonizers of Virginia. In the main, they were of the same English stock and came from the same walks of life. However, there were religious differences, with corresponding divergences in their outlook upon life and in their manner of living. These differences, together with those of climate and geography, were sufficient to create two distinct cultures. The northern colonies were more compact, versatile, and democratic. Less emphasis was put on agriculture and the pursuit of the aristocratic way of life than in Virginia.

The first company to build a settlement at New Plymouth in 1620, were Separatists, or Pilgrims, who, in conflict with the Established Church of England, had suffered persecution and hardships. Members of one congregation had fled to Holland and had lived there for twelve years practicing their austere faith. Of the one hundred and two who finally made the voyage in the Mayflower to Plymouth, thirty-five were of this body, and the remainder were from London. They were poor folk, too poor to outfit an expedition to America without assistance, and therefore were forced to mortgage themselves to a group of London merchants for a term of seven years. For the most part they were artisans and laborers, small farmers and petty tradesmen. With few exceptions, the company were people of little formal education. Nevertheless, they were well equipped in many ways to cope with the strange conditions of their new home. They were full of fierce energy, determined and unyielding. Men and women alike were accustomed to grinding toil and rough living. There was nothing either in their religion or in their experience to lead them to expect ease and untroubled times in this world. In fact, their interpretation of the Bible encouraged them to welcome trials and hardships as tests of their faith. They were a unit in thought and purpose. This fact alone gave them tremendous advantage over the oddly assorted Jamestown company. They set themselves to the tasks of building, clearing, and planting, casting no backward glances at the England they had left. They earnestly went about the business of working out their destiny in the New World. In all things they saw the hand of God and never doubted that they were carrying out His will.

The Pilgrims' leaders gave considerable thought to the question of clothes. Their revolt against all excess and worldly show found one of its principal expressions in dress. Their garments conformed in general shape to the prevailing fashions, but they stripped or attempted to strip them of all ornament. Braid, ribbons, laces, large decorated buttons, all things suggesting the loose-living gallants of the royal court, were inveighed against. They eschewed handsome materials—silks, satins, velvets—in favor of broadcloths and fustian.

These Pilgrims had emigrated at a time when European fashions were rapidly changing. It was a period of transition which witnessed the lengthening and loosening of the doublet, the passing of trunk hose and the ruff, and the advent of the falling collar (page 70 *et seq.*). Pinched for money as they were, it is probable many of them landed on these shores dressed in the doublet and trunk hose of the older fashion. Moreover, during the first ten years of the settlement, communication with England was so rare that little in the way of new fashions would have been brought to Plymouth. Then, too, the early years were filled with such struggle and adversity that makeshift garments of hide and fur must have been worn much of the time. The thirty-five Pilgrims from Holland, however, undoubtedly showed some hint of the broadness and greater fullness of the Dutch manner in their garb.

The dress of the women (page 84 *et seq.*) showed the same tendency; a modification of the stiff and rigid lines of the previous generation. For the women there was a greater looseness and freedom in the treatment of the skirt and bodice. Heavy cloaks and hoods were an important part of the dress of the Pilgrim women, but gloves seem to have been considered an extravagance. These first Pilgrims came with an ample supply of simple clothing, much better equipped in that respect than in the matter of tools and household gear.

They suffered during the first year of the settlement, enduring the ice and snow and biting cold of the New England winter. Weakened by the lack of food, disease and exposure to the harsh winter made them lose almost half their number. They built a log meeting house on a hill, a stout, fortresslike structure. It was used for both prayer and a haven in time of danger. Around it were clustered their little cabins and sparse fields of Indian maize. The dark forest pressed closely on three sides. A Dutch traveler of the time gives this picture of their life:

> "Upon the hill they have a large square house, with a flat roof made of thick-sawn planks, stayed with oak beams, upon the top of which they have six cannons, which shoot iron balls of four or five pounds, and command the surrounding country.

*The lower part they use for a church, where they preach on
Sundays and the usual holidays. They assemble by beat of drum,
each with his musket, or firelock, in front of the captain's door;
they have their cloaks on, and place themselves in order, three
abreast, and are led by a sergeant without beat of drum. Behind
comes the governor in a long robe, beside him on the right hand
comes the preacher with his cloak on, and on the left hand the
captain with his side arms and cloak on, and a small cane in
his hands; and so they march in good order, and each sets his
arms down near him."*

During the early years the lonely settlement was always like a small
armed camp. It hugged the shore, and the unexplored wilderness hemmed
it in. All their neighbors were Indians. The nearest Europeans were those
with the Dutch trading posts along the Hudson, and their nearest English
neighbors had settled on the banks of the James. Yet, the Pilgrim colony
grew and prospered in a modest way. New colonists came out; the settlement spread beyond the confines of the town and into the surrounding
country. The colonists opened a profitable trade with the Indians and
took to fishing. However, the Pilgrim colony never became a factor greatly
influencing the development of New England. It lacked material wealth,
and its numbers were too few. In 1630 their total was 250 persons, and
near the end of the century, they numbered nine thousand Soon they
were absorbed into the larger Massachusetts Bay Colony and lost their
identity. Nevertheless, their humble and simple history is of tremendous
importance in the development of America for they were the first Englishmen to maintain a community without aid and by their own exertion in
the North American wilderness.

Ten years after the Pilgrim landing, a much more important migration began to spread along the shores of the bay to the north. It was
the beginning of the real Puritan exodus from England that was to quickly
overshadow the Plymouth settlements and to shape the destiny of New
England. The newcomers were akin to the Plymouth people in many
ways. They possessed the same tendencies toward more primitive forms
of worship, toward simplicity of life, and plainness of dress. They looked
upon the business of living as a somewhat grim and difficult thing. They
were not, as were the Pilgrims, or Separatists, in open revolt against
the Church of England, but reformers inside its ranks who wanted to
purify the church from within. Yet these religious distinctions between
these groups, however large they may have loomed in England or in the
earliest years of the colony, quickly lost their importance under the new
conditions in America. In practice, at least, the theological distinction
between Puritan and Pilgrim, Nonconformist and Separatist, gradually
ceased to exist.

A distinction of greater importance was the difference in class and
culture. There was a great deal of wealth among the Puritans. They were

largely of what was considered the English middle class, landowners, merchants, scholars, yeomen, and tenant farmers. Some were landed gentry, preachers, and professional men. A high proportion of these men had intellect and learning.

They came well equipped, bringing with them stores of all kinds for their own use and for trade with the Indians—tools and farming implements, livestock, and seed. The wealthier ones brought with them servants, laborers, and household gear, and they felt well prepared to set up their establishments in the New World. It was their plan to transfer their estate almost bodily to Massachusetts and to erect in New England a social order corresponding to the one they had left behind.

Their wealth and rank were reflected in their dress. There was less difference between their dress and that of the average Englishman than is generally supposed. It was by no means always possible to tell the majority of Puritans by their attire. In the main, it was sober and restrained. However, the garments of many people of entirely different religious persuasions were similar. Puritan preachers inveighed against the extravagance of fashion and exhorted the flock to abandon the use of lavish and costly materials. The church published lists of prohibited garments and the ruling body enacted sumptuary laws that attempted to regulate attire in accordance with station and wealth. The populace was surrounded by prohibitions and restrictions at every step of their daily life—more than it was humanly possible to observe. Certainly, a combination of vanity and natural resentment against this restraint caused many to come into conflict with the zealous preachers and their adherents, who attempted to fasten upon New England society their own narrow and rigid convictions.

The sermons of the time are filled with tirades and invectives against those who "arrayed themselves in fine raiment." The court records are crowded with the names of persons summoned for violation of the laws restricting dress. The great numbers of people fined or reprimanded, and the great difficulty and often the impossibility of enforcing the sumptuary orders, leads one to believe that the law was little respected.

It is a fact of supreme importance that only about one-fifth of the population of early Massachusetts had membership in the Puritan church. Because church membership was the qualification for suffrage, this minority controlled the destiny of the colony. In turn this comparatively small number of church members and voters was dominated by its preachers and leaders, a group of vigorous minded and aggressive zealots. It is from the ranks of these zealots that the characteristics have been taken which make up the picture of the stern Puritan as he is usually conceived (Plate 15). This iron-lipped, solemn figure, sturdy, dignified and unbending, in stiff broad-brimmed hat, black or sullen-colored doublet and breeches, coarse stockings and heavy square-toed shoes, was a real one. He was a type that appeared early on the New England scene, and who played an important role in its history. Unfortunately, for strict historical accuracy, he has come to stand for the typical Puritan. Perhaps this image persists because his extreme restraint offers such an obvious contrast to the ringleted and beribboned courtier, or possibly because of the opportunity he offers for caricature. Whatever the reason, this image has been reinforced through the years by pictures and the written word. It is difficult to remember that his numbers were few; that he was an extreme and eccentric type; that even in the New England of the seventeenth century he was not a common figure.

Confusion regarding seventeenth-century New England dress emanates from two sources: The Pilgrims and Puritans are lumped together, even though in dress, as in some other facets of their lives, they were two distinct and sometimes quite dissimilar groups. (Some costumes for plays and historic pageants go so far as to lump together the Quakers, Pilgrims and Puritans . . . a remarkable feat!) Possibly the most immediate source for our present-day distorted view of seventeenth-century New England is our present-day tendency to see that society as populated only by Puritans, and the most fanatical strand of Puritans at that.

Although an oversimplification, New England society of the period may be divided into four basic groupings:

The controlling body consisted of ecclesiastics, allied with a small, but powerful, Puritan merchant class. It is this group which, by law, decrees, and preaching, attempted to set the general tone of ethics and morals in the colony, including its dress In the main, they did not prescribe in specific terms the dress that should be worn, but what they deemed unseemly. The dress of the clergy tended to be severe, and conforms to our present day image of "Puritan dress." But the Puritan church-goers did not generally conform to the manner of dress of their spiritual leaders.

The second group consisted of merchants and merchant adventurers. As time progressed, they came to dominate New England trade. These men may have been Puritans, or they may have belonged to other Protestant sects. But their dress was, by and large, that of the Virginia colony and the high fashions of England and not the severe garb of the' Puritan zealot.

The third stratum of seventeenth-century New England society was made up of yeomen, tenant farmers, freemen, servants, sailors; what was later called the "Third Estate." Their clothing was similar to that worn by their counterparts in the mother country, except for adaptations caused by the difference in climate and materials available. (See page 55).

The fourth group consisted of African slaves, whose clothing, at first, was any kind of "hand-me-down" available (See page 52).

New England society was, therefore, far from monolithic, and its dress cannot be restricted to a small segment, or described in the usual oversimplified terms. It was also a fluid society in which the various groups sought allies in order to gain dominance. When the Puritan zealots began to lose control, they resorted to witch hunts in order to reassert their power. The witch hunt served as a warning to the rising merchant class. The fact that many of the victims were innocent bystanders or belonged to the "third estate" is not surprising. The bully does not always tackle his most powerful opponent but selects the weaker element, which he can destroy with impunity in the hope that others will then bow to his demands.

The divisions within and dynamics of early New England society, are generally ignored in "costume" histories and in school textbooks. Plays and films also invariably perpetuate the image of the drabness of all seventeenth-century New Englanders, and theatre costume designers follow suit. By such means, the essential character of that period is totally distorted. Dress—which should epitomize a historical epoch—becomes the instrument for giving visual expression to these distortions. In the introduction to this book, there was reference to the popular image (preconception) as one of the factors which tends to obscure source material. The clothing of seventeenth century New England is a perfect case in point.*

The great bulk of the New England population reflected their social rank and their wealth quite accurately in their dress. It was a system ingrained in the European scheme of things; and the newcomers of that time, Puritans and well-to-do merchants alike, did their utmost to continue it in America. The dress of these early colonists was not essentially different from that of the Virginians described in the preceding chapter. It is not essentially different from English dress of the same time. In fact, the dress of the Bay Colonists always followed prevailing modes, rejecting the most exaggerated and fantastic forms, eliminating excrescences and obtruding decoration, and avoiding the blatant and the conspicuous. In short, it was and is exactly the kind of restraint exercised by sober persons of any time or place.

The arrivals of the 1630's came well stocked with clothes current in England. These garments were cut in the fashion that had been slowly evolving since the latter years of the reign of James I and were now well established (page 70 *et seq.*). Trunk hose, in the main, had been replaced by full, knee-length breeches; the ruff was still worn by the older generation. The doublet was loose and longer. The wide sombrero-like hat was still worn and was to be popular until almost the middle of the century. The footgear was still square-toed shoes tied with ribbons, or boots of varying lengths and widths, often turned down in bell-like flaps.

Dress worn by women (page 84 *et seq.*) bore many points of resemblance to that worn by men. The bodices were becoming lower in the neck and higher at the waist, with short tabs like the doublet. Generally,

---

* In later volumes we may deal with the special problems of the designer of the theatre costume. Suffice it to say at this point that the first loyalty of the designer must be to the author's intent, and only then to historical accuracy. This does not mean that the costume designer must *per se* ignore the facts. Knowing them well, within this framework, costumes can still be freely conceived, giving the designer full range for his creative imagination. Historical truth need not become an artistic strait jacket.

the changes were in the direction of less rigidity. The sleeves were looser and often gathered in a single puff. The farthingale had vanished, and the skirt was gathered full at the hips and allowed to hang freely to the ground. The broad, falling collar had replaced the whisk and ruff, except among the more conservative of the older generation. Veils and hoods were worn outdoors, or a broad-brimmed hat similar to that worn by the men.

This migration of the thirties was the beginning of a Puritan colonization that was almost without interruption for a hundred years. The Bay Colony grew rapidly in numbers and wealth and spread over its borders into the surrounding territory of Rhode Island, Connecticut, New Hampshire, and Maine. With this growth came a change in the economic life of the colony.

The wealthy Puritans had hoped to establish a colony of farms, of large landed estates owned by themselves, and small freeholds to be distributed among the yeoman class. There were, however, certain factors outside their calculations. The geography and climate of New England conspired against a purely agricultural colony. The winters were long and relentless. It was difficult to wrest a living from the stony and grudging soil. The rivers were short, difficult to navigate, and did not provide easy penetration into the interior, as did the rivers of the South. Therefore, the early settlements stayed close to the coast. Here, with many bays and harbors offering suitable shelter, with great fishing banks close at hand, and a seemingly inexhaustible forest to furnish ship timber, it is not surprising the early New Englander was drawn to the sea, to fishing and to trade.

He was drawn not only to the sea but into a variety of pursuits promising gain and development. He built rude sawmills at the fall line of navigable streams to fashion timbers for the shipyards and planks and beams for the trim new houses, that were replacing the old log dwellings. Higher up the rivers, or on the banks of their swift tributaries, were erected mills for grinding maize and wheat, tanneries and, later, mills for fulling the homespun cloth. Sea-water was evaporated for salt. The New Englanders dug in the swamps and lowlands for bog iron. These activities may seem slight and unimportant in the light of present-day industrial development; but they were the first faint beginnings of New England industry and trade, the growth of which was to affect so tremendously the future life and history of these colonies.

These small industries and the first tentative shipping ventures were, through the middle years of the century, already helping to shape the social and political character of New England. They were developing a practical-minded, adaptable, self-reliant man of many trades, who could competently solve the problems constantly occurring.

In this colony, geography and climate had made the development of large plantations with their attendant landed aristocracy impractical, encouraging instead, small holdings, and the yeoman farmer. The diversification of trade and industry, while it permitted the growth of a small wealthy merchant class, depended for its success upon a large body of independent, skilled artisans, and of intelligent, capable, midde-class clerks and tradesmen. African slaves were available in almost unlimited numbers but were only used to perform menial tasks. Indentured white servants were in demand, but in a land so lavish in opportunities many became freemen after the expiration of their terms. Since this group of free laborers was healthy, ambitious, and free from poverty, it gradually won the balance of power, holding in check the usurpations of the clergy and the wealthy.

It made for a much more democratic society than that forming in the South. Although it was by no means true that all freemen were political equals, the barriers between the classes were passable, and early New England society never became as set and clearly defined as did that of the South.

Then, too, any aristocratic tendencies in the social fabric were checked by the New England system of land ownership. Each community was virtually self-governing, the land passing into the hands of the town corporation, and from it into the possession of the individuals composing the community. Usually these individual allotments were small, and there were always certain lands held for the common use.

By the last quarter of the seventeenth century, New England was dotted with hundreds of these self-governing and self-supporting communities. The village clustered around the steepled church which faced the trim village green. About the green were spaced in ample grounds the homes of the more prosperous citizens; a tavern with its stable, sheds, and painted sign; a square, log or boarded schoolhouse; and, perhaps, the platform and framework of the town pillory. Upon either side of the highroad leading away from the green were other frame houses, cottages, and huts, shaded by some of the forest trees left standing, or by young English elms or willows brought as seedlings from the home country. Even in 1675 New England villages had an air of quiet spaciousness and dignity.

The log homes of the earlier days were fast disappearing. Lumber was abundant, and sawmills had become fairly numerous. Thus, the new homes were built of sawn planks or clapboards. Most of these homes were of the cottage type, with one story, an attic, and a broad sweeping roof covering the kitchen and sheds in the rear. Often the house was linked to the barn. The roofs were frequently thatched, particularly in communities close to the sea, where the salt marshes afforded a liberal supply of suitable reeds. The more pretentious houses were of two stories, with the second story projecting over the front of the first with turned pendant ornaments at the corners. These New England builders copied, as best they could, the houses of England as they remembered them. Behind the houses were the kitchen gardens, the orchards, the cleared fields bounded by low stone walls, the meadows and grazing land, and the strips of virgin forest, whose giant pines were fringed with a lighter growth of birch and dogwood.

Within, the houses were dark. Although some glass was in use, oil paper was the most common way of keeping out the elements. In the evenings handmade candles and the flickering log fire in the fireplace gave but a dim yellow light. Earthen floors were still common, although the better houses had floors of heavy sawn planks, often carefully sanded. The walls were of boards, or of clay mixed with chopped straw. Against these rough, peasant textures was placed the limited furniture of the home—the chests, cupboards, and heavy chairs. Some of these pieces were brought from England. In fact, many of the wealthier immigrants had brought all of their household goods. Their furniture, of course, was in the rectangular, heavily underbraced style current in the England of James I and Charles I. Most of the somewhat scanty supply of furniture in New England, however, was homemade. Her joiners and cabinetmakers were not without skill and taste, and they succeeded in copying the imported pieces in a rougher and ruder form that often had a striking character and flavor of its own. There were few gracious lines in these early pieces, but they reflected the temperament of New England of the seventeenth century. They were as sturdy as the persons who used them.

In addition to the imported furniture and the work of the local cabinetmakers were the things fashioned by the farmer himself. He made stools, benches, and rude tables. Because metal was scarce, most of the articles for household use were contrived from materials at hand. Plows, shovels, rakes, and almost all farm implements were of wood Churns, trays, firkins, tubs, and troughs were made of the same material. Pewter was not common. There was no glassware, and pottery was rare. Cups and bowls were made of gourds. Shells were used for spoons or dippers, and the trenchers, tankards, flagons, and basins were wooden. During the long winter evenings, the men of the household whittled and wrought, exercising considerable ingenuity in the working of native materials into shapes of use and, often, of beauty.

As in the case of the furniture, the stores of clothing brought over by the new arrivals and that imported from the London merchants were insufficient to supply the needs of the colony. Clothing had to be supplemented by native products. Almost from the first, homespun materials were made. In some of the first fields to be cleared of forests and rocks, flax was grown. By the latter half of the century almost every farm had its blue-flowered flax patch. The gathering and preparation of the flax were difficult and tedious. Before it was ready to be spun into thread, over twenty different operations were necessary, all requiring considerable skill and experience. The greatest dexterity was needed in the spinning of the yarn into thread on the small flax-wheel. Finally came the bleaching, washing, and weaving. The home-woven linen of the time was a sturdy, closely woven material, so resistant to hard wear that linen covers, testers, and even shirts and bands were willed as heirlooms down through several generations.

Woolen materials began to be made almost as early as linen. In 1643 a contemporary writer says: "They are making linens, fustians, dimities, and look immediately to woolens from their own sheep." Sheep were brought over in many of the early boats, and in 1644 there were estimated to be three thousand in the colony. Their numbers grew rapidly after that date, for sheep-raising was encouraged by special legislation. The spinning and weaving of the wool were stimulated by giving prizes and bounties, and by the formation of classes and schools. Perhaps these artificial means were not required, for the great necessity for warm materials and the growing prosperity of the colony were enough to insure the development of the industry. So rapidly did it grow, indeed, that by 1675 New England was actually exporting wool to France and Spain.

The homespuns were at first heavy and coarse and of uneven texture. But a generation of weaving developed the skill and perfected the process. Soon, much of the broadcloth manufactured by the women in their homes was of such excellent quality that it could be favorably compared with English imports.

For dyes they used the flowers, roots, and barks of the countryside and other materials at hand. Very few dyes were imported, except indigo for blue, which began to be used in quantity during the late years of the century. Brown was easily obtained from the bark of the red oak, hickory, and maple trees, or from walnut hulls. A very deep shade of brown was obtained from the low-spreading alder. Yellowroot, barberry root, the petals of St. John's wort, and sassafras gave various shades of yellow. Crimson was obtained by boiling pokeberries with alum; for violets or purples, pokeberries, elderberries, sumacberries, and the petals of the purple iris were used. Indigo mixed with goldenrod blossoms gave a fine green. Fustic and copperas were also used for the yellows. This fine array of hues dispels the idea that dress in New England was altogether a drab and sullen affair. These colors, if not brilliant or gay, were at least warm and cheerful. When one remembers that on the bills of lading scarlet cloaks are constantly mentioned, the Puritan emerges as a more colorful figure than he is usually supposed to be.

The excitements and troubles of the Commonwealth and the Restoration in England scarcely moved him. He accepted in a moderate way the changes in fashion they brought; the extremes he ignored. Thus, the development of his dress from the days of the first landing was an orderly progression without eccentric outward divergencies.

I. DRESS OF THE PILGRIMS: MEN
1620–1630

There were marked distinctions in the dress of the Pilgrims from that of the Puritans. The Pilgrims, with the exception of their leaders, were simple folk, whose ideas went toward plainness and restraint in clothing. Doubtless, at the time of their sailing for America, new innovations were beginning to be seen in the dress of the wealthy circles. But these changes were surely not seen in the clothes of the emigrating Pilgrims who did not allow their thoughts to dwell upon worldly things and who were accustomed to hard work and simple living. As their wardrobe was generally supplied to them by the company of London merchants to whom they had mortgaged themselves, it must have presented considerable conformity and similarity in appearance. As it was selected with a view to meeting the rigors of pioneer life, strength, durability, and stoutness were its chief characteristics.

DOUBLETS.—The doublets, though not quite as shaped, were similar to those worn by the first settlers of Virginia (Fig. 24 A B). They were fairly long-waisted and had a short skirt of tabs. The sleeves were moderately close and were probably fastened to the armholes of the doublets with points. Where the sleeve and doublet met at the point of the shoulder the joint was masked by a jutting piece of material called a wing. The doublet was buttoned down the front and, as a rule, was muted in color.

FIGURE 24

Among the Pilgrims, however, were a number of men who were not of the same deep religious convictions. These came to the New World not to escape religious persecution, but to seek adventure. Miles Standish was one of these persons (Fig. 25). Naturally, the dress of these adventurers was not restrained as that of the Pilgrims. In fact, it too was quite similar to the dress worn by the first settlers of Virginia. Their doublets were long-waisted, buttoned down the front (Fig. 26 A C, or held by clasps (Fig. 26 B). A leather belt was buckled around the waist. Wings (Fig. 26 A B) or the crescent (Fig. 26 C) masked the juncture of the sleeve and doublet. The sleeves, fitting close, were composed of a different material (Fig. 26 A). Sometimes the underseam was left open for several inches up from the wrist. It could then be worn open or be fastened with buttons. The skirt of the doublet could either consist of tabs (Fig. 26 C) or be plain (Fig. 26 A B).

The Pilgrims, as well as the adventurers, were provided with leather jerkins, which could either be worn separately or under the breastplate (Fig. 25). The dress was completed by a sword, bandolier of strong "neats' leather," powder flask, musket, burgonet, and boots.

BREECHES.—The breeches of the Pilgrims were made of strong cloth, canvas, or leather and were generally what we call the knickerbocker type (Fig. 24 A). They were either buttoned or fastened by a small band knotted below the knee. However, some members of the community preferred the full trunk hose so common during the reign of James I (Fig. 24 B), while others might have worn any of the styles worn in Virginia (Chapter II).

FIGURE 25

FIGURE 27

FIGURE 26

CLOAKS.—Great cloaks of three-quarter length (Fig. 24 A) or longer (Fig. 24 B), made out of some warm material and frequently lined with fur, protected the settlers from the New England winters. Skins of animals, bartered from the Indians and made without tailoring, were undoubtedly thrown over the shoulders to serve as mantles.

LINEN.—A simple band tied with cords (Fig. 24 A. Fig. 26 A B), or a pleated ruff (Fig. 24 B. Fig. 26 C), was worn around the neck. At the wrists plain, turned-back linen cuffs were worn (Fig. 24 A. Fig. 26 B).

HEADGEAR.—The Pilgrims wore hats of the broad-brimmed type with high crowns, around which they placed a simple band (Fig. 24 A B). The adventurers, if a group name can be given these independent men, had the sense of *panâche* and adorned their hats with plumes (Fig. 26 A B). For defense they wore burgonets (Fig. 6 C E) or morions (Fig. 6 B D) if they had them.

HAIR.—The hair was worn cropped closely to the head (Fig. 24 A B) or slightly long over the ears (Fig. 26 A).

FOOTGEAR.—The foot covering of the Pilgrims and Puritans was shoes. These shoes were of leather, heavy and sturdy, and of about ankle height. They were fastened over the instep with shoestrings (Fig. 24 A). Heavy woolen stockings covered the feet and legs, and were fastened under the breeches, just above the knee (Fig. 24 A). Boots, of course, were worn by some Pilgrims.and by the other members of the colony. They could be worn with the tops turned down (Fig. 24 B), or they could be pulled high up over the knee and thigh.

ACCESSORIES.—Swords were worn on a belt around the waist (Fig. 24 B. Fig. 25) or were suspended from a baldric. The baldric was worn over the right shoulder to support the sword and scabbard on the left side (Fig. 26 A). The bandolier, powder flask, and gun were usually handy when the men went to work in the fields or ventured far from the settlement. The older men carried canes. Heavy, serviceable gloves of rather crude make were worn for comfort; they were never carried merely for style as in the South.

II. DRESS OF THE PILGRIMS: WOMEN
1620–1630

The little band of one hundred and two Pilgrims, under the leadership of Elder Brewster, landed in Plymouth Harbor in the cold, bleak winter weather of late November of the year 1620. Of this group, by far the greater number were men. Even though the season was late, and winter fast closing in, several weeks were lost before a suitable place for landing and home building could be found. The men went ashore, where they built the crude log huts and cabins, their future homes. Meanwhile the women and children remained aboard the *Mayflower*. Only a short time after the Pilgrims landed in New England, another scene was to be enacted far to the South. In this connection it is interesting to note that in the year 1621 the Virginia Company of London sent from England a number "of respectable young women" to Jamestown, Virginia, to be the wives of the planters. Both the women who came to Virginia looking for husbands, and those accompanying the Pilgrim Fathers as wives and daughters, emanated from about the same class in English society, though they were not of the same religious belief. Thus, in a large sense, one realizes there must have been considerable similarity in the cut and general style of their clothes. However, the garments of the Pilgrim women were far plainer. Probably, too, the Pilgrim women who had spent twelve years or so in Holland leaned a little more toward Dutch styles. It is interesting that the Dutch influence—the short-waisted bodice and full skirt—was also popular at home in England. Falling bands and ruffs were worn by both the Pilgrim and Virginia women, as well as cuffs at the wrists. There is in fact a greater similarity between the dress of the Pilgrims of the 1620-1630 period and their Virginia counterparts of the same period than between these and their Puritan sisters who did not reach these shores in large numbers until many years later.

BODY GARMENTS.—As noted, the Pilgrim women seem to have preferred the short Dutch waistline (Fig. 27 A). Although a dress with a long waistline, the bodice tapering to a point in front, was not uncommon (Fig. 27 B). The bodice was made to fit, but it does not seem to have been much boned or artificially stiffened. There was a closefitting sleeve (Fig. 27 A); there was also a tendency for the sleeve to become fuller from the elbow to where it met the bodice at the shoulder (Fig. 27 B). There seems to be no indication that the farthingale was worn, but skirts were made quite full. The skirt may or may not have been open in the front to show an under-petticoat.

LINEN.—Ruffs of fairly large dimensions encircled the neck (Fig. 27 A). In place of the ruff, a broad falling collar of linen could have been worn (Fig. 27 B). A shawl was sometimes worn over the white linen collar (Fig. 27 B), or simply the shawl alone could be folded around the neck and over the shoulders. Plain linen cuffs were turned back from the wrists (Fig. 27 A B).

HAIR.—The hair, which was dressed quite plainly, was brushed back from the forehead and brought into a twisted knot at the back of the head. The hair was usually covered, indoors or out, with a hood (Fig. 27 B) or coif (Fig. 27 C).

CLOAKS.—It is often impossible to determine whether a garment should be classed as a hood or as a cloak, since so many cloaks were made with head coverings attached. These could, for better protection, be pulled up over the head. These long hoods, or cloaks, "covering the face, head and all the body," were excellent for a cold, wintry climate such as New England. They were usually lined, either with a bright colored material or with fur. Being both warm and comfortable, they were exceedingly popular. It can be readily understood why each Pilgrim woman provided herself with a garment of this type. Small hoods covering the head, tied with a bow-knot under the chin, and not attached to the cloak, were the most favored of all head coverings among the Pilgrim women (Fig. 27 B). Cloaks of various lengths without the hood attached were extremely popular and quite common. They were usually worn with the small unattached hood. These cloaks, so conducive to warmth and comfort, never seem to have lost their popularity until the nineteenth century.

HEADGEAR.—Some of the tall-crowned, woolen hats with straight brims, which were extensively worn in England when the *Mayflower* sailed for America, may have been worn by Pilgrim women. They were, however, costly and inconvenient for travelling on shipboard. Hoods, or head scarves, and low-crowned felt hats, equally common in England, were probably worn for such extensive sea trips.

FOOTGEAR.—Shoes were seldom seen, for they were hidden by the long, full skirts. They probably resembled those worn by the men—shoes with blunt toes, laced over the instep, and provided with wooden heels.

ACCESSORIES.—The numerous small accessories, such as lace, handkerchiefs, feathered fans, masks, paint, powder, and patches, so associated with the clothing of women of the time, are noticeably absent. Small muffs and warm, heavy gloves, however, may have been used.

III. NEW ENGLAND DRESS: MEN
1630–1675

As we have seen, there is very little reason to believe that the majority of the Puritan men and women of New England, once they were established in the New World, dressed very differently from the Cavaliers and their wives in the South, the exception being those garments affected by climatic conditions. However, during the early days in England, Puritan reformers preached at great length against extremes in dress, advocating simplicity of attire as one of the most important precepts of the Puritan church. By the time the Puritans came to America, in 1630, many of the more rigid reforms had disappeared. These laws concerning dress never seem to have been very permanent, nor were they ever strictly followed except by the most religious and zealous members of the Puritan faith. Indeed, a comparison of the list of clothes provided for the Puritans by the Massachusetts Bay Colony, with the wearing apparel dealt out to the early Virginian settlers by the London Company, leads one to the conclusion that the Puritans were better provided for than the early Virginians, both in the quantity and quality of their garments. This is further supported by the fact that, in going over the early portraits of the founders of America, it is next to impossible, having only clothing as a guide, to separate Puritan from Cavalier, as they were so similar in dress and general appearance. Therefore, it seems that the Puritans as a religious group reacted only against excess in dress and absurd extremes in fashion. It was this attitude toward dress that seems to have been their guide in the selection of their garments. It is not strange, then, that the rather foppish fashion of petticoat-breeches never made a great appeal to many Puritans. On occasion petticoat-breeches made their appearance in New England when worn by visitors from abroad or from Virginia. As a part of Puritan dress, they hardly existed.

As soon as the colonists had established themselves in the New World and had emerged from the first years of toil and home-building, with prosperity crowning their efforts, they turned their attention to dress. Liberty in the New World was taken by many as an opportunity to freely express their desire for fine clothes.

Thus, from the beginning, one finds the colonists sending to England for the latest fashions in doublet and breeches, in bodice and skirt. It appears, however, that the latest modes did not meet with the approval of the critical New England magistrates. This caused the enactment of a series of sumptuary laws, which were formulated with the intent to restrain the rapidly growing desire for expensive and fashionable attire. That the sumptuary laws were hardly successful and were continually violated, is known by the number of persons who were "presented" in court. There is almost no record of successful sumptuary laws in occidental history, though they have been tried again and again. Although they were reprimanded, and at times fined, love of fine clothes overcame fear of the court. Finally, these sumptuary laws, as usual, became only a statute and were rarely enforced. When, however, the vast number of sermons preached by the ministers of that day is reviewed, one is struck by the persistence with which they continued their tirades against the "overwhelming love of fashion" among the "lambs of their flock." In studying the portraits and in reading contemporary accounts, one finds that the Puritans "arrayed themselves in fine raiment" and "walked with outstretched necks and wanton eyes mincing as they go."

It may well be that the terms "plain" and "sad" used for describing colors, have misled many into thinking the Puritans wore only black, gray, and dark brown. But, upon investigation, it is found that these "sad colors" were muted, or "tired" colors, for that is what the term "sad" originally meant. Russets, browns, scarlets, stammel reds, Bristol reds, Kendal greens, Lincoln greens, watchet blues, purples, and oranges are the colors often referred to in reports of the period, besides many more whose terms are now obsolete.

Thus, one finds the colonists did not make any decided change in their dress when they left England for the New World. What change was made seems to have taken place here in everyday working clothes, where heavier and warmer clothing was worn and stronger and stouter materials used. For Sundays, holidays, and best occasions, clothes of the finest materials and of the latest cut and fashion were brought forth. Dress was more or less of an indication of social and class distinction, as zealously guarded in the colonies as in the mother country.

DOUBLETS.—By 1630 the doublet, as worn by the Cavalier and well dressed Puritan had become an easy-fitting, comfortable garment, with a high waistline and long skirts pointed in the front, or cut straight all the way around. The waistline was decorated with points, and the sleeves were full and open on the front seam, and masked at the shoulders with wings or shoulder puffs (Fig. 10 B). The doublet of the plainer dressed Puritan followed the same general lines and cut as the garment described, though the fashionable high waistline was lowered. Compare Figure 28 A with Figure 10 B. The absence of the vertical slashing of the body of the garment can also be noted as well as the bow-knots around the waist.

FIGURE 28

At times, the doublet, without an apparent waistline, sloped away into a pointed front (Plate 15). Where the waistline was retained, the skirts descended to about the hip or mid-thigh (Fig. 28 A). The doublet might be either buttoned down the front to about the waistline, from where it remained unfastened (Plate 15), or it might be brought together with laces, starting at the neck and ending at the waist (Fig. 28 A). The front seam of the sleeve was occasionally left open but was provided with buttons and buttonholes with which it could be fastened. Also the jutting wings at the shoulders were retained, masking the joint between sleeve and doublet (Fig. 28 A). Most likely, doublets were made of a coarse, durable material, or even of leather "lined with oiled skin leather."

Prior to the revolution of 1649 in England, which resulted in the beheading of King Charles I, plain attire was very much favored by the Roundheads, those ardent followers of Oliver Cromwell who so strenuously opposed the Cavalier and Royalist faction. The term Roundhead seems to have come into existence about 1640. They were a fanatical religious group who cut their hair short, in contrast to the long locks worn by the Cavaliers, and stripped their garments of all decoration. It was a revolt of sober-minded people against the extravagances of the court life. Of this sect, however, few seem to have come to the colonies during the period of the Commonwealth in England. Many sought refuge here, however, after the restoration of the monarchy in 1660. It appears that among many of the Roundheads the extremes in plain dress were not carried as far as is generally supposed. Roundhead fashions were somewhat reflected in New England, and Figure 28 B will convey a clear idea of this type. This figure shows a doublet cut straight, without much shaping at the waist. The lower portion was cut in long, straight tabs edged with buttons. It was also buttoned down the front. Sometimes the doublets were sleeveless, in which case a plain or striped sleeve of an under-jacket or a shirt would be seen. These sleeves, of a different material from the doublet, were separate articles, fastened to the armholes of the doublet by means of points. Jutting wings masked the joints between doublet and sleeves. It is not necessary to repeat again in detail the development of the fashionable doublet worn at this time in New England; it is similar to that worn in the South. We would refer the reader to Chapter II, Section III, where it has already been dealt with at length.

The leather jerkin must have been as popular in New England as it was in the South. It was suited for hard, everyday wear and afforded good protection from Indian arrows. It could be worn either separately or, as so often occurred, under the breastplate. For a fuller description, see Chapter II, Section III.

BREECHES.—Breeches have been fully treated in Chapter II, Section III, and all the types described were worn by many of the Puritan men, with the exception of the petticoat-breeches which never seem to have been popular in New England. There is little evidence that such breeches were worn anywhere in the colonies. No portraits showing them are known. Records, if any, mentioning the purchase or shipment of petticoat-breeches, rhinegraves, or other variants are not available, and any actual American artifacts have not come to notice. Elisabeth McClellan in her book *Historic Dress In America* tells of a certain Captain Creedon who astounded Boston by appearing in a pair. An illustration by Darley for Lossing's "Our Country" shows Carteret setting foot on New Jersey and sporting the simpler type of petticoat-breeches illustrated in Chapter II. On this evidence of legend and artist's concept must rest the appearance of this garment in the colonies.

With the majority of the Puritans, and especially among the plainer dressed members, we find "knickerbockers," or knee breeches. From a tight waistband, they spread out fairly fully over the hips, descending to below the knees, where they were confined by a band. A bowknot of ribbon (Fig. 28 A) was usually affixed to the outer side of each band. They were fashioned from a serviceable material, even from canvas or leather. After 1640 another style of breeches became almost as popular as the knickerbocker. The new breeches were of a straight, cylindrical shape. They terminated at the knee without being gathered and were decorated around the bottom of the leg opening with small tabs or loops. Along the outer sides were vertical stripes or bands, ending just above the knees in a cluster of loops (Fig. 28 B and Page 77).

STOCKINGS OR HOSE.—The stockings brought over by the Puritans were either tailored of cotton or woolen cloth, or they were knitted. Later, when the spinning wheels were found in every home, the tailored stockings must have given way to the heavy homespun stockings knitted from woolen yarn. They appear to have been quite varied and gaily colored, mention being made of green, blue, yellow, brown, and gray stockings. Stirrup hose and turned down stockings were not popular in New England.

CLOAKS.—Warm heavy cloaks or capes of varying lengths, reaching to about the hips (Fig. 28 A), or to the ankle (Fig. 28 B), were worn by both men and women, whether Cavalier, Pilgrim, or Puritan, from the first moment of landing in America until well into the early years of the nineteenth century. They were made very full on what appears to have been a semicircular pattern, often gathered to a band that went around the neck. Generally the cloak was provided with a collar that was worn turned down or turned up around the neck (Plate 15). It was thrown over the shoulders and held in place by a band or cord tied across the chest (Fig. 28 B). The cord holding the cloak in place could be worn either over or under the linen band. Many, especially among the younger men, wore the cape in the more rakish Cavalier fashion. This was accomplished by placing the garment over the left shoulder, and from there allowing the open neckband to fall diagonally across the back. It was secured in the desired position by bringing one end of the cord, by which it was fastened, across the chest, under the right arm, and then tying it to the other cord (Fig. 29 A). Cloaks made of warm materials were colorfully lined with fabric or fur.

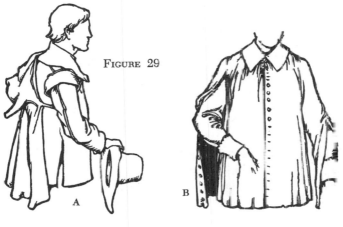

FIGURE 29

A   B

Among other articles of clothing, the Puritans were furnished with a garment called a mandillion, a loose cloak or coat worn as an outside protection, over the doublet. Fairholt, in speaking of this garment, says that the mandillion was "worn upon the doublet, either buttoned or open. It had no sleeves, but two broad wings on the shoulders, and hanging sleeves at the back." Planché calls this garment "a loose jacket or jerkin," and quotes Stubbs as follows:

> "Then as they be divers in colors, so they be divers in fashions; for some be made with collars and some without; some close to the body, some loose, which they call mandilians, covering the whole of the body down to the thighs, like bags or sacks that were drawn over them, hiding the dimensions and lineaments of the same."

A garment called a mandillion is found in the collection of costumes in the South Kensington Museum, London, and is evidently of the type and cut worn by the Puritans in New England, as shown in Figure 29 B. This garment was fastened down the front with hooks and eyes, others could be closed with buttons. To give protection to the wearer in the cold New England winters, the mandillion was lined with cotton. The long sleeves are shown hanging at the back. Through the upper opening appears the sleeve of the doublet. The falling band as a rule, was worn on the outside of the garment. The mandillion hung straight and fairly full from the shoulders, reaching to about mid-thigh. The long, hanging sleeves might be done away with, and in their place might be supplemented the "two broad wings on the shoulders."

The mandillion has caused a confusion of identification in studies of American dress of the seventeenth and eighteenth centuries. The mandillion at times had a collar which, by the end of the seventeenth century, was called a "cape." The mandillion with a "cape" became a coat worn by workmen. Before the middle of the eighteenth century this coat, now called a "frock," was being worn by "gentlemen" for sport, country wear, shooting, boating, and riding. A sort of cousin to this coat developed; a riding-coat called a "redingote" which also had a cape. From the redingote, in a somewhat extreme style, the "cape coat" was developed. Several capes were "layered together," the smallest cape on top, with each cape under it being larger. The cape coat became very popular.

The term "frock" was originally used to designate a monastic garment that covered the entire figure and had a hood-like effect. It may have been a sort of "rochet." A shortened version in velvet was said to have been worn by Henry VIII while he courted Anne of Cleves. The monastic frock was adapted to a work garment of linen by farmers, porters, and the like, by the last third of the seventeenth century and was called a "smock-frock." "Smock" was originally a woman's "over-the-head-shift" which, since its medieval beginnings, had gradually become elaborately decorated with embroidery. This embroidery gradually took on a special form which today is called "smocking." Out of these two words—smock and frock, we still retain an indicative usage. "To strip a woman to her smock" means to leave the one garment next to her skin. When we strip a cleric of his position we "unfrock" him.

To sum up: the mandillion acquired the workable sleeves of a frock and so became the frock, a coat, which, by the 19th century was a "frock-coat"; the monastic frock became a smock-frock by the end of the seventeenth century and was shortened both in name and length in varied ways throughout the eighteenth century. Today it again seems to be a smock—a garment worn as a work "cover-up" and which buttons in front like its one ancestor. It is worn by both sexes.

LINEN.—Under the doublet, a linen shirt was worn. The shirt was put on over the head, and it was opened nearly to the waist. It had no fastening except possibly at the neck where it was gathered. Or, it might have been frilled alongside the opening, below the neckband. The stock and waistcoat held the frills in place. Lacking frills, the cravat served to mask the opening. Nothing was worn under the shirt. The open shirt is seen in Plate 16. It was cut full in the body and sleeves. The Puritan usually wore a stiff collar of linen or cambric; the style, shape, and size of which varied considerably with the individual, and which was called a "fallingband" (Fig. 28 A). It has been stated that the smaller the band, "the greater the religious enthusiasm of the wearer." Bands, however, were not the only neckwear of the Puritans. Many references to ruffs are made in the old inventories. While ruffs do not appear in many of the paintings of the early settlers of New England, a splendid example is shown in the portrait of Governor John Winthrop (Plate 1 B), whose ruff is starched, carefully laid in pleats, and beautifully edged with lace. An even later example, and probably of one of the last gentlemen to wear the pleated ruff, appears in the portrait of one of the Bowdoin ancestors, dated 1647 (Plate 1 A), whose large ruff is made up in a triple box pleating.

The falling band was sometimes made up of several collars worn one over the other. Band strings, or cords, were used to fasten the collar together in the front. At first they were not much in evidence, but, gradually, after 1640 the strings were ornamented with tassels of silk, lace, or with small tufts of ribbons (Plates 5, 6). About 1665 the cravat appears, tied in at the throat with a ribbon bow (Plates 8, 12). Later, the ribbon was discarded, and the cravat tied into an ample knot with the ends falling longer and more freely (Plate 17). The severe New England magistrates would not tolerate the fashion of edging the bands with embroidery, or otherwise enriching them, and enacted sumptuary laws forbidding this "excess" in fashion. As previously mentioned, there were many in New England whose desire for fine and, at times, eye-catching apparel could not be restricted by laws. They followed the latest fashions, wearing the lace collars and bands described in Chapter II, Section III.

Examples of this are the portraits of John Freake and Thomas Savage (Plates 18, 19) wearing rich lace collars. From under the sleeves of the doublet, the sleeves of the linen shirt edged with ruffles at the wrist are seen. The early Puritans are often represented without the turned back cuffs at the wrists (Fig. 29 A). When they are shown they are usually perfectly plain (Fig. 28 A B), or, as in the portrait of Governor Winthrop, are edged with lace to match the ruff or band (Plate 1 B).

DRAWERS.—Apparently, drawers were worn as a nether-garment. At least, they are mentioned in clothing lists. But it is noteworthy that they are always numerically less than other garments listed. An inventory of the period reads: "four suits, one pair of drawers, five pairs of stockings." The stock of one store had a ratio of a pair of drawers to a dozen cravats.

FOOTGEAR.—Puritans wore shoes much more often than boots. In fact, one of the earliest sumptuary laws in New England was directed against men of moderate circumstances, forbidding them to appear abroad in great boots. Each Puritan was provided with four pairs of shoes. These were cut with a dip at the ankle, rising to a high tongue in front, and tied over the instep with shoestrings. They tapered to a square toe and were provided with wooden heels (Fig. 28 A). When boots were worn by the New England settlers, they were of the type shown in Figure 17 A B C and Figure 28 B.

HAIR AND BEARDS.—The real Puritans cut their hair short to the shape of their heads, in opposition to the long locks of the Cavaliers (Fig. 28 A. Fig. 29 A). Yet many of the New England colonists, after 1640, wore their hair fairly long, or to about the nape of the neck (Fig. 28 B.). During the time of Charles I, the pointed chin beard and mustache were common. The fashion of long hair falling to the shoulders persisted during the reign of Charles I, and lasted until the periwig became the fashion (See Chapter II, Section III). Perhaps instead of his own long hair, what appears to be the early form of the periwig is seen in the portrait of Mr. Freake (Plate 18). However, in the portrait of Sir George Downing (Plate 10) the great black periwig, with the mass of curls split at the side, falling over the chest in front, and down the back, is seen. These were the popular type of periwigs following the fashion set by Charles II, albeit reluctantly.

HEADGEAR.—The hats were broad in the brim with a high crown, usually of felt. A band of ribbon encircled the crown and was held in place by a small silver buckle (Fig. 28 A). This was characteristic Puritan headgear, though there were many who wore hats after the Cavalier fashion, even to the point of decorating them with feathers and plumes as described in the chapter on Virginia. Beaver hats, always an expensive head covering, were fashionable for those who could afford them. Even as early as 1634, there was an attempt made to regulate by law that only men of considerable means would be allowed to wear beaver hats. It is hardly necessary to mention that this ruling, like all sumptuary laws, was never very effective. Almost any one who could buy a beaver hat wore one. Besides the high-crowned black felt and beaver hats, Monmouth caps, fur caps, and plain knitted hats, as well as hoods, were all worn upon occasion. There were also a number of men in the settlements who went about partly armed, wearing jerkins or buff coats with breastplates or gorgets over them. Instead of wearing hats, they covered their heads with iron helmets or burgonets.

ACCESSORIES.—Walking canes (Plate 19), gloves (Plate 18), snuff-boxes, swords shoulder-straps, rich baldrics (Plate 10), as described in Chapter II, Section III, were about the same in New England as in the South.

ARMOR.—Armor worn in the middle years of the seventeenth century is shown in a portrait of Sir Edmund Andros (Plate 20) who was born in London in 1637 and came to New York in 1674. Next to him is a portrait of the Earl of Southampton wearing a gorget to protect his neck. To the lower left General Brog, in an engraving whose inscription indicates it was taken from a portrait done in 1635, wears pauldrons at the shoulders. The Earl of Warwick, to the right, has not only this protection but is well-guarded to the knees. He has brassards on his upper arms and lobster-tailed tassets over his thighs. For a further description of armor, see Chapter II, Section I. As part of the military equipment of the settlers in America, one finds in the "List of Apparel" furnished to the New England colonists such items as partisans, halberts, muskets, swords, corselets, pikes, and half-pikes.

FIGURE 30

The early Puritan governors usually wore over their doublets a great gown that hung quite full from the shoulders and was not shaped to the figure. It was fastened with buttons down the front (Fig. 30 A). There were openings at the sides through which the arms were thrust. This sometimes formed a short sleeve reaching halfway to the elbow. This type of sleeve was decorated on the outside with bow-knots. From these openings appeared the sleeves of the doublet. The upper seam of the doublet sleeves were slashed, exposing the sleeves of the linen shirt. The linen cuff was turned back from the wrist. The linen band appeared on the outside of the gown at the neck. A coif, or small cap, was worn on the head, covering the ears and descending to about the nape of the neck. Over this again was worn the high-crowned hat with a broad sombrero-like brim.

The everyday working dress of a smith or artisan is shown in Figure 30 B. He has taken off his doublet and is wearing a shirt with sleeves rolled above the elbows and a "waistcoat of green cotton, bound with red tape," as mentioned in the records of the Massachusetts Bay Company. This artisan also wears knee breeches, coarse woolen stockings, leather leggings, and stout leather shoes. Over these he wears a leather apron roughly shaped out of a hide. An "Ells shear linen Handkerchief" is knotted around his neck. On his head he wears the knitted Monmouth cap. In the good New England tradition, the same outfit was worn in the cold of winter and the heat of summer.

IV. NEW ENGLAND DRESS: WOMEN
1630–1675

Women's fashions did not change as rapidly in the seventeenth century, either in England or America, as they did later in the eighteenth and nineteenth centuries. While new styles were introduced from time to time, it did not always follow that the older styles were altogether discarded. As a matter of fact, the garments in these early years of the settlement of our country were made out of "honestly woven" material that endured for years; these garments were worn as long as the material lasted, frequently doing service through three generations. There are other factors to be taken into consideration. One must remember that fashion news was not then circulated by the use of fashion books, as it was two centuries later.

It is even doubtful whether at this early date the "fashion babies," or dolls dressed in the latest styles, had yet found their way into the shops of the mantuamakers in Boston, Salem, or Plymouth. Probably the most direct method of keeping in touch with the latest styles abroad was to import garments from England. It may well be that the proud and happy possessor of these new importations, whether dress, bodice, hood, or cloak, allowed her neighbors to profit by using them as models. Moreover, it appears that while the shops in all the important centers carried a large stock of substantial as well as rich and costly materials. they had no ready-made clothing. Ready-made clothing was not to be had until the middle of the eighteenth century for men, and not until somewhat later for women.

When the complicated conditions affecting dress during those years are reviewed, it appears that in spite of sumptuary laws, fines. sermons, and pamphlets intended to control undue extravagance in dress the New England women revealed their love of fine clothes by their defiance of the laws and of the magistrates. As soon as their position in the New World afforded the opportunity, they arrayed themselves in silk dresses, fur-lined "tiffany" hoods and plenty of lace and ribbons.

However, in the early days clothing, at least for general and every-day occasions, seems to have been quite restrained in New England. This was probably even more apparent in Plymouth than in Boston and Salem.

BODICE and SKIRT.—From 1630 to 1640, the gown was made out of a good serviceable cloth, the bodice shaped to the figure. Below the waistline, there would be a series of small tabs. The skirt was cut long and full. On occasion it was turned under and looped up toward the back, showing the underskirt, or petticoat (Fig. 31 A); or the skirt could hang perfectly straight (Fig. 31 B). By 1645 the bodice often came to a point in front (Fig. 32 A) and probably was rounded in the back. It was worn over a full-gathered skirt. The sleeves might be of equal full-ness throughout their length, terminating halfway between the elbow and the wrist, where a large linen cuff was turned back over the sleeve. The bodice occasionally had a V-shaped opening in front, filled in with a contrasting material, above which the edging of the linen chemisette was seen.

FIGURE 31

A　　　　　　　　B

The development of the bodice and skirt, as worn by the more fashionably dressed New England women, was the same as that already described
in Chapter II, Section IV, which discusses the dress of Southern women.

LINEN.—Broad collars of linen were turned down around the neck
of the gown. They could be either plain (Fig. 33 A), with a delicately
scalloped edge (Fig. 32 A), or, at times, edged with lace (Fig. 32 B).
The bands were sometimes worn over a low-cut bodice (Fig. 32 A). For
out-of-door wear a kerchief was folded and placed around the neck over
the linen collar, the two ends being allowed to hang down in front, the
opening held together by a bow or bows of ribbon (Fig. 31 A. Fig. 33 B).

FIGURE 32

A   B

The falling band was sometimes made up of two or more collars, one
worn over the other (Fig. 32 B). At the wrist were turned back linen
cuffs matching the falling bands. During the 1630's they were quite plain;
but from then on they were apt to be provided with a more decorated
edge. Aprons of white holland, trimmed with lace, or of other materials
and colors, were brought over by the first Pilgrim and Puritan women from
England. They were extensively worn, not only as a protection to the
gown but also as a decorative part of the costume. By the middle of the
eighteenth century, beautifully made aprons were an indispensable part
of a lady's wardrobe.

HEADGEAR.—"Coifs," hoods, and high-crowned hats similar to those
worn by the men were the head-coverings of those days. The coif (Fig.
31 A), a tight-fitting headdress, or cap, was often worn under the hat.
When the coif was less tight-fitting it was called a "pinner." In this period,
the same name, "pinner," was applied to a "modesty piece" tucked into

the front of a décolletage, and to the bib of an apron when it was pinned to the dress. Hoods could be attached to the cloak or worn separately. Throughout the colonies, the hood was the head covering most universally worn by women in all stations of society. Because they were becoming, it is only natural that the women made them as attractive as possible, using silks, especially tiffany, a thin gauzelike silk, and often lining them with fur. These lovely hoods were so effective that the magistrates became disturbed, and at a very early date enacted laws restricting the use of silk and proscribing certain gay colors. The simplest hood, if it could ever be called such, was made out of an oblong strip of material thrown over the head; the ends were twisted, brought forward and tied under the chin (Plates 13, 14; Fig. 33 A). It seems the Pilgrim women came to this country with their heads protected by hoods. However, the Puritan dames possessed not only hoods but hats, some of them probably the high-crowned hats with straight wide brims (Fig. 31 A Fig. 32 B) which were so popular in England at the time. As a rule, these woolen hats, when worn by the women, were placed over the small coif or cap (Fig. 32 B).

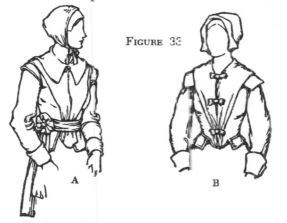

FIGURE 33

A   B

CLOAKS.—Cloaks and capes of heavy cloth or fur were worn in the colonies from the very first settlement, and retained their popularity well into the eighteenth century. These cloaks worn by the Puritans did not differ from those worn by the Pilgrim women and described in Chapter III, Section II. Besides the cloaks, there were narrow coverings of silk gauze or other material placed around the neck and known as tippets. The winter tippet was made of fur, which gave its warm protection to the neck and shoulders. Muffs were generally carried (Fig. 31 A. 32 B). They were made either of cloth or fur, or of cloth edged with fur. If a fur tippet was worn, the muff was usually made to match.

MASKS.—Masks were worn as a protection against the wind and cold at a very early date, not only in New England but generally throughout the colonies. They were made of black velvet or of white or green silk. They were either held up against the face by the hand, or held in position by fasteners passing over the ears. A common method was to fit them with a mouthpiece, consisting of a cord with glass buttons on the ends. The buttons were held between the teeth, thus holding the mask in place.

There are not many portraits of women of these early days, and one turns with great interest to those still in existence. The portrait of Penelope, the wife of Governor Winslow, is exceedingly interesting (Plate 21). It hangs in Pilgrim Hall, Plymouth, Massachusetts, and shows the horizontal décolletage with a suggestion of the linen chemise fringing the opening. One notes the cluster of curls at the sides of the head, fashionable in the 1660's.

There is an interesting portrait of Mrs. John Freake (Plate 13), shown with the simple hood over the head and tied under the chin. The elbow sleeves are decorated with bow-knots, and from under the sleeve appears the linen sleeve with its ruffle. Around her neck she wears a beautiful lace collar. Another Plymouth portrait in the same group is that of Elizabeth Paddy Wensley (Plate 14), wearing the long stiff-boned bodice popular at that time. Her head is covered with the same type of hood as is worn by Mrs. Freake. The round neckline, long-waisted bodice, and the way the sleeves are puffed and tied at elbow length is typical of good style in the England of 1655. The fullness of the skirt as it appears in the painting is of a somewhat earlier date. Mrs. Freake is more up-to-date, if not more "chic," for she is wearing a collar which didn't come into style until the middle 1660's. In any case, these portraits show a quality of dress which ranks these New England ladies with their peers in Virginia and New York.

A house built in 1643—Pigeon Cove, Mass.

CHAPTER IV

The Dutch In New York

1623-1675

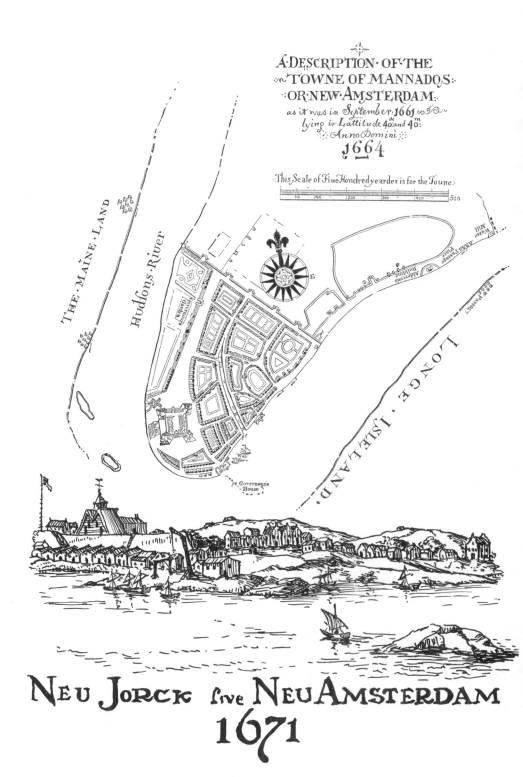

A DESCRIPTION OF THE TOWNE OF MANNADOS OR NEW AMSTERDAM as it was in September 1661 lying is Lattitude 40: and 40: Anno Domini 1664

This Scale of Fiue Hondred yeardes is for the Toune

THE MAINE LAND

Hudfons River

LONGE ISLELAND

NEU JORCK five NEU AMSTERDAM 1671

CHAPTER IV

The Dutch In New York

1623-1675

The Dutch occupation of New York was a commercial venture fostered by the Dutch West India Company, which planted the Dutch flag in the Hudson, Delaware and Connecticut valleys. The Company's mission was to pour wealth into the pockets of the shareholders by settlement and conquest, trade, carrying slaves to these shores, and by legalized piracy upon the gold ships of Spain. It was only in this last pursuit that it found the profits thus sought.

Official incompetence as well as mistaken policy is usually given as the cause of the slow growth of the Dutch settlements and their failure to attain any stability or lasting power. However, there were other contributing causes. Holland, with a population of but two millions, could not send a sufficient body of settlers to claim the territory from the greater number of English settlers. Neither did economic pressure make the Dutch look toward North America as a shore of opportunity and release. Holland had newly won her independence, and her virtual monopoly of sea trade had brought her such a degree of prosperity that her people were not inclined to leave the comfortable certainties of Holland for the arduous uncertainties of the New World, North and South; for the Dutch had made equally futile attempts to colonize Brazil.

Holland's first gestures toward settlement in the North were no more than the establishment of trading outposts. There was one such settlement at Fort Nassau, later renamed Fort Orange, now the present site of Albany, New York. At that time it was deep in the fur country. Another trading post, this one on Manhattan Island, began as four log huts. Encouraged by the returns rewarding the early fur trading efforts, a more serious attempt at colonization was made in 1623, when a shipload of some thirty Walloon families settled at Fort Orange, along the shores of Long Island, and on Manhattan Island. Two years later more families came, bringing a supply of farming implements and a hundred head of cattle. With the arrival in 1626 of a governor and another band of settlers, the newly christened town of New Amsterdam began to have a look of substance and activity.

As in all new settlements life in those early years was difficult and primitive. A line of log huts was thrown up behind the protection of the Battery, and wharves and storehouses were built to handle the bundles of furs that came down the river. The little farms lying to the north of the fort along the island were soon able to supply the growing community with greens, fresh vegetables, milk, butter, and eggs. Contemporary letters of the time often voice complaints of the lack of comforts and necessities. Nevertheless, the growth of New Amsterdam progressed with little of the suffering and despair that had been the portion of both Jamestown and Plymouth. It was as yet too workaday a community to indulge in extravagant dress. But the Dutch and Flemish fondness for color was not curbed by any churchly diatribes. Thus, the early New Amsterdam scene was far brighter than the early Puritan strongholds to the north.

Except for the more colorful materials of which they were made, the dress of these early Dutch settlers differed very little from those of the Pilgrim band. The doublet, the few remaining examples of the trunk hose, and the breeches were the same, except for a certain squareness and fullness in the cutting. The Dutch, too, were addicted to the excessive use of decorated buttons and were fond of elaborate ruffs and richly embroidered collars. With the entire life of the colony revolving around the fur trade, it is natural that furs should have played an important part in their dress. Their doublets and cassocks were often lined with it, and it appeared as trimming upon their gowns and cloaks. In winter they wore cloaks, hoods, and caps made entirely of skins.

New Amsterdam grew slowly in population, but the appearance of the little town changed quickly. The outer walls of the bastion of the fort were faced with stone, and behind them a replica of a small Dutch community began to appear. Warehouses for the West India Company were built of stone brought from the northern part of the island. Then came a brewery, a bakery, a horse-mill, and later the inevitable windmills. Brick was shipped from Holland, and houses were erected in the characteristic Dutch fashion. Their high gables, often picked out in patterns of yellow, red, and black brick, faced the street. A gilded weathercock surmounted the peak of each shingled or tiled roof. Glass in small diamond panes, mounted in leaded casements, was found in all but the poorest homes. These windows were small, but the doors were wide and spacious. The door was cut into an upper and lower portion. The upper portion, with its polished knocker, swung back in fine weather. Each house had its stoop, usually flanked by highbacked benches, where the family sat on summer evenings, the women knitting and sewing, the men smoking their long pipes. Behind each house was a garden with fruit trees and beds of tulips, hyacinths, larkspur, pinks, gillyflowers, and wild saffron. These gardens were often walled in or enclosed with hedges; the more prosperous burghers built summerhouses and arbors. There were also benches and tables where meals could be served in warm weather.

The more costly Dutch home had a wide hall from the front to the back, with rooms on either side. The guests bed with its curtains and valance of camlet often stood in this wide hall. The floors, during the earlier half of the seventeenth century, were usually sanded and stroked into quaint patterns by the broom. The fireplaces were large and cheerful, with their brass fenders, fire screens and tools, their scrubbed brick or stone hearths, and their curious tiles set in the chimney breast. There was more furniture in the New Amsterdam homes than in those of New England. Every ship brought crates of chairs, chests, and tables, and there were skilled hands among the local craftsmen. In the early half of the century, furniture was of sturdy, substantial build, carved and turned in the Flemish manner. Spanish furniture, decorated with tooled leather and studded with elaborately wrought nailheads, was sometimes found. This was spoil taken from Spanish merchantmen and gold carriers. Every Dutch family aspired to have at least one great cupboard or "kast." In it were placed the most treasured articles in the house—silverware, glass, and fine porcelain. A huge chest, carved and sometimes covered with leather, was used to store the linen. A long, oak, drawing table, somewhat of the extension variety; some heavy, domed beds, high-backed chairs, benches and settles completed the usual inventory of furniture.

Looms and spinning wheels were included among the furniture. Every household had from two to six spinning wheels for wool and flax. Looms, too, were in common use, and piles of homespun cloth and snow white linen indicate the industry of the active Dutch maidens. Hoards of home-made materials were thus accumulated in the settlement, sufficient to last many generations. It was the passion of every Dutch housewife to accumulate a great store of fine linens, both for use and as dowries for her daughters. Her huge kasts and chests were crammed with pillowbeers, towels, napkins, cupboard cloths, tablecloths and heaps of uncut linen awaiting the shears and thread. Of New Netherlands women, it has been said that the worthy Dutch matrons arrayed themselves in their best linsey jackets and petticoats, and putting a half-finished stocking into the capacious pocket which hung from their girdle, with scissors, pincushion and keys outside their dress, sallied out to a neighbor's house to spend the afternoon. Here they plied their knitting needles, discussed the village gossip, settled the affairs of their neighbors to their own satisfaction, and finished their stockings in time for tea. The maidens spent much of their time making petticoats of rich stuffs and many colors, quilting them in fanciful designs and elaborate figures.

It was a busy, comfortable, and unhurried life in early New Amsterdam. Yet here too, as in every other colony, there existed that sharp contrast between the sheltered existence of the town dweller and the perils and strains of the pioneer. Compare the substantial homes of the New Amsterdam burghers with this contemporary description of the shelters of the new settlers. "Those who have no means to build farmhouses according to their wishes, dig a square pit in the ground, cellar-fashion, six or seven feet deep, as long and as broad as they think proper, case the earth inside all around the wall with timber, which they line with the bark of trees, or something else to prevent the caving in of the earth; floor this cellar with plank and wainscot it overhead for a ceiling, raise a roof of spars clear up, and cover the spars with bark or green sods so they can live dry and warm in these houses with their entire families for two, three, and four years, it being understood that partitions are run through these cellars which are adapted to the size of the family."

The new settlers who inhabited shelters of this sort in the outlying districts were harried by Indians and were subject to all the rigors of frontier life. In one respect they were more fortunate than their brothers in the other colonies; they had the support of the West India Company, with its supplies of livestock, farming tools, and seed. Their dress was simple and sturdy, homespun or leathern breeches and doublets for the men, fustian or linsey-woolsey skirts and bodices for the women. In winter both the men and women wore garments made of skins. In the fields they wore wooden clogs, or sabots. The men often wore an overfrock of rough linen, called a "pattrock," sometimes hanging loose, sometimes belted at the waist.

As early as 1629 a new departure in policy by the West India Company brought about an interesting change in the structure of New Netherland society. Because immigration was lagging, the company offered a large land grant with almost sovereign power of administration to anyone who at his own expense would transport fifty persons to the colony and establish them on the land. Many wealthy merchants seized this opportunity to become "patroons" and in a sense rivals of the Old World nobility. A number of these great families, like the Schuylers and Van Rensselaers, acquired an enormous amount of wealth and power, holding their new feudal state until well after the Revolution. They, together with the rich merchants of New Amsterdam, constituted a strong aristocracy of wealth. The gap between them and the humble tenant farmer was a wide one, wider than in the northern or middle colonies. It corresponded to the relation between the planter and the poor white in the South.

As the century entered its third quarter, both the wealth and numbers of this class increased. New Amsterdam had become a humming, commercial city. Its harbor held ships of all nations, and its wharves were heaped with goods from a hundred strange seaports. The fur trade was still flourishing; the little farms along the river and the Sound were sending in an abundance of farm products. A steady stream of wealth was finding its way into the hands of many. The prosperous New Netherlander developed a taste for the rarest, finest, and most costly things. His home was filled with silk and cotton hangings and other goods from Eastern looms, lacquer boxes and cabinets, Venetian and Bohemian glass, porcelains from the Orient, and furniture made from exotic woods.

Dress gained in richness and color. The finest fabrics from the looms

of Europe and the Orient were used to make clothes for the New Nether-
landers. The new fashion of the "coat" was appearing. The younger men
of wealth preferred those of the brightest colors, lined with flashing silks
and satins. Silver buttons and ribbons were used recklessly. Gold braid
and loops of silver were sewn on the beaver hats, down the outer seam
of the breeches, and on the cuffs and collars.

Old inventories and wills reveal a corresponding sumptuousness in
the dress of the women. There are long lists of clothing such as "blew
silk petticoats," lace cornets, silk lutestring scarfs, scented gloves of colored
leather, petticoats and calico stomachers. Spelling was still a personal
manner of expressing the sound of a word in writing, and the names of
colors, cloths and items of dress could be written in many different ways.
"Blew" is the hue which we spell "blue" today. A lace cornet was a cap
formed of lace. The lace might be of any variety suitable to make a
somewhat stiff cap, with a flattish top and sides which were sometimes
described as looking like "a hound's ears." Lutestring or lustring was a
soft, pure silk material with a semilustre. Calico was at that time any
kind of cotton material that came from Callicut, in India. Sometimes
designs were "painted" on it, which today we might describe as "hand-
printed;" then it was called "calmendar." Excellent materials were used in
the clothes—velvets, satins, taffetas, silks, serge and "sarsenets." Sarsenet
is variously described as a thin, gauzy material, a soft silklike lutestring
or as a silk with a twill weave.

Among the fashionable colors were "fawn," "mauve," "rose," "Fire
color," "dead-leaf color," "amaranth," and "scarlet." The women in New
Netherland wore an abundance of jewelry: chains of gold, strings of pearls,
brooches, pins, rings, bracelets, and earrings. The use of hair ornaments
was distinctly Dutch, and travelers of the time always remarked upon
this feature of the costume of the Dutch women of the former New Amsterdam, which had now been renamed New York. Another characteristic
Dutch custom was the wearing of a "chatelaine" of gold or silver at the
waist, from which hung keys, bodkin, thimble, scissors, and various scent
boxes and trinkets.

During the latter portion of the century, there was in New York a
color and flavor of the sea and of the Old World that was not to be found
elsewhere between Maine and Carolina. With the commerce of the
world crowding her docks, and the tongues of a score of nations clamor-
ing along her quays, the little Dutch town still preserved its placid Low
Country air. Although she was, even in the seventeenth century, the most
cosmopolitan town in America, the leisurely Dutch way of life was pursued.

After the occupation by the English in 1664 she resisted for a
long time the encroachments of new and strange habits. In Albany and
among the Hudson settlements the Dutch atmosphere persisted into the
nineteenth century. In "The American Language," Henry Mencken wrote
that, until our own time, Dutch was the first language in some of the
remoter parts of the Hudson Valley.

I. DUTCH DRESS: MEN
1623–1675

In continuing the study of the dress of the early settlers of New York, a knowledge of both English and of Dutch dress is necessary.

Upon investigation, it is found that the dress of the Dutch and English during the sixteenth, seventeenth, and eighteenth centuries, affected as it was by the same influences, had a marked similarity. Especially is this true of the dress of the upper and middle classes who resided in the more populous cities.

The Spanish influence in dress, that had held sway for so long a time, setting the fashion for western Europe and England, gradually waned after 1620. From France during the next decade, 1620-30, came the so-called "Cavalier" style in dress, a style which rapidly spread through western Europe, affecting equally the styles of the Low Countries and those of England.

The Dutch in the New World did not oppress their people with religious intolerance, but allowed those within Dutch jurisdiction freedom of thought in matters spiritual. Therefore, there was no interference by the authorities, nor the effort to control dress by sumptuary laws, which was attempted without complete success in New England.

A study of Dutch dress in the New Netherlands begins in 1621, the year the Dutch West India Company was given control of Dutch trade activities in America. Yet it was not until 1623, three years after the landing of the Pilgrims at Plymouth, that the colony really began to take permanent form. Of the thirty families sent over to these shores then, nearly all were Walloons, who were "protestant refugees from Belgium." In common with many of the immigrants to the New World, they were a most industrious people, skilled in many trades, and equipped to meet the hard struggle for a livelihood in the New World. From all accounts, they wore the same dress as the Dutch. As has been seen, there was little if any difference in the dress of English and Dutch gentlemen of the upper and middle classes. In the main, body garments, breeches, linen, hats, cloaks, footgear, followed the same development and evolution in styles in the Low Countries as they did in England. This being so, it will not be necessary again to go over in detail the garments of these years. This has already been done in the Virginia section, Chapter II, Section III, where the main features of this type of dress are discussed. In this section the dress will be treated more generally, stressing those features more essentially Dutch.

Figure 34 shows the dress worn by the early Dutch settlers. This may be a drawing of one of the Walloons who came over in 1623. The doublet is quite shaped to the figure, with a low waistline to which is attached a series of small tabs coming to a point in front. In this drawing the three-quarter length cloak hides the wings, or rolls, at the shoulders. The sleeves are tight-fitting and plain instead of the more elaborately slashed type, as is becoming to his station. In his great, full-gathered breeches one sees a last example of the trunk hose. The stockings are cross-gartered around his knees and tied in bows on the outside. Under the doublet is the linen shirt, the upstanding collar of which, with a scalloped edge, encircles his neck. The hat has a large sombrero-like brim and a moderate crown.

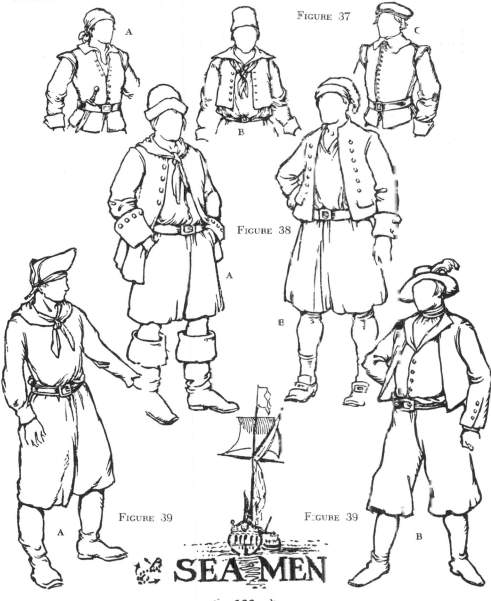

FIGURE 37

FIGURE 38

FIGURE 39

FIGURE 39

SEA MEN

As has been noted, the patroon system was established in 1629 to stimulate emigration. The material advantages were so great under this system that it was not long before patroons in the Hudson Valley had thriving estates. The dress of the patroon is shown in Figure 35 A. The doublet, which is less shaped to the figure, has a high waistline and a fairly long skirt. The waistline might be left plain or decorated with points. The sleeves could be plain or full and slashed in the upper arm, coming to a tight sleeve over the forearm. A falling ruff of fairly good size surrounds the neck. The breeches, instead of those seen in Figure 34, are the full-cut ones of the knickerbocker type. These great baggy breeches were extremely characteristic of the Dutchman and were made in a variety of shapes. They seem also to have been quite varied in color, and were elaborately trimmed along the outside seam with buttons, stripes, and ribbons. The buttons used were covered with cloth, but, occasionally, silver buttons worn by those who could afford them were seen.

FIGURE 35

FIGURE 34

A

B

The Dutch were very particular in the selection and care of their neckwear. Standing collars, whisks, ruffs, bands, and later, lace collars, were made out of the best materials. They were always carefully washed, starched, and the sets skillfully pleated. The ruff was retained by the older men until quite late. They are seen in Dutch paintings dating as late as 1650. At the wrists, and turned back over the doublet sleeve, were the cuffs made to match the neck pieces. Under the doublets were worn the shirts. Mention is made of plain shirts, lace shirts, white and blue shirts, calico, Holland, and flannel shirts.

"Stockings," writes Esther Singleton, "were of great importance, and were generally of the same material as the trousers. Sometimes they were elaborately embroidered or trimmed. We read of silk, cotton, woolen, satin, flannel and roll stockings; stockings of white, black, blue, and above all, scarlet. The stockings were held in place by garters; the garters contrasted with, or matched the stockings. There were garters of satin, silk, or cloth."

The hat had a broad brim and a round low crown. Around the crown was placed a ribbon band or a metal chain of gold or silver. It might be further trimmed with a fine feathered plume. There were also tall, conical crowned hats with straight, flat brims.

Cloaks of the same general line and cut as those worn by the Virginia Cavaliers formed a very important part of the Dutchman's wardrobe. Esther Singleton writes, in "Dutch New York," published in 1909: "To wear a cloak with elegance was the mark of a gentleman; and it was not an easy thing to throw it over the shoulders in the proper folds and to keep its graceful lines." Men of substance, such as the burgomaster, wore it to church and to the meetings of the Council, and kept it on as they did their hats while paying a call. On arriving home the cloak and sometimes the hat were removed. The slippers were substituted for the heavy shoes. Many of the cloaks were richly trimmed with gold or silver lace, or embroidered; but as a rule, they were handsome cloth lined with silk and sometimes ornamented with buttons.

Boots were of course worn, but like the Pilgrims and the Puritans, stockings and shoes were more usual.

Citizens of position carried swords suspended from belts or baldrics. The shoulder belts were often embroidered and provided with silver buckles. Walking-sticks, canes with silver or ivory heads, were common.

There appeared to be many military features in men's garments as a result of the Thirty Years' War. That long, bloody struggle in which England and Holland crushed the power of Spain came to an end with the Treaty of Westphalia in 1648. Many of these military features seem to have originated in the Low Countries. As an instance, from 1625 to 1640 we find many Dutchmen appearing in the buff coat or leather jerkin when on military duty in the colonies (Fig. 35 B). It is usually provided with long, flaring skirts overlapping in front. They were held together either by lacings, points, or by a broad sash tied around the waist with a large bow on the left side. The leather jerkin might be made either with or without leather sleeves. When made without sleeves, as is the case in the illustration, the sleeves of the doublet worn underneath it would be exposed to view. Later, after 1640, the long, flaring skirts gradually shortened until they disappeared. The gorget, or breastplate, was often worn over the buff coat. The full breeches were tucked into long boots, or the tops of the boots were turned down and cupped. A shoulder strap slung over the right shoulder supported the sword, which was suspended on the left side. This Dutchman wears a large sombrero-like hat, decorated with a sweeping feathered plume. A brace of pistols might be thrust into the wide sash at his waist.

By 1660, a cassock-like coat was quite generally worn. It was collarless, with medium sleeves turned back in large cuffs. It was buttoned down the front, and the skirt reached to about the knees. Cassock, as a name, had been used for a military coat and to designate a clerical garment. But it no longer described the garment in general use among laymen. It was called a coat or a "Brandenburg." After about 1680 it will be called a "surtout." This coat seems to have been popular with the Dutch. At the neck is the stiffened linen collar in the form of a whisk. In place of the whisk, the cravat or neckcloth might be worn. About 1655 to 1660 the cravat gradually replaced the falling band (Fig. 36 B). The breeches were cylindrical, reaching to a little below the knees.

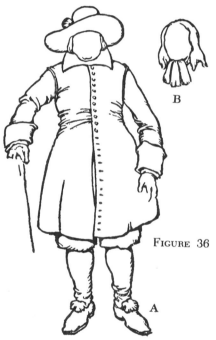

FIGURE 36

A Plumbago Drawing,
Flemish in style, about 1625.

The dress of a workingman of the seventeenth century consisted of a loose-fitting doublet of coarse but stout material, probably of "homespun, linsey-woolsey, canvas, or leather." It would undoubtedly be sleeveless. Therefore, the medium full sleeves of the shirt, coming to a band at the wrist, would be seen. At the shoulders were small wings. The doublet was provided with buttons and buttonholes down the front. The breeches, of the same material as the doublet, were in the fashion of the full Dutch knickerbockers. The stockings were of "hand knitted yarn." Over his short hair, the workingman would wear a knitted cap, or a felt hat with a medium brim that could either be rolled up or pulled down over the face.

II. SEAMEN'S DRESS
1623-1800

New Amsterdam had been a trading settlement from the beginning, its chief object being to carry on commerce, especially in furs, for the enrichment of the traders and merchants of the Dutch West India Company. As early as 1643, due to the great activity in the fur trade, New Amsterdam had become one of the most cosmopolitan cities in the New World. It is stated that at that time eighteen different languages were spoken in the city, so varied and heterogeneous was its moving population. The slave trade, likewise, flourished throughout the New Netherlands, where it was looked upon as a respectable, as well as most profitable, enterprise. By 1750, when it had been New York for nearly a century, it was indeed a busy place. Hundreds of sailing vessels of all types could be seen along the waterways partly surrounding the settlement. Along the old waterfront the great bowsprits of the ships in port extended well over what is now Pearl Street. Towering beyond, rose a forest of masts and spars.

As the commercial activity of the Dutch had made New Amsterdam one of the shipping centers of the New World, it was here probably more than anywhere else that seamen were seen in greatest numbers. This accounts for this chapter being selected as the one in which to describe seamen's clothing. The development of the dress worn by seamen from the period of this chapter, 1623-1675, to the end of the eighteenth century will be described.

Along the waterfront and scattered through the city, the masters and sailors of the merchant ships might have been seen in their picturesque clothing. Although they were of all nationalities, their dress was quite similar. In Figure 37 C one sees a master of a sailing vessel of about the first years of the settlement of New Amsterdam. His doublet fits close, buttoning down the front. The projecting wings are seen at the shoulders. A leather belt is buckled around the waist. At the neck is seen the small falling band of the linen or cotton shirt. The cuffs are turned back from the wrists. He wears a flat cap with a small projecting brim, rather like the original Monmouth cap. His breeches, if seen, would be of the full knickerbocker type (Fig. 35 A). Heavy woolen stockings would be worn either with boots or shoes.

A common seaman of the time is seen in Figure 37 A. The doublet is of the same general cut as the one just described; but instead of being made of cloth, it is probably canvas. It is open from the neck to below the chest. The collar of a coarse cotton shirt appears turned down at the neck, while cuffs are turned back at the wrists. The doublet might also be sleeveless, in which case the sleeves of the cotton shirt would be seen.

In the belt a knife is thrust either at the side, cr as is so often the case, at the back. A handkerchief, usually of a bright color, is tied around his head and knotted at the side. Over this is worn a heavy knitted cap. In Figure 37 B a sailor of a later date is seen. The doublet is now a small, sleeveless jacket, cut very short and worn open down the front, although provided with buttons and buttonholes. The shirt, with its turned down collar and turned back cuffs, was made quite full. The jacket was very short, and the shirt was full enough to fall over the waistband of the breeches. The full-cut canvas, heavy linen, or cotton breeches were of the shape seen in Figure 38 A B. A neckcloth or handkerchief was knotted around the seaman's neck under the collar. A brimless, high-crowned hat of truncated form made of the fur of some animal, adorned his head.

A sailor's dress, dating from about 1680, is seen in Figure 38 A B. In place of a doublet, there is a short collarless coat or seaman's jacket. It is worn over a linen shirt, which also appears to be collarless. A hand-kerchief is knotted around his neck. The full white canvas trousers, some-times called "skilts," are belted in with a wide leather strap at the waist, and they reach to about the knees. Round-crowned hats with upturned brims, knitted caps, handkerchiefs tied around the head, earrings, knives, cutlasses, and pistols thrust into belts were additions to the dress. Heavy stockings and shoes or boots composed the footgear. As often as not, the coats were taken off, the sailors appearing in shirts and unbelted skilts, with a red or colored handkerchief tied around their necks. The crews of the ships putting into the different ports along the eastern seaboard of the New World, of course, would be similarly attired.

The dress of the common seaman from about 1745 to 1776, as shown in Figure 39 A, would consist of the very wide-open breeches extending to about the knee. He might wear either a tight-fitting shirt or a knitted jersey. The wide breeches were belted in around the waist. The feet and legs were thrust into heavy knee-length boots. There was usually a hand-kerchief tied around his head, presumably a red one. Over this he might wear a knitted cap or, more probably, during the years in question, "a flat cocket hat." The hair would be plaited in a short, straight pigtail, the ends tied with a ribbon. About 1765 one finds the "hats of glazed leather, or woolen thrums, closely woven and looking like rought knap." In Figure 39 B one sees again the clothing of a common seaman, taken from a print dated about the time of the Revolution. The great, loose breeches are beginning to lose the very wide flare which may have given rise to the term "skilts.' The word seems to combine "skirt" and "kilt," and is most descriptive. Although sailors' pantaloons are seen, skilts of knee length are still characteristic dress of the common sailor. A vest, buttoning down the front, and with large, turned back lapels is tucked inside the waistband of the breeches. The opening at the neck reveals a shirt gathered in small pleats to a band encircling the neck. A stock, or cloth, is worn around the neck.

III. DUTCH DRESS: WOMEN
1623-1675

After the Dutch were firmly established in America and had begun
to flourish and grow wealthy, almost immediately their homes reflected
this growing prosperity. The wives of the rich merchants of New Amsterdam furnished their houses in the latest fashion. When possible, they
had furniture made in the Colony. In the great trading ships of the East
India companies, both Dutch and English, came the fine stuffs from far
Eastern looms, not only materials for hangings, upholstery, and curtains,
but silks, painted calico and other fine quality cotton goods for dress.

The dress of the Dutch women in the colonies followed the same
development in fashion as that of the Cavaliers' wives in Virginia.

The woman in Figure 40 A is one of those who came from Holland in 1623. The bodice is boned, still showing the rigid effect of the
old Spanish influence. At the shoulders are the slashed puffs. The bodice
is cut with a square opening at the neck, revealing the chemise. Rising
from the neck of the bodice is a starched standing linen collar. The skirt,
gathered up around the figure, shows a fine petticoat. The hair is brushed
back and carried over a pad, on top of which is placed a characteristic
Dutch cap.

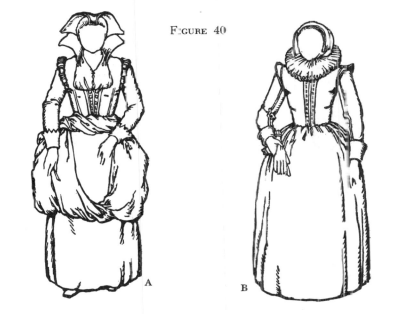

FIGURE 40

A   B

In Figure 40 B one sees the dress of a woman of fashion of about the year 1629. She is probably the wife of a patroon. Note the tight-fitting Dutch bodice, which is evidently boned and laced. Small wings are shown at the shoulders. The skirt is cut very full and shirred at the waistline and worn over the bodice. The ruff, of which the Dutch ladies were very fond, seems to have been worn well into the middle of the seventeenth century. In the example shown, a round ruff made up of fine pleats and extending well out over the shoulders and high in the back is seen. In order to keep them in shape after they were starched and ironed, they were fastened on gold and silver wires. Ruffs were an extremely expensive part of the dress. Not only were they made out of the finest quality of cambric and edged with lace, but took a huge quantity material. When all the pleats were smoothed out, they were said to measure sixty yards. The care of fine ruffs must have entailed considerable work and effort. The making, undoing, washing, starching and ironing, and remaking was no common work, and many Dutch ladies attended to the making and doing up of their ruffs themselves. A favorite ruff of the Dutch ladies, was one in which the pleating varied across the front by a section that was either straight or of a slightly reversed curve (Fig. 41 A). As can be seen from the illustration, the ruff is worn over a falling lace band that spreads well out over the shoulders and is held together in the front by a jeweled pin or bow-knot. The skirt is gathered up under the arm to show the petticoat. These handsome petticoats were made out

FIGURE 41

of the finest materials such as silks, damasks, velvets, and satins. For everyday wear, linen or cotton was used. Petticoats were among the most prized articles of a lady's wardrobe. The hem was often trimmed with silver, gold, or silk embroidery. Over the skirt was worn the apron. The apron served not only to protect the skirt but was a fashionable feature of the dress. Naturally, aprons thus worn were made of fine materials, although plainer ones for everyday wear might have been used.

The Dutch seem to have been very fond of jewelry, especially of diamonds. "They sparkle in rings, lockets, earrings, chains and pendants of various descriptions." Mention is also made of gloves both for men and women.

A loose jacket was brought over from Holland, where it was very popular; it was made of silk, velvet or other cloth (Fig. 41 B) and trimmed with fur or swansdown around the neck, down the front, and around the bottom. This jacket was introduced about the middle of the seventeenth century. Its popularity is shown by the many paintings in which it is seen.

The clothing of a Dutch workingwoman in her everyday garments consisted of a bodice that fitted quite loosely, with long sleeves reaching to the wrists. Over her shoulders was placed a folded kerchief. A long skirt was worn over a petticoat that came to a little above the ankles. An apron of some serviceable material was tied around the waist. While working, in order to have greater freedom, the overskirt and apron were caught up and fastened around the hips.

A Long Island New York house of about 1715.

A View of the City of New York
about 1773

CHAPTER V

Growth And Change In The Colonies

1675-1775

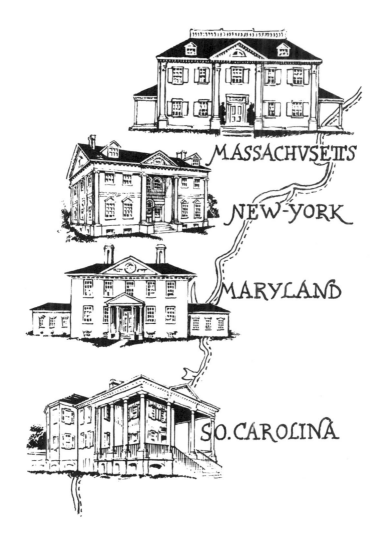

Vassall-Craigie-Longfellow House, Cambridge, Mass. 1759. Apthorpe House, New York City, about 1755, (Destroyed). Tulip Hill, West River, Maryland, 1755. Nathaniel Heyward House, Charleston, South Carolina, 1750.

CHAPTER V

Growth And Change In The Colonies
1675-1775

During the last quarter of the seventeenth century, the coastal plain was rapidly being put under cultivation. The expanding seaboard cities needed not only the produce of the hinterland, but they needed also to develop new markets for the European goods which their merchants imported in an ever increasing flow. To accomplish this, networks of roads were built which thrust deep into the countryside. New packet ship routes were added to the already existing routes. The lines of communication between the agricultural community and the cities were thus strengthened, and trade was soon moving readily from colony to colony. All this gave new impetus to the westerly movement of settlers fighting their way into Indian Territory. By the eve of the armed revolt against England, the more daring had penetrated the Allegheny Mountains, and one of the barriers to expansion was nearly breached.

The area of the coastal plain, with its increasing number of plantations and acreage for freeholding farmers, was then producing a great stream of provisions, much too large to be consumed at home. Tobacco from Virginia and the South, and corn, flour, furs, hides, flax, and hemp from the middle colonies, and lumber, turpentine, and fish from the Massachusetts Bay Colony were sent to England and the Continent, as well as the West Indies and the other colonies. In return came money and credit and all the rich and costly things for the home or person the older civilization could supply. Wealth also poured in from the many young and flourishing industries in the middle and northern provinces, which manufactured linen and woolen materials, felt hats, stockings, bar iron, candles, paper, and rope. In New England, where, by the middle of the eighteenth century, seventy ships were to be built and launched annually, entire communities were already being made prosperous by the still limited foreign and coastal trade and by the fishing carried on in New England bottoms. Under the stimulus of this prosperity, villages grew into towns, towns into cities.

As the seventeenth century ended, Philadelphia was still a tiny town of a few hundred houses; Charles Town and New Port were even smaller. New York had barely five thousand inhabitants; while Boston, the largest community in the colonies had perhaps seven thousand inhabitants. In 1760, though the colonies were still basically rural and were to continue so for another century, the urban population, concentrated in the five major cities, had grown fivefold.

Coincident with this growth of the cities and its attendant wealth came a society actuated by the manners and aims of European aristocracy, a society that attempted to reproduce the life of England and the Continent. Much of the simplicity and ruggedness of the early days was passing and a type of town life was coming into being, one which was quite a contrast to the agrarian society of the hinterland. In the colonies there was as curious a blend of both sophisticated civilization and primitive life as could be found anywhere.

One can visualize the North with its emphasis upon well-cut garments, New York with traces of its Dutch bulkiness, Philadelphia with its satins and interest in high fashion. In the tidewater country the clothes were fashionable but with more reserve, contrasting with a kind of gaiety in Charleston. When General Oglethorpe established his Georgia colony in 1733, it was made up of probationers who were working off sentences for varied crimes committed in the mother country. No frivolity in dress was encouraged, certainly, for the duration of the sentence. The somewhat darker hue of the Georgians' clothing may too have reflected the somber clothing of their Spanish neighbors.

It is during this century of expansion that the source materials for the study of American dress begin to increase. In the previous era of the early settlements the evidence is discouragingly scanty. The pictorial records—they are the most valuable of all records in this study—are few. The information to be gleaned from letters, diaries, books, invoices, and acts of legislation is not too abundant. Many of the conclusions regarding the early dress must be drawn from inference and deduction, and from knowledge of European sources.

The first newspaper was published in 1690, and, although short-lived, others followed. From their quaintly worded advertisements, it is possible to check quite accurately the arrival of new fashions and to trace the growth of native manufactures. The monthly journals appearing toward the middle of the century also contained occasional bits of information, but they are much less valuable sources than the weekly newspaper. European travelers in the colonies were fairly numerous, and, fortunately for us, many of them were observant men who published their impressions. These travel accounts, like those of the Abbé Robin, Burnaby, and Chastellux, are packed with comment on the life, manners, and dress of the time. They are doubly valuable since they constantly compare life in the colonies with European standards. Also, there exists a wealth of documentary evidence in the form of letters, sermons, court records, diaries, bills of lading, handbills, and account books.

There is a corresponding increase in graphic material. Toward the middle of the eighteenth century, many engravings and wood blocks appeared in the papers and journals, on handbills and stickers. The technique of these early illustrations is usually crude, and the facts they present are sometimes misleading, owing to the indifferent skill of the artist. Yet they furnish many valuable clues for the student of dress. It is the painters of this period, however, that give us the bulk of reference material.

The portrait was the popular artistic expression of the time, and in the largely Calvinistic atmosphere of the colonies only a medium so utilitarian as portraiture could flourish. (Comment on the painters of these portraits will be found on pages 274 *et seq.*)

I. DRESS OF THE MEN
1675–1775

About the year 1370, one finds a change in the dress of the men throughout western Europe, England, and America. This change marked the beginning of the triarchy of coat, waistcoat, and breeches which, in one form or another, has lasted until the present day.

COATS AND WAISTCOATS.—The coat is usually claimed to have been developed from the "Eastern fashion of vest . . . after the Persian mode," as mentioned in Evelyn's Diary in the year 1666. Referring to this, Kelly and Schwabe state: "The peculiar costume known as a vest after the Persian fashion, adopted in October 1666 by Charles II and his court, was an ephemeral mode and had little or no lasting influence. It was introduced as a counterblast to the craze for French fashions, which after as before retained their supremacy." For the best information concerning this new fashion in vests, which made its appearance in the Court of Charles II, turn to the October entries in the Diaries of

Evelyn, Pepys, and Rugge for the year 1666. It is interesting to find them all giving the identical information relative to the King and the Court adopting the new dress, which all refer to as the "Eastern fashion in vests."

Evelyn made an entry in his Diary on October 18, 1666, which reads as follows:

> "To Court. It being the first time his Majesty put himself solemnly into the Eastern fashion of vest, changing doublet, stiff collar, bands and cloak, into a comely dress, after the Persian mode, with girdles or straps, and shoestrings and garters into buckles, of which some were set with precious stones, resolving never to alter it, and to leave the French mode, which had hitherto obtained to our great expense and reproach. Upon which, divers courtiers and gentlemen gave his Majesty gold by way of wager that he would not persist in this resolution."

FIGURE 42

It appears, therefore, that the fashion for "Persian vests in the Eastern fashion" was more or less limited to court circles abroad, and was of such a short vogue that the vests could hardly have appeared in America. They can be dismissed without further comment.

What seems to have been more probable is that the coat of this style and cut, appearing about 1670, was developed from a garment then called a "cassock" and not from the "Persian vest" (Fig. 42). The cassock, in turn, had been derived from the earlier military garment the leather jerkin with long skirts (Fig. 35 B). An authority states: "The cassock is collarless, reaches to the knee, and has full turned up sleeves" In support of this, Planché defines the cassock as "a long loose coat or vest." In referring to an illustration of Fairholt's of a hackney coachman, taken from a broadside of the time of Charles I, now in the British Museum, and called by Fairholt a cassock, Planché adds: ". . . which is certainly nothing more or less than a loose coat, with buttons all down the front, and large cuffs, the prototype of the coats of our great grandfathers."

FIGURE 43

A   B

It appears that after the coat and the nearly always attendant waistcoat became fashionable in England about 1670, they were quickly adopted by the coteries about the local governors of the colonies. In a sense, the group around each governor was a miniature "Court," and in its small way, aped the Royal Court of England. Thus one finds the first coats following the lines of the cassock, cut straight and without being shaped in at the waist, and extending to about mid-thigh, or a little below (Fig. 43 A). Coats were provided with buttons and buttonholes down the front, but as a rule, they were only buttoned to about the waist-line. From there down, they remained open. At the elbows were found the broad, turned back, split cuffs, usually of a different material from the coat. Below the broad cuffs protruded the full sleeves of the shirt. Such sleeves were gathered to a band at the wrists, from which the ruffles fell over the hands. The pockets were usually horizontal, placed low down and covered with large flaps. The vest was exposed when the coat was open, and reached to a little below the waistline.

The next change in the coat was shortly after 1670, when it began to be cut a trifle more full in the skirt and commenced to be more and more shaped in at the waist (Plate 23; Fig. 43 B). It was also gradually lengthened until it reached to the knees, or a trifle below. The vest, follow-ing the same lines, was lengthened until it was only a few inches shorter than the coat. Though the vest was provided with buttons and button-holes all the way down, it seems never to have been buttoned, at this time, all the way to the bottom. It was fashionable to allow the coat to remain open. In the back the full skirts were split in two openings, one at each hip. The openings were provided with buttons and buttonholes, so they could be closed if desired. The pockets were still set very low in the coat and vest and were either provided with large flaps or edged with braid or galloon. It was in these great pockets the men carried silver combs for their periwigs, snuffboxes and handkerchiefs, usually of lace. Handkerchiefs were called "muckinders" at that time. The word "hand-kerchief" or "handkercher" was then used to describe a neck cloth. By the end of the century, the neck cloth was called a "neckerchief," and "handkerchief" returned to its original meaning and is so used today.

The horizontal pocket seems to have been more generally preferred than the vertical one. While sleeves of elbow length were worn through-out the century, there was a tendency to lengthen the sleeves until, by the last decade of the century, it was quite common for the sleeves with their turned back cuffs to reach almost to the wrists. Both vests and coats were collarless.

Many men preferred wearing the coat without the vest (Plate 24 A; Fig. 44 A), a style borrowed from France, where it was, especially among the younger men, a fad which lasted into the early years of the eighteenth century. Discarding these heavy vests must have been a great comfort in the summer months, especially in the South. The coats were allowed to remain open, and the full linen shirt hung over the waistband of the breeches. As a matter of fact, the coats rarely seem to have been fastened, the buttons and buttonholes being more for adornment than for utility. The buttonholes were carefully cut and laid around in gay colors, embroidered with silver and gold thread, and bound with vellum, kid, or velvet.

At the beginning of the last quarter of the seventeenth century, the coat was being more and more fitted to the waist. This fashion increased with the years. When the last decade of the century was reached, the skirts of the coat were enlarged and stiffened. This resulted in the skirts

of the coat being gathered into pleats that radiated in fan-shaped forms
from a button on the hips. As will be seen, this style of enlarged skirts
gathered into radiated pleats in the back lasted until about 1750, when
it gradually went out of fashion. These buttons, by now more or less
ornamental, had been copied from the buttons used on riding-coats, so
that the coattails could be buttoned to them, thus keeping the coattails
out of the way when the rider mounted his horse. They could, of course,
be used the same way on the street coat. Cord loops were placed at the
corners of the skirts for that purpose. This must have been convenient
for everyday wear and for walking as well as for riding.

FIGURE 44

During the first half of the eighteenth century, there was no marked
change in the style of the coat, except in the narrow turned down collars
which occasionally appeared on coats in the late thirties (Fig. 45 A).
Other changes occurred during those years, but they were concerned with
minor details. The features already explained in the dress of the fashionable man became more and more pronounced. The coat and vest from
1700 to 1750 remained about the same length (Plate 25; Fig. 44 B), the
coat extending to the knees or a little below, the vest remaining several
inches shorter than the coat. As a general rule, neither the coat nor the
vest was provided with a collar (See Chapter III, Section III, for comment on the collar).

Apparently, the young, although they wore coats similar to those of adults, were considered "smarter" in an informal style. In 1747 George Washington ordered a coat "with lappels and a collar" for his step-son.

Between the years 1715 and 1720, the coats with the full skirts gathered into radiated fan-shaped pleats from the hip buttons were further emphasized by stiffening the skirts of both the coat and vest with buckram to give them "a lamp shade outline as if to rival the ladies' hoops."

From the beginning of the century, the general tendency was for sleeves to lengthen toward the wrists, where they were turned back in deep split cuffs. The cuffs were usually held in place by buttons. William Heath says: "The cuff of the George the First coat, had three buttons with three notched holes, otherwise there was no ornamentation, and the material was as plain and economical as decency permitted."

It was during these years that the pockets of both the coat and vest were raised considerably higher. We are told that, "the opening of the pockets was much reduced and sank to about the point at which a man could easily put his hands into them, as if the very tailors felt the movement in favor of thrift, and the pleasure of clutching one's money."

Many of the waistcoats were richly ornamented down the front, and around the skirts, with embroidery in the form of running vines interspersed with clusters of flowers. There was also rich embellishment around the great pocket flaps and the buttonholes. Buttons were selected with great care. They were made of paste, "were rich in colored enamels and jewels, in odd natural stones of lovely tints, such as agates, carnelians, bloodstones, spar, marcasite, onyx, chalcedony, lapis lazuli, malachite."

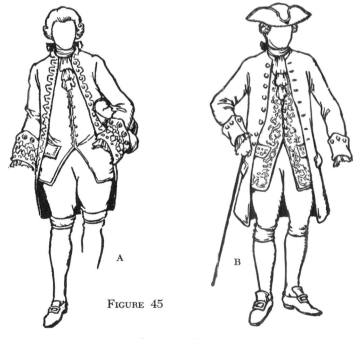

A   B

FIGURE 45

Between the years 1750 and 1760, the buckram skirts of the vests and coats gradually lessened in width and exaggeration until they finally went out of fashion. Fairly plain coats with closer fitting skirts took their place. Horace Walpole is quoted as saying ". . . the habits of the time shrunk to awkward coats and waistcoats" (Fig. 45 A B). The coat, which in the beginning came together in the front (Fig. 43 A), was gradually left more and more open, until it sloped away from the neck toward the waist, thus decidedly increasing the opening (Plate 27; Fig. 45 A B). There was still, however, a trifle of fullness left in the skirts. Less material was used, especially lace and embroidery. Instead of the quadruple skirts with multitudinous folds, which were the delight of the days of William and Mary and of Queen Anne, a man's coattails were now reduced almost to the dimensions of the modern frock coat. However the numerous folds were represented by three narrow ones, which hung at each side of the skirts apparently suspended from a button

The large turned back cuffs (Plate 27; Fig. 45 A), that by now reached the wrists with only a slight ruffle of lace showing from under them, were worn until about 1760. Gradually the smaller cuff was coming into favor, and after 1760 cuffs became small and tight (Plate 28; Fig. 45 B).

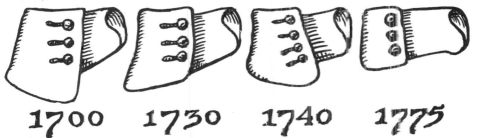

The boot-cuff or boot-sleeve, as it was sometimes called, which was a style of the 1730's, persisted for many years. The portrait of Governor Moses Gill, painted in 1766 (Plate 29) shows a late model of a boot-cuff. His is a closed cuff in the English style. Some portraits painted in the Hudson Valley, when the boot-cuff was high style, show a semi-open or "slit" sleeve. This may have been a local style or the aberration of a single artist. See Plate 24 B for an example.

It was also about this time, 1750 to 1760, that the great pocket flaps were much reduced in size.

The vest was left unbuttoned a short way down from the neck in order to show the carefully arranged cravat. It was then buttoned to about the waistline. From this point the skirts sloped rapidly toward the sides. The vest was considerably shortened, the skirts coming to about mid-thigh (Plates 27, 28, 29; Fig. 45 A B). Thus one sees a gradual "shrinking" of the coat and vest into smaller garments, which lasted until the Revolution.

FIGURE 46

Plates 30, 31, and Fig. 46 A, depict the shift from full to narrow styles in the men's clothes and in parts of the women's dresses such as the sleeves. By the eve of the Revolution, the coat had lost most of the fullness and amplitude which characterized it until a little past the middle of the century. The front of the coat dropped in uncurved, slightly oblique lines to about the knees. The coattails still radiated with a few folds from the two buttons that had been moved more to the back (Fig. 46 B). The cuffs were much smaller, and they may or may not have had buttons on the upper edge. The waistcoat was considerably shortened. It buttoned on a straight line to a little below the waistband of the breeches, where it slanted off at a decided angle, forming a short skirt (Plates 28, 32 A, 33; Fig. 46 A C).

BANYANS.—The dress of these years of which we are speaking, picturesque and charming as it was, was not altogether comfortable. The long, tight-fitting vests, the heavy and excessively hot wigs, the greatcoats with large turned back cuffs, and ruffles of lace at the wrists and neck, did not provide a dress that was comfortable and conducive to lounging. Without doubt, as soon as the man came into the privacy of his own home, the coat, the wig, and sometimes the vest, were taken off and laid aside for a more comfortable garment. This negligee was not only needed for lounging. It should not be forgotten that the long summer months of exceedingly hot weather must have made wigs and coats, especially in the South, almost unbearable. Men undoubtedly went about their business clad in a linen shirt and breeches, or wore at most a vest over the shirt. To fill the need for a more comfortable garment that could be worn as a negligee, a gown was introduced called either a "morning gown," or a "nightgown." This garment, in America often termed a "nightgown," did not refer to a sleeping garment but was a loose, comfortable robe worn as a dressing gown or negligee. The sleeping garment, when one was worn, was usually known as a "night rail." It is of interest to find that this morning gown was just as popular in many of the countries of Europe as it was in America; this was especially true of both England and France. It appears that early in the eighteenth century a new garment similar in cut and form came to the colonies from England and was known as a "banyan," the name of a loose garment worn by Hindu tradesmen and adopted as early as 1670 by English soldiers stationed in India. It became exceedingly popular with the colonists, particularly in Philadelphia and the South where the summers were hot. It was a handsome article of dress and, for those who could afford the expense, made out of the richest silks, brocades, velvets, and other fine materials.

All banyans were not made of silks or damasks. There were many who could not afford such rich materials or wanted a less expensive garment for general wear. They could be obtained, therefore, in cheaper materials such as striped and figured cottons, and they would probably be lined with colorful materials.

The banyan made of brocade or velvet and provided with a heavy, warm lining was for winter wear. For summer, there were unlined banyans of "soft Chinese silk." What a welcome relief these cool, loose garments must have been after the heavy coats with their deep turned back cuffs and stiffened skirts! Banyans were worn alike by men, women, and children. Not only were they worn in the house, but during the summer months merchants and lawyers went to their countinghouses and offices attired in this dress. In the South the masters and overseers of the plantations went the rounds of their vast estates dressed in these cool and comfortable garments.

As can be seen in the portraits of Edward Bromfield, the young genius who contributed to the technical uses of the microscope, Ezekiel Hersey (Plate 34), and Nicholas and Thomas Boylston (Plate 35), banyans were an important enough garment to have been worn by them while having their portraits painted. They are made of rich figured silks, with a lining of plain silk. The plain silk of the lining, as a rule, formed the long, rolling, kimono-like collar, as well as the full turned back cuffs of the fairly ample sleeves. The banyans were made the same inside and out and, thus, were often worn reversed. With the banyan is usually associated the turbanlike headdress that was worn over the shaved head when the wig was removed. (See turbans under the caption Headgear.)

CLOAKS AND OVERCOATS.—From the beginning of the period, capes and cloaks were no longer fashionable garments, nor of as much importance as in previous times, when the wearing of a cloak in the "grand manner" was part of the training of a gentleman. It is true, however, they were seen from time to time during the entire eighteenth century. They were worn especially by travelers in cold weather either when mounted on horseback or when traveling as passengers in the great lumbering coaches. In either case, a traveler could bundle himself up to his eyes in a warm, heavily lined cloak. The cloak was now more like a great mantle, worn wrapped around the figure instead of being thrown over the shoulders. In the late 1730's and during the 1740's the "gathers" at the neck, which had made the former cloak so clumsy were eliminated, and it now became a tailored cloak made in four pieces and shaped to the neck. It had a single or double cape collar and a vent in the back for riding. It was called variously a "roquelaure," a "roguelo," or a "roculo."

FIGURE 47

In place of the cloaks one finds, for general wear, the long, loose overcoats coming into fashion (Fig. 47 A). They were provided with great cuffs turned back in the same manner as those upon the sleeves of the coat. Around the neck of the overcoat was a fairly large flat collar. Sometimes the collars overlapped, then the outer collar could be pulled up around the head and face and buttoned down the front, thus giving protection from the cold. The overcoats were commonly belted and buckled in at the waist.

Shortly after the middle of the eighteenth century, overcoats provided with double or triple capes are seen (Fig. 47 B). They were also double-breasted and provided with large "lappels" that turned back in front of each shoulder. These overcoats were provided with a back-vent for riding. Called a "surtout" by the tailor, after about 1740 it acquired the nickname of "wrap-rascal" in deference to the style set by highwaymen.

There is little doubt but that the earlier types of fur and leather coats, such as the deerskin coats of the huntsmen, were still worn. The over-coats were spoken of as "mooseskin" or "raccoonskin" then, just as we do today.

BREECHES.—By the end of the first decade of the seventeenth century, the voluminous trunk hose had been sewn to a waistband which was fastened together in front by points. The rear of what had been two separate hose was sewn together from the waistband to below the crotch. The codpiece dropped out of fashion for the very fullness of the newly formed "breeches" usually concealed the opening left in front. As the full-ness gave way to the slimmer lines of the next decade, means of closure were introduced. At the very first, a few more ties or points were added to those holding the waistband together. Soon, a buttoned flap, sewn vertically to the middle of the sides of the opening, was added. This was extended to a full line of exposed buttons and buttonholes by the end of the first quarter of the century. Until the middle of the eighteenth century this was the usual way of fastening breeches.

Petticoat breeches (Fig. 15 A B C) were undoubtedly worn on occa-sion in some sections of our country, probably in the South or among the Dutch in New York. They were very definitely out of fashion by 1680. In no part of this country did they ever threaten the general popu-larity of the gathered breeches which we have come to call "knicker-bockers" after Diedrich Knickerbocker, the fictitious name under which Washington Irving wrote "A History of New York" in 1809. The very voluminous breeches (Fig. 43 A) became more moderate during the mid-dle years of the seventeenth century. By 1675 they had lost much of their fullness and were gathered more tightly about the knees (Fig. 44 A B).

For the next seventy-five years the only change in breeches was a gradual tightening. By the middle of the eighteenth century the breeches were getting so tight that a new means of closing them was developed, and the "fall closure" appears. This is the squared flap over the opening (see the drawing by Thomas Rowlandson, Plate 16) which persists in breeches worn by sailors today. The fly front did not occur in the eighteenth century. During the last years of the century, the breeches were made "not tight to the leg, but just full enough for comfort." They were cut, however, full in the seat and were gathered to a tight waistband (Fig. 46 A). These tight-fitting breeches came down over the knees and were fastened in place on the outside of each knee by a buckle (Fig. 46 B D), or with small buttons, usually four or five in number (Plates 27, 28). Other than the buckles or buttons at the knee, these breeches were not embellished. As a rule, the breeches matched the coat in color and material, although unmatching breeches of a neutral color and con-trasting material, such as black velvet, were occasionally worn.

After the close-fitting knee-breeches once came into fashion, there seems to have been very little change in their cut and fit (Plates 27, 36, 37, 38) until the even more tight-fitting riding breeches of the last quarter of the century led the way to pantaloons. In fact, as long as the coat or the vest was full skirted, the breeches were hardly visible (Plate 39; Fig. 43 B). It was not until the skirts of the vest had disappeared and those of the coat had retreated towards the rear that the tightness of the breeches became apparent. The self-portrait of Matthew Pratt (he is seated and holding a drawing board, Plate 40 A) reveals just how tight the breeches had become by the last quarter of the century.

LINEN.—Shirts made of materials which ranged from the finest Holland linen to coarse cotton or calico were worn under the vest. Or, as has been seen, they were often worn without a vest in the early years of the eighteenth century. This negligee effect was a short-lived fad, not a true fashion (Plate 30; Fig. 44 A). In those early years the quite short coat sleeves terminated in great cuffs which extended back to the elbow. This revealed a length of shirt sleeve which ended at the wrist in a ruffle of lawn or lace. There was an interesting variety of cuffs on the coat sleeves of this period. In Plate 42 the round cuffs of 1720 are shown, those of 1746 in Plate 43. This was a commonly worn style for it appears in many portraits which bear dates from the 1720's to the middle of the century. Plate 43 shows slit sleeves of 1745.

Examples of such cuff treatments may be seen in a few portraits of about that date. The open sleeve, which developed from the slit one, became the popular style. Plate 44 depicts the open sleeves of about the middle of the century. The buttoned "open sleeve" of mid-twentieth century coats is a survival of this style. Its precise forerunner is shown in the portrait of Dr. Alexander Shearer (Plate 32 A). Similar cuff treatments are shown in Fig. 44 B and Fig. 45 A B.

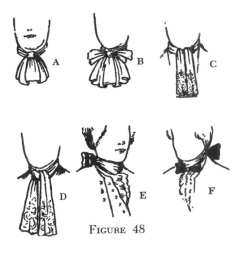

FIGURE 48

As has been noted, the cravat and the falling band were worn contemporaneously, though never at the same time. The cravat was introduced into the colonies about 1660, gradually supplanting the falling band. Mrs. Earle implies an interesting economic condition when she mentions that, "Governor Berkeley, of Virginia, ordered in 1660 a cravat which was to cost five pounds. Such rich (sic) neckware as that could not have been found in New England at this date." When cravats were first worn, the neckcloth encircled the neck and was tied under the chin with "short-spreading ends" (Fig. 48 A). Sometimes the ends of the cravat were brought together and fastened at the throat with a ribbon bow (Plates 9, 11; Fig. 48 B).

The next change took place in the 1680's when the cravat fastened at the neck with the ribbon bow was no longer fashionable. The tie-ends of the cravat were lengthened and arranged to fall freely down the front in two long ends. Sometimes the ends were tied to fall over the neckband (Plate 45; Fig. 48 C), and on other occasions a simple knot was evident, with the two ends hanging down the front (Plate 46 A; Fig. 48 D). Older men remained loyal to this fashion well into the eighteenth century (Plate 46 B).

After 1692, the Steinkirk cravat (Fig. 44 A) appeared among the fashionably dressed men in France. It was soon accepted in England and in both countries was occasionally worn by the women as well. From England, or from France, this fashion was introduced into the colonies, where it was worn by the young bucks and dandies. Here is an interesting example of the way a new style may be brought about. Quoting from Planché:

"The battle of Steinkerque, 3rd. August 1692, introduced a new fashioned cravat, . . . It was reported that the French officers, dressing themselves in great haste for the battle, twisted their cravats carelessly around their necks; and in commemoration of the victory achieved by the Mareschal de Luxembourg over the Prince of Orange in that day, a similar negligent mode of wearing the cravat obtained for it the name of Steinkerque."

Later, the long loose ends were thrust through a buttonhole of the coat. It does not appear, however, to have lasted in fashion much beyond the first quarter of the eighteenth century (Plates 42, 47).

By 1715 the fashion of lace frills had arrived. The neckcloth appeared without evident ties and was soon being made of a band of pleated material buckled in back of the neck. The lace frill, attached to the shirt, was arranged immediately below the "stock," as the neckcloth now came to be called. The frill served not only as a decorative opening in the front of the shirt, for without an arrangement of this kind, the bare chest was always visible (Plate 48 A; Fig. 45 A B). This style of frill gradually supplanted all others in general popularity. In the early nineteenth century this eighteenth century style was referred to as a "jabot" but there seems to be no evidence that it was so called contemporaneously.

From France and the court of Louis XV came a most attractive and becoming fashion known as the "solitaire." The solitaire was a ribbon of black silk attached to the bag in which the back hair of the wig was placed (Fig. 52 D). When it first came into fashion the ends of the solitaire were carried around to the front of the neck and were tucked into the shirt or were lost among the lace frills (Plate 31; Fig. 48 E). The ends could also be caught in at the throat by a brooch. Around the 1740's, it was usual to bring the two ends of the solitaire forward, tying them in a bow-knot under the chin (Fig. 48 F). The carefully arranged wig, with its bag and solitaire, the jeweled buckle of the stock, the beauty of the frills of the jabot, and the fine ruffles worn at the wrist were all the marks of the gentleman.

COIFFURES.—In the Virginia chapter, Section III, mention was made of the great periwigs that came into fashion about 1660. In spite of the great discomfort, untidiness, and the previously mentioned expense that accompanied the fashion of wigs, the style grew in favor.

Dating portraits with any degree of accuracy by the style of wig worn is not always possible. There was considerable overlapping in the different varieties, the older men often keeping to their periwigs and full bottomed wigs long after those with queues, bags, and pigtails had become fashionable.

By the early advertisements and accounts of these years, it is noted that a good wig, usually made up of human hair, was very costly and at times hard to procure. This resulted in barbers using horsehair, goat hair, and even "hair from the tails of cows," as substitutes in the cheaper grades of wigs.

Nor did the expense end with the buying of the wig, as great care was necessary to keep it presentable and in good repair. This was usually done by the barber, who was often paid as high as "eight or ten pounds a year" for the care of a single wig. It is not surprising, then, that an article so generally in demand as a wig could easily be disposed of at a good profit, and was therefore especially attractive to thieves. It is doubtful if wigs were snatched from the heads of their owners as they walked along the streets of Boston, New York, or Philadelphia, as it reportedly occurred in London. But shops and private houses were broken into; the much coveted wig being the loot in mind. Various advertisements offering rewards for their return appeared in the newspapers throughout the eighteenth century.

By 1670 the periwig had assumed quite large proportions (Fig. 20 B), the curls falling down the back and clustering over the shoulders. By 1675 it became huge and quite artificial in appearance. What is probably the most exaggerated form came into favor approximately around 1690, its chief characteristic being a well defined part in the center with a high peak on either side of the part (Plate 46 B; Fig. 20 C), the ends of the wig being separated in such a way that a cluster of curls hung over the front of each shoulder. Such an arrangement was seldom seen after 1735.

THE PERUKE.—As the periwig continued to grow during the last years of the seventeenth century into a most cumbersome affair of corkscrew curls that hung well over the shoulders, the size and weight must have caused much wearisomeness and discomfort. There is little doubt but that toward the end of the seventeenth century the colonial gentlemen tied their voluminous curls while they were hunting and riding, as did their English and French cousins.

About 1685, therefore, for informal occasions the periwig gave way to a less cumbersome wig known as the peruke (Fig. 49). The peruke was used for traveling, riding, and everyday wear. It was known as the campaign or traveling wig. Both the periwig and peruke continued in use until the middle of the eighteenth century. After 1735 the great curled periwig was no longer considered fashionable, and when it is found in portraits after this date, it is the older men, especially those in the professions, and not the younger, who are wearing them.

The peruke, campaign, or traveling wig, then, is a less cumbersome wig worn in place of the curled and loosely hanging periwig. With the peruke, the curls were carried farther back instead of surrounding the face. The rear, side locks were turned up into bobs or knots and tied with ribbons (Plate 49 A). A drawing of the portrait of Governor Ward shows him wearing the peruke (Fig. 49 B). The fullness was carried more to the back; the long lappets and curls, formerly hanging over the shoulders in front, were done away with.

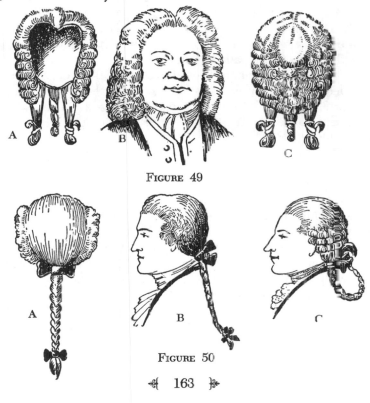

FIGURE 49

FIGURE 50

Occasionally one sees a portrait of a gentleman wearing his own hair, unpowdered, as in the painting of Thomas Van Alstyne done in 1721 (Plate 45). Evidently, even in the heyday of monstrous periwigs there were men who objected to the weight, expense, and discomfort of a wig, and the untidiness that resulted from the use of hair powder.

THE RAMILLIES WIG.—The peruke, the traveling wig, and the short bob were all modifications of the great periwig. This tendency to further reduce the size of the wig is apparent as the eighteenth century advances. In Europe in the year 1706 the Battle of Ramillies was fought between the French and the English. The soldiers, with the evident intention of freeing themselves of the cumbersome full wigs, are said to have plaited them in a queue. They then fastened the plait with a black tie at the end, and one at the nape of the neck where the plait began. This wig was known as the Ramillies wig (Fig. 50 A). It had quite a vogue in Europe and soon, due to its comfort and popularity, found its way into the colonies. The Ramillies wig, which must have appeared in America as early as 1706 or 1707, is one of the earliest forms of the plaited queue (Plate 39).

PLAITED QUEUE WIGS.—Ramillies wigs were not at first considered for full dress, being used only for the hunt, riding, and the day's business. Yet these wigs were the models for smaller and neater, fashionable ones. Queue wigs, which usually had one tightly plaited "pigtail," and "tie" or sometimes "tye" wigs, with a ribbon bow holding in a long curl at the nape of the neck, were "high style" by 1730. This arrangement of the hair permitted a puff or wave which rose from the hairline and extended upwards to the top of the head. Somewhat exaggerated versions of this wave were called "toupets."

Similar waves in the hair just above the ears were called "pigeon wings." Rolled puffs or curls at the sides of the head were other variations (Plates 32 A, 40 B C D E, 49 B C; Fig. 50 A B). The plait, if long, was sometimes looped up and fixed at the back of the wig by combs or a ribbon tie (Fig. 50 C).

From 1730 on, in newspapers, gazettes and advertisements, or in the many diaries preserved to us from this period, one finds, as Dion Calthrop so aptly states, "a veritable confusion of barbers' enthusiasms." The many names for wigs were derived from slight tricks of fashion in the arrangement of curls, puffs and queues. One can only surmise from these names what many of these wigs were like. There was one called "the comet" which probably referred to a wig with a long tapering queue. The "cauliflower" was surely an arrangement of curls. Many of the names such as "vallancy" with its sense of a crown, the "brush," "the staircase," convey very amusing images of the period. A fashion note in a 1734 issue of "London Magazine" complains, "I have seen a prim young fellow with a Cur or Adonis as they call the effeminate wigs of the present Vogue, plaister'd rather than powdered." Some of these named wigs were no passing fancy. Writing the "Spiritual Quixote" in 1773, Richard Graves mentions "a fine flowering Adonis."

Wigs, without doubt, demanded more care than any other part of the gentleman's wardrobe. On Saturdays they had to be sent to the barbers, where they were brushed and curled. Small rollers of pipe clay, called sometimes Bilboquets or more commonly roulettes were used. The curls were sometimes wound tightly around these while they were very hot. The more destructive way was to wind the hair around the cold roulettes and then heat the whole wig. Late on Saturday afternoons the barbers' boys would have been seen hurrying from the shops to deliver the wigs to important customers for them to wear that night, or on Sunday. In the larger houses, such as "Stenton" in Germantown, near Philadelphia, powder closets are still to be seen. Here, in that period, gentlemen donned the freshly delivered wigs and, with great cloths draped around from neck to feet and cones of paper or glass to protect their faces, were "powdered" by their valets. Both the closets and the powder are used differently today.

The wigs of the majority of men, however, did not receive the same careful attention. In fact, many of the wigs worn by the men who were not wealthy must, from all accounts, have been sorry affairs. Often the discarded head coverings of the upper classes were won in public lotteries, or were bought at one of the many second-hand wig shops. They were brushed and combed back into some semblance of their previous grandeur, to do duty in a simpler walk of life.

In the colonies the gentlemen of fashion followed closely the latest styles in wigs in London and Paris. Orders from the colonies for wigs in the newest styles were on the books of the English wigmakers, to be sent to their patrons in America as soon as the new styles appeared. This was not confined to any one section of the country, but was more common in the New England States, the Central, and Southern States. Thus, it was only a matter of weeks before the latest fashions in England appeared in the colonies.

The different varieties of queue wigs appearing almost simultaneously, after 1725, can be placed under certain divisions for the convenience of study. One must realize all these styles were worn at the same time (Plate 50).

TYE OR TIE WIGS.—A very popular type of the queue wig, and one appearing quite often in old colonial portraits, was the tye, or tie wig (Fig. 51). It was dressed, up until the middle of the century, with the early form of the low toupet. It was full at the sides, with the back curls gathered into a bunch and tied with a black ribbon bow at the nape of the neck. About the middle of the eighteenth century, the toupet was not worn as flat over the head as formerly, but it was now much higher, being dressed in quite a formal manner (Fig. 51 B).

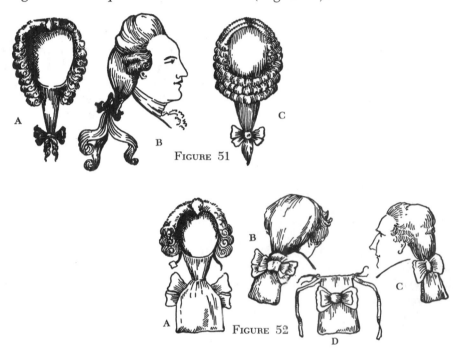

FIGURE 51

FIGURE 52

BAG WIGS.—The bag wig was evidently a very convenient as well as fashionable way of wearing the hair. The back hair was placed in a square or rectangular bag. The bag was then drawn tight with a drawstring at the nape of the neck and a black bow tied around the closure (Fig. 52). The bag served not only as a decoration but also protected the coat from the grease and powder of the wig. Until 1740 pigeon wings (Fig. 52 C) were worn over the ears, but after that date were replaced by puffs and rolls (Fig. 53 A). Around the 1740's, the bag was often so large that it practically covered the shoulders of the wearer (Fig. 52 A). It was also to the bag that the silk ribbons of the solitaire were attached (Fig. 52 D).

PIGTAILS.—Pigtails were either one (Fig. 53 C) or two (Fig. 53 B) in number. They were tightly wrapped in a spiral manner with black silk ribbons. They were tied at the nape of the neck with a ribbon bow. The hair hung free at the end, coming from out of the spiral wrappings. They

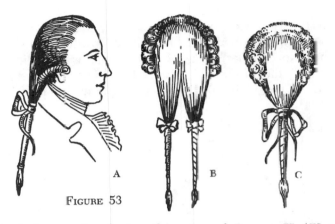

FIGURE 53

were particularly popular during the reign of George II (Plate 40 D E).

Gradually, about 1770, many men ceased to shave their heads. Wigs, with the exceptions of those retained by professional men, went out of fashion. Men again wore their own hair, although it was dressed in much the same manner as the wigs—with puffs and rolls, with queues, pigtails, and bags. The hair, however, was still usually powdered. Powder, which had been worn for over one hundred years, finally went out of fashion following the tax on hair powder in England in 1795.

HEADGEAR.—By 1670 the brims of the hats had increased greatly in size. This tendency continued until, by 1675, the brims of the hats measured in width as much as six to eight inches. In fact, the brims were so broad that through constant wear they lost their stiffness and had a tendency to fall about the face. To correct this the brims were rolled up, either at one side, in the front, or in the back (Fig. 53 A). They were also looped up and cocked in various ways. In this manner, the cocked hat was introduced into fashion. A large feather, or plume, was usually placed around the crown. Hats continued to be decorated in this way until about 1680. Yet, from the very beginning of this period the fashion of plumes, ribbons, and feathers began to wane in favor of the edge of the brim being bound with braid, galloon, or even lace. After plumes were discarded, another very fashionable way of decorating hats was to place a fringe of ostrich feathers along the brim (Fig. 44 A).

Cocked hats continued to gain in favor. First the hats were cocked up on one side, then, on both sides. By 1690 they were cocked up in the back and both sides—the familiar three-cornered hat (Fig. 45 B). The three-cornered hat was never called a "tricorne" in English-speaking countries of the day. By 1700 they were generally worn, retaining their popularity until after the Revolution.

The cocked hat, as a rule, was more often carried under the arm than worn upon the head (Fig. 45 A). We are told, "they are cocked up at all angles, turned off the forehead, turned up one side, turned up all around," until the whole appearance of the wearer might be changed from day to day by varying the angles of his cocked hat. The edge of the brim of the cocked hat was usually trimmed with metal lace or galloon. The peak in front continued to rise until in the 1740's it reached its greatest height in the "Kevenhuller" (Fig. 46 A). There was a slight dropping of the peak until the 1760's; this moderately high peak lasted until the middle of the 1770's. Plate 50 gives a good picture of hats and wigs in 1776.

From a drawing done by Marcellus Laroon in his old age, England, 1768.

For indoor wear, there were the negligee caps and turbans. They were worn with the morning gowns or banyans, which they usually accompanied. The turbans became so popular that not only were they worn for negligee but on many informal occasions as a blessed relief from the hot wigs. In order to understand this continual wearing of caps and turbans and wigs, one must realize that the head under the wig was kept closely shaven. With this protection removed, the wearer seems to have been extremely sensitive to cold and drafts. Therefore, men wore nightcaps upon retiring and whenever the wig was removed; whether indoors or out, some kind of head covering was immediately donned. This was usually the turban (Plates 34, 35). The turban, then, was for informal wear and was used to supplement the uncomfortable powdered wig. How important a part of the dress it became, to reiterate, can be judged by the number of fashionable gentlemen who continually sat for their portraits dressed in banyan and turban. The turban was usually worn perched upon one side of the head in a "very jaunty manner." Small felt-brimmed hats and round caps edged with fur were worn in place of the cocked hat by travelers and by the sporting and riding fraternity.

STOCKINGS.—Stockings worn in the early part of this period had their tops hidden under the baggy bottoms of the breeches. The stockings were evidently fastened to stay up by a form of garter made of a cloth band or ribbon. If the garter did show below the bottoms of the breeches, a decorative knot of ribbon was attached to each garter on the outside of the leg (Fig 43 A). As the breeches grew longer and tighter below the knee, wealthy men brought the tops of the stockings over the bottoms of the breeches and above the knees in a style known as "roll-ups." The style began to wane about 1735 and finally, before as "roll-ups." The style began to wane about 1735, and from then until the middle of the century, roll-ups were definitely out of style—a style that had an unusually long life for the eighteenth century.

During the first half of the century, stockings were varied of hue, frequently of russet or green. By the 1770's white silk was *de rigueur*. Elaborate embroideries on the stockings at the sides of the ankles called "clocks," and sometimes of silver or gold threads, were often used on dress occasions. The style lasted until 1790.

In 1731 there appeared in "The Boston News Letter," an advertisement for "stirrup hose." Stirrup hose were provided with wide tops, and at that time were no longer in general use. They were probably used to pull on over the stockings and knees of the breeches to protect them from the boot-saddle when riding horseback. Knitted homespun stockings, leather stockings, cloth stockings, and "good knit worsted stockings" are all mentioned during this period and were worn by men and boys who could not afford the expensive silk hose. Other varieties are, "Diced hose, masquerade hose, silk clocked and chevered hose, fine four-threaded Strawbridge knit hose, yarn hose, ribbed, pointed cheveled worsted hose, Jersey-knit hose."

FOOTGEAR.—At the beginning of this period under consideration (1675), shoes still retained their red heels and the tongue rising high up over the instep (Fig. 43 A). Shoe roses were no longer seen. In their place the shoe was fastened by strings or ties (Fig. 43 A), or by buckles (Fig. 44 A). The buckles were small at first (Fig. 44 A), being strapped high up on the instep, and were either square or oval in form. In fact, from 1680 on, buckles seem to have replaced all other forms of fastening and gradually became larger. With the high-heeled, high-tongued shoes, is generally found the square ending to the toe. This fashion lasted throughout the first quarter of the eighteenth century.

From 1720 on, the high tongues were gradually shortened, and the decidedly square toes gave way to a shoe with a more natural and rounded shape to the toe (Fig. 44 B). About 1740 the short-tongue, natural shaped shoe with a large buckle over the instep took that shoe's place (Fig. 45 A B. Fig. 46 A).

Boots were not a part of fashionable everyday attire during this period, but were worn more for riding, traveling, and hunting. The favorite boots of the last part of the seventeenth century and the first part of the eighteenth century were the heavy, cumbersome, rigid "jackboots." They came into fashion on the Continent about 1660. However, it appears they did not come to the colonies until several years later. By 1675 they were generally worn. The jackboot (Fig. 54 D) was made of stiff leather from the ankle to just below the knee, where it flared into a large cup. They were usually provided with large spur leathers over the instep, and to these leathers the spurs were attached. They seem to have gradually lost favor with the gentry toward the close of the first quarter of the eighteenth century. From about 1720 on, jackboots diminished in size and rigidity until a new boot was evolved, built on the same lines. The new ones were lighter and more flexible, fitting more to the shape of the leg (Fig. 54 A). These new boots were so flexible that a small strap was often buckled around the boot just under the knee to hold it more securely in place. The spur leather was still worn over the instep.

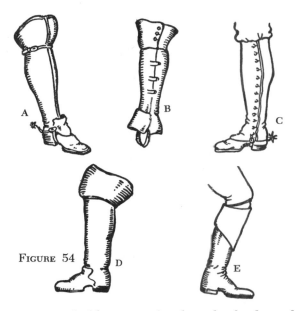

FIGURE 54

The boots were probably worn for horseback through the 1770's. From these light jackboots, about 1700, leggings of leather called "spatter-dashes" evolved (Fig. 54 B). Buttons and buckles down the side made them fit close to the leg. They were worn over the shoes. Where the legging met the shoe, the joint was masked by a large spur leather, making it difficult not to confuse them with the regular jackboot. Even higher spatterdashes were also worn extensively (Fig. 54 c). They buckled under the shoe and buttoned up the side. Mention is made of "Thread and cotton Spatterdashes." Spatterdashes were used to protect the stockings in wet and stormy weather and were worn especially by sportsmen until the end of the century.

Top boots made their appearance some time in "the latter half of the century," and because of their elegant appearance became exceedingly popular with young bloods. The lower part of this boot (Fig. 54 E) fitted tightly over the leg and was made of black leather, usually polished. The top of the boot, that came from a little below the knee to the middle of the lower leg, was either brown or white leather. So exceedingly trim were these boots that they became a part of the "walking dress."

PUMPS.—Low-heeled shoes with pliable soles were designed for running footmen, who went alongside a carriage. These pumps, usually buckled, were sometimes laced over the insteps. The beaux of the 1730's and the 1740's, thinking them smart, copied them. This is a form of shoe that has been with us ever since—as a style for little girls, then for mature women, and currently for younger women and girls.

SLIPPERS.—The slipper was designed to replace the boot at home. Its style has not changed from that day to this (Plate 34 B).

ACCESSORIES.—The baldric, in the wide and elaborate form that seemed to dwarf the sword, does not seem to have been worn into the eighteenth century. Its place was taken by a simple sling made on the lines of the baldric, or by a "frog," which was attached to a belt worn under the vest. The loops of the frog extended just sufficiently below the edge of the vest for the scabbard to be slipped freely in or out of them. To retain some of the decorative quality that had formerly been contributed by the baldric, the hilt of the sword was often embellished with a large bowknot of ribbon.

Muffs, both large and small, and made out of fur, cloth, and cloth edged with fur, were carried by men throughout this period.

Most gentlemen "took" snuff, and the handsome snuffbox was to the man of fashion what the fan was to the fashionable lady. A corner of a fine lace handkerchief would protrude from one pocket of the coat. In the other pocket was the great comb for putting the periwig in order; this was often done in public.

During the 1740's the fashion for carrying a watch with a fob attached first appeared. The fob ribbon hung out of the pocket in which the watch was kept, or it implied the presence of a watch in that pocket. From the end of the ribbon hung a cluster of seals, often exquisitely cut in steel or gems.

II. DRESS OF THE WOMEN
1675–1775

During the last quarter of the seventeenth century, America was beginning to develop the wealth that made the eighteenth century, until the Revolution, one of the most prosperous and comfortable periods in her history. A growing maritime commerce between Boston, New York, Philadelphia, and Charleston cemented a relationship between these different sections of the country. Different elements—the Puritans of New England, the Dutch of New York, the "world's people" of Pennsylvania, and the aristocratic landowners of the South became unified in ideas of dress and fashion. Commerce and intercourse were extremely active and continuous between the colonies and the mother country. London dictated styles and fashions to America until the eve of the rebellion. Speaking of the dress in the colonies, Frank Alvah Parsons says:

> *"The instinct for dress, the fundamental desire for show and personal attraction were no different; the determination not to be outshone and the admiration for the latest and prettiest fashions from England were almost universal, and even where there was a pretence to plain living and an outward expression of piety through its manifestation, the author fails to find any considerable number of instances of individuals who resisted falling into the ways of the world at the first perfectly good opportunity. The few isolated instances are so small in number, that 'the exception proves the rule.'*
>
> *"As the eighteenth century advanced, the Colonies naturally grew in wealth, their commerce (particularly with Britain) increased, and the awakening of a national consciousness resulted."*

In this striving to imitate the English styles, the fashion dolls, dressed in the latest modes, played a large and most important part. It was by means of dressed dolls that many of the newest fashions first made their appearance in the colonies. Fashion "babies" were dressed by the mantua-makers of Paris; from there they were sent to the eagerly waiting women of London. These dolls helped set the new styles for the fashionably dressed English ladies, together with new dolls supplied by the London milliners, who were the dry goods dealers of the day. They purveyed the dolls—whoever made them. The dedication to hats was a later development. Many of these dolls were sent to the colonies. In this way many new fashions were brought from France and England to America. After these dolls had served their purpose, and their little gowns were no longer capable of stimulating the feminine taste, they were given to children to play with. Many of them were destroyed, of course, partially accounting for the comparatively few survivals of this host of small invaders.

The most fashionable dress worn by women in this present period was the "sacque." This garment, hanging from the shoulders over the large hooped petticoat, passed through various changes. It retained its popularity from about 1720 to 1777. The most usual dress, however, and one continually seen throughout these years, was a dress with a long-waisted bodice. It came to a point in front, the neck bared by a medium horizontal or round décolletage, the skirt full. In fashion at the end of the third quarter of the seventeenth century, this was the basic style for more than a hundred years. Many examples of this dress appear in eighteenth century portraits (Plate 51; Fig. 23 A B).

BODICE.—The bodice was still low-cut and low-waisted, coming to a point in front. If it fastened in front, the opening was embellished with bowknots (Fig. 55 A). The opening around the bosom was generally softened by allowing the border of the chemise to appear above the edge of the bodice, or by fixing in front of the décolletage a "modesty piece," a bit of ruffled lace or lawn to cover the "pit of the bosom." Around the rest of the neckline a "tucker" could be used. This was a false ruffle, basted to the shift or sewn directly to the edge of the closed robe itself. Sometimes, for modesty or allure, a fine scarf or a folded kerchief covered the bosom. The lace band or lace collar did not last beyond 1690 (Plate 14; Fig. 55 A).

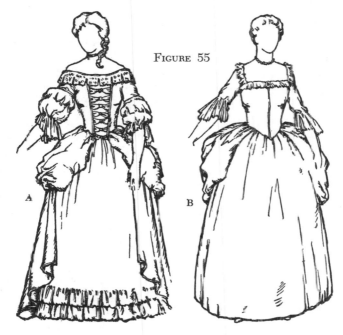

FIGURE 55

A   B

From these later years of the seventeenth century until about 1715, a kind of gathered ruche of the same material as the dress was frequently used in a band along the robings, the edge of the overskirt, and the hemline of the petticoat. This was the French "falbalas," called in England and the colonies, a "furbelow." Though in this period the word was never applied to anything but the sort of banding just described, "furbelows" came to mean any showy ornamentation.

The furbelow was out of style from 1715 until the middle of the century. It then returned to fashion until the end of the 1770's.

Sleeves reaching the wrist were no longer fashionable after 1660. Elbow length sleeves or ones that ended midway between the shoulder and the bend of the arm took their place (Plate 14; Fig. 55 A B). Appearing from under the sleeve of the bodice was the full sleeve of the fine chemise, ending in a ruffle of lace. Sometimes ruffles were sewn to the bodice sleeves and served to conceal the plain chemise sleeves underneath. Though the chemise sleeve was supposed to be unseen and therefore ended in a plain band, it was made long enough to cover the elbow, which was then considered ungainly. Without this protection a careless gesture might have revealed a naked elbow. Whichever type of sleeve was worn, the ruffles at the elbow remained in fashion throughout the period (Plate 51).

The long waisted bodice might have been decorated down the front with a band of lace (Plate 14) or it might have been left open to reveal a "stomacher." The stomacher was a piece of cloth in the form of an inverted triangle. Usually contrasting in color and material to the bodice, it could be worn in three ways. In its most elaborate form, the stomacher was stiffened by long pins of whalebone or carved ivory which were inserted into vertical pockets. These could be withdrawn for greater comfort in informal moments. That these informal moments were somewhat less than private is indicated by the beauty of the "busk(pins)," for they have since been collected as works of art.

A less expensive way, though a less comfortable one, to stiffen the stomacher was to line the triangle with cardboard. The stomacher was then attached with pins or some such means under the widely opened edges of the bodice. In another variation, the unstiffened material was pinned to the front of a "busk." The busk, sometimes called "stays" into the twentieth century, was a "corset," the eighteenth century name for a similar garment worn by men. The two side edges of the stomacher were hidden by the robings at the edges of the bodice. Lacings which held the bodice in place, or appeared to do so, were very stylish. A more elaborate decoration consisted of a graduated series of ribbon bowknots called "échelles" (Plates 53 B, 54, 64; Fig. 55 A).

Later forms of the bodice, from 1700 to the Revolution, differed only slightly from the earlier styles. They were longwaisted and worn over a tightly corseted figure. Sometimes they descended to a point in front (Plates 53 A, 55, 68 A). Again, they might be rounded about the waist

(Plate 51). The bodice was often fastened down the back, leaving the
front perfectly plain, except where it is relieved by a lace ruffle at the
opening of the décolletage (Plates 51, 56, 57), or softened by the lawn
chemise (Plates 57, 58, 59, 60). A ribbon bowknot was commonly placed
at the top of the bodice in front. A ribbon might also be tied around
the waist in a bowknot, usually a little toward the right side. The sleeves
of elbow length were similar in arrangement throughout these years with
only slight variations. The fine linen or lawn sleeve, with its accompanying ruffles and laces, appeared from under the bodice sleeve and fell in
rich clusters around the elbow and over the forearm (Fig. 55 B, 56). The
ruffles of lace, shorter on the upper part of the arm, were usually graduated in length (Plates 53 A, 68 A). Besides these charming elbow sleeves,
wrist length sleeves became popular about 1770.

SKIRTS AND PETTICOATS.—The skirt in the year 1675 was still
gathered, as formerly, into small close pleats about the waist (Fig. 23 A).
It was usually open in the front, exposing the petticoats. When worn in
this manner, it was fashionable to loop the skirts up about the hips, holding it in place with knots of ribbon (Fig 55 A). Until the introduction
of hoops and panniers, the fullness of the skirt gathered up about the
hips was further exaggerated by a small bustle. Both skirt and petticoat
at this time were provided with a train.

A Section of The Petticoat or The Venus of 42 and 94

The left-hand engraving is by Hogarth (1742.) The right-hand engraving by Lady
C.C.1 . . . (1794.)

Hoops came into fashion between 1710 and 1715. Planché says: "It is in the reign of Queen Anne that the hoop starts forth again as a novelty." Sir Roger de Coverley in "The Spectator," 1711, describes the new fashion thus: "You see, sir, my great, great, great grandmother has on the newfashioned petticoat, except that the modern is gathered at the waist; my grandmother appears as if she stood in a large drum, whereas the ladies now walk as if they were in a go-cart." The hoop skirt was a circular arrangement of whalebone. The whalebone hoops started at the waist, gradually becoming larger as they descended. They might have been attached to a canvas petticoat. Later, about the middle of the century, they were made in two side-pieces to enable the wearer to handle them more easily.

It appears that the whalebone hoops were quite round and funnel-shaped at first. During the next few years they became more and more flattened in front and back, projecting out in varying widths on both sides over the hips (Plates 61, 62, 63, 64; Fig. 55 B, Fig. 56). Instead of forming a circle, the shape of the skirt was now more oval, a fashion worn throughout the period.

With the introduction of hoops, the trains gradually disappeared until in a few years the skirt and petticoat touched the ground evenly all the way around. From 1730 on, the skirt and petticoat were usually of ankle length, especially for everyday wear. For dress occasions they reached the ground (Fig. 55 B. Fig. 56.)

FIGURE 56

The skirt is often shown closed (Plate 65 A). When the skirt was open in front it might be gathered full over the hips, from there hanging free, revealing a V-shaped section of the petticoat (Plates 35 B, 66; Fig. 56). Another manner of wearing the open skirt was to gather it up in the old manner and fasten it in panniers at the side (Fig. 55 B).

GOWNS.—When the bodice and skirt are made in one piece, it is called a gown. The skirt of the gown was worn hanging down fully over a hooped petticoat (Fig. 56) or looped back over the hips and revealing the petticoat (Fig. 55 B). The bodice of the gown, however, did not differ from the bodice made to wear separately with a skirt. The décolletage, from the early years of the eighteenth century, tended to a round (Plate 67) or a square cut neckline (Plate 68 A). When the bodice was left open in front, it was worn over the stomacher (Plate 55; Fig. 56). The stomacher was embellished with embroidery, a pattern of lacing, or the échelles down the front. A band of lace, as a tucker, was the favored way to edge the décolletage.

A wrapping gown worn in the early years of the century was called a closed robe. In the middle years of the century, 1735 to 1755, almost exactly the same type of gown was worn in public and it was then called a "roundgown" (Plate 69 A C D).

From about 1720 until the end of the fighting in the war with England, a most fashionable dress was the "full gown," called a "sacque," that hung from the shoulders, its fullness spreading out over the hooped petticoat. Of French origin, this sacque is generally spoken of as the "Watteau gown," and the box pleating in the back as "Watteau pleats." Perhaps a more suitable name for the gown would be the "robe à la française." In Plate 71 there are three robes drawn by Antoine Watteau about 1721. These three appear to be a form of "undress." The one to the left (71 B) is a wrapping gown. Below it is a local variant, à la Piedmontese (71 D), and to the right (71 C) a gown called "à l'Anglaise," and very probably the source of the "Watteau pleats." The dress at the top (71 A) is the fashionable version for street wear, the true "robe à la française." This dress first appears in a series of paintings by Nicolas Lancret. The first recorded date for their exhibition was 1741. The fullness of the gown in the back was brought into a series of box pleats, attached to the top of the bodice at the neckline, very much as they were in Watteau's "Robe à l'Anglaise." From there the pleats descended to about the line of the waist, becoming part of the fullness of the skirt, also as in the Watteau drawing (Plate 70 A; Figs. 57, 58). A shortened version of this style, worn over the gown as a jacket, also appeared in the same years. Called the "Pet-en-lair," or sometimes "Petenlair," it is rarely seen in American portraits. However, an early version of the style, perhaps imported as a garment from France, is clearly shown n Plate 54. Perhaps it was an "undress" and so was quite a rarity in portraiture. Popular in the 1750's, the Pet-en-lair went completely out of fashion in the 1770's.

FIGURE 57

FIGURE 58

The sacque was worn in three ways: open all the way down the front with the stomacher and petticoat showing; closed from about the waist down (Fig. 57 A); in some instances, closed all the way. The ruffled sleeves followed the general fashion, coming to the elbow. When the sacque was closed, it was often made to fit close in front down to the waist, with the two pleats hanging down the back and merging below the waist with the fullness of the skirt (Plate 55; Figs. 57 B, 58 A). Later in the period, the box pleating instead of hanging freely from the neckline was brought in and sewn almost flat to the back of the bodice.

The portrait of Mrs. Thomas Newton (Plate 70 B) shows a very stylish version of a sacque of about 1770. The overskirt has the lower front corners pulled up underneath the fullness of the skirt in a manner which was described as "rétroussé." The slits through which the corners of the overskirt were pulled were commonplace in the straight hanging skirt, providing access to pockets in the petticoat without lifting aside the skirt. Sometimes these slits were emphasized with embroidery or by appliqués about them; more frequently, they were concealed in the fullness of the skirt. Pockets in petticoats used when travelling, and in the fuller skirts worn by elderly women, persisted into the twentieth century. When the opening of the pocket was vertical, it was inserted in a seam, in a way similar to that used for the pockets in a man's trousers.

From France came a new gown, the "polonaise," that was to be exceedingly popular as well as fashionable in the colonies during the years prior to the Revolution and the early years of the new Republic.

FIGURE 59

A　B

True, it was less fashionable in France than the "robe à la française," for the robe remained the gown of ceremony until their Revolution wiped out the hoops. The bodice of the polonaise fit closely to the tightly laced figure and came to a point in front (Fig 59 A B). Two pleats or ruffles came from the back of the neck over the shoulders and descended into a rounded front. The full skirt in back, instead of hanging at full length, was usually looped up with ribbons, forming three festoons in back with the center one slightly longer than the two at the sides (Fig. 59 B). The petticoat, after being hooped out from the waist, fell quite vertical (Fig. 59 A). It reached to a little above the ankle; the hem was usually embellished with a wide box pleating. The bodice was laced over a stomacher, with a "silk cord through eyelet holes." The gown was cut low, baring the shoulders (Fig. 59 A). The neck, however, was often covered with a folded shawl or fichu of lace.

RIDING HABIT.—The first means of traveling and of communication between the different settlements in the colonies were either by following the streams and rivers in boats and canoes, or on foot, threading the forestways along old Indian trails. Gradually, the trails and blazed paths through the forest widened into roads, making horseback riding possible. Even after carriages and stagecoaches came into general use, horseback riding remained by far the most popular way of getting around until the close of the eighteenth century.

The usual way for women and children to ride about in the early days was seated on a "pillion," for no woman rode alone until late in the seventeenth century. The pillion, however, remained in general use until the end of the eighteenth century. The pillion was a leather or padded cushion on a wooden frame, measuring about a foot and a half in length and ten inches or so in width. A sort of platform stirrup, or footboard, hung from the offside. The pillion was strapped to the horse's back behind the saddle. A metal handle, or strap, was fastened to the framework of the pillion, to which the rider could cling for safety. In place of this, the pillion rider sometimes steadied herself by placing her arm around the rider, or by clinging to a heavy leather belt strapped around the man's waist for this purpose. The manner in which a woman rode "apillion" became a study in "correct form," akin to the way in which she "sat sidesaddle."

There was no riding dress especially designed for women in those early days. They protected their garments from being splashed with mud and dirt by donning a cloak and pulling over their skirts a garment which could be called a "safeguard," weather skirt, or riding petticoat, which was made out of some stout material, usually a heavy linen. Safeguards seem to have been worn as a protection as long as women rode horseback. While the safeguard served for all general purposes in the colonies, there appeared late in the seventeenth century advertisements in the London papers, as well as in writings, in letters, and diaries, descriptions of a new, fashionable dress especially designed for hunting and riding. This riding habit soon found its place in the wardrobe of the well-dressed woman of America.

One of the earliest descriptions of an outfit that might be considered as being made especially for riding appears in Pepys's Diary under the date of July 13, 1663. Pepys, while strolling in the park, saw Charles and the Queen riding by, and upon his return home made the following entry relative to the riding habit worn by her Majesty: ". . . a white laced waistcoat and crimson short pettycoat, . . . in this dress, with her hat cocked and a red plume." In a newsletter of the year 1682 the ladies of the English court are described as taking the air on horseback "attired very rich in close-bodied coats, hats, and feathers with short perukes."

Planché also refers to an English riding-dress that was advertised for sale in 1711, the costume consisting of "coat, waistcoat, petticoat, hat and feather all well laced with silver."

Many advertisements appeared in the London newspapers of the eighteenth century, advertising lost or stolen garments. Among fashion descriptions, the following, published in 1712, describes a lady's riding dress: "A coat and waistcoat of blue camlet trimmed and embroidered with silver, with a petticoat of the same stuff, by which alone her sex was recognized, as she wore a smartly cocked hat, edged with silver and rendered more sprightly by a feather, while her hair, curled and powdered hung to a considerable length down her shoulders, tied like that of a rakish young gentleman, with a long streaming scarlet band."

Still another early reference made to the riding "habit" appears in 1727, which reads: ". . . riding habits with hats and feathers and periwigs." During the eighteenth century, riding habits were called by various names; the "Brunswick," introduced in England about 1750, was the one most generally worn. As in the case of those previously described, it was made in the masculine mode of coat and waistcoat.

Along with other imported clothes, came riding habits. The two women in riding habits (Fig. 60 A B) illustrate the equestrian dress which is similar to the description given. In Figure 60 A the coat has masculine lines and is brought in close to the tightly laced waist, with skirts that flare out over the full petticoat. The sleeves are turned back into great elbow cuffs, held in position by loops and buttons. Under the coat is worn, in place of the waistcoat, a low-cut bodice. A cocked hat, decorated with lace and plumes, very mannish in character, is worn completely hiding the hair in front and at the sides.

FIGURE 60

A riding habit decidedly more masculine in appearance is shown in Figure 60 B. The coat, tailored with straighter lines, is not brought in so tightly to the waist, and it is worn over a waistcoat that is a few inches shorter than the coat. At her neck is a stock with the two ends of the cravat hanging down over the waistcoat. A cocked hat rests upon a peruke, or upon her own hair dressed to resemble that of the fashionable man. To complete the masculine look, the back hair was occasionally placed in a bag such as men wore on their wigs, and the solitaire that held the bag pulled into the neck and tied over the cravat. For a description of women's riding dress up until the opening of the nineteenth century, see Chapter VII, Section II.

CLOAKS.—The cloak, in one form or another, was popular in America from the time of the first settlements until the opening years of the nineteenth century. Cloaks were so extremely comfortable and warm, so easily thrown about the shoulders, that even when more fashionable garments such as coats, jackets, Pet-en-lairs, and pelisses came in, they continued to be worn. Those worn during the eighteenth century were of a scarlet color, lined with gay and colorful materials. A certain confusion sometimes exists regarding the difference between the cloak and the hood with a cape attached. It is difficult at times to distinguish by name and description the various forms. The long cloak of about three-quarter length or longer, with or without a hood attached, varied hardly at all from the style of the early seventeenth century and was worn all through the eighteenth century (Fig. 61 c). Still another style, and an exceedingly popular one, was in the form of a short cloak made of silk, with a hood attached. Called a "capuchin," it was worn throughout the eighteenth century. It resembled the medieval capuchin, a hood which had been patterned after those worn by the Capuchin friars. The actual cloak had two long points hanging down in front (Plate 72 A; Fig. 61 B). Then there was a cloak in the form of a shawl, called a "rocket." Country women bundled themselves up in these West Country Rockets. These were large rectangles of a serge-like material or linsey-woolsey doubled together. Steamer rugs and stadium blankets are modern survivals of these rockets and have the same characteristic fringelike ends known as "fags." The tobacco shreds sticking out of a handrolled cigaret were known as "fag ends," and from that, cigarets get the nickname "fags." Unlike the modern versions, the rockets were apparently of solid colors, with white favored for summer, scarlet for winter. There was also a scarlet cloak, usually of a woolen material, called a "cardinal." It was evidently a cheaper, but warmer garment than the capuchin. The "pelisse" became popular about the same time and in the following way: In 1730 a small scarf, called a "manteel," was worn, sometimes with a hood attached.

FIGURE 61

Within a decade the front ends of the manteel were made longer until finally they could be crossed at the waistline in front and tied around it in the back. The cape section remained short. In this newer form the manteel was now a "pelerine." One is illustrated in Plate 68 B. Then the sides were lengthened and it became a somewhat loose mantle with side slits through which to thrust the arms. This was the "pelisse," and it became very fashionable indeed. Some versions had a broad flat collar, some retained the original hood, and some were provided with sleeves. The more expensive pelisses might be trimmed with fur (Fig. 61 A).

Several variants of the pelisse were developed and though they attained a brief popularity, none remained in favor as long as did the pelisse. One of the variants was a short, full jacket with elbow length sleeves and a broad turned-back collar. Another was a more cape-like version of the pelisse, called a "polonese," which was popular briefly about 1750. During the last two decades of the century, the cloak became simply a long rectangle. We would call it a stole. The cloak, in this fashion, was wrapped around the shoulders and over the arms. It became very stylish and is seen again and again in portraits (Fig. 66).

COIFFURES.—The hair, which had been dressed from 1660 on with wired out curls that hung from the side of the head (Plate 21), was brought closer to the face during the 1670's. This manner of dressing the hair persisted during the first years of this period until the new fashion of arranging the hair over the brow and closer to the side of the head came in about 1680 (Fig. 62 A). Gradually, the hair was dressed higher and higher, until by 1690 it was dressed over a wire frame, rising in two tall peaks above the brow. At the same time it was brought much closer to the side of the head (Fig. 62 B). One or two long curls hung from the back of the head over the shoulders. This mode of dressing the hair, decidedly French, was introduced into England and from there into the colonies. In America it never seems to have in any way approached the exaggerated height it assumed in France, and often in England.

Shortly after 1700, the style of high coiffures gave way to a fashion in which the hair was dressed close to the head and off the face. This popular fashion lasted until the late 1760's (Plate 51, 56). The only slight variation occurred when the hair was dressed over a roll in the form of a pompadour (Fig. 62 C). Long loose curls might fall over the shoulder. Plates 59, 60 A, 73 give an excellent idea of how the hair was dressed during this time. In Europe, powder for the hair, used sparingly in the opening years of the eighteenth century, increased as the years progressed. In America, however, it was only occasionally used until the middle of the century. From 1750 on, it became quite popular especially for dress occasions, until it went out of fashion in 1795.

About 1760 the hair was dressed in a high pompadour with a symmetrical arrangement of curls at the sides and over the top of the head. Pearls were usually worked into the coiffure. One or two curls might hang from the back of the head over the neck and shoulders (Fig. 57 A).

Drawing by Henry Fuseli, 1775.

Drawing by Godfrey Kneller, 1715.

A

B

C

FIGURE 62

French caricature, 1785.

Gradually, toward 1770 the colonial ladies dressed their hair higher and higher (Plate 73 A) in imitation of the great coiffures worn by the French and English women. In France, where the fashion originated, and where after 1775 it was carried to the most unheard-of exaggerations, there are numerous drawings, cartoons, and paintings from which to visualize these exotic headdresses. And we know England of the time intimately, for such great artists as Hogarth, Rowlandson and Darly laid all bare. In America, however, one has to depend mostly upon extracts from diaries and letters, from advertisements of the various articles needed for headdresses, which appeared in the newspapers, and from the few existing books treating with the "art" of hairdressing. While undoubtedly the ladies of America followed from a distance the fashions of France and England, there is no evidence leading to a belief that they at any time copied these towering coiffures to the same extent. French ladies, or their hairdressers, were continually inventing new styles, and the names given to these new coiffures were frequently ridiculous. The hair was dressed "butterfly fashion," "sportsman in the bush," "foaming torrents," "coiffure coiled sentiments." One style was the *pouf au sentiment,* made up of various ornaments such as birds, butterflies, and cupids. The ornaments were cut out of cardboard, assembled together with twigs of trees and even vegetables into varied compositions and somehow fixed in place over the mass of waving curls of hair. This coiffure was much in fashion in court circles. "The comet of 1773," states Augustin Challamel, "gave its name to a certain headdress in which flame-coloured ribbons played a striking part. The *coiffure à la Belle Poulé* consisted of a ship in full sail, reposing on a sea of thick curls." He further states that "the scaffolding of gauze, flowers, and feathers was raised to such a height that carriages were not lofty enough for the ladies. The occupants were obliged either to put their heads out of the windows, or to kneel on the carriage floor so as to protect the fragile structures." The bodies of these enormous creations were formed of tow, over which the hair was drawn in great curls, rolls, and bobs, with false hair added. Next the whole was freely plastered over with powder and pomatum, and finally it was decorated with huge bows, ribbons, feathers, and flowers.

The variants in the mode of hairdressing are apparent in Figure 62. At the upper right of the figure is a drawing by Sir Godfrey Kneller made early in the century. The rise in height of the hair after the 1760's is evident in the drawing to the left by Henry Fuseli, made about 1777. In the caricature at the bottom of the figure, though they are exaggerated, the headdresses are nevertheless accurately rendered.

One of the most astonishing circumstances connected with headdresses during the span of this curious style was the agony and distress gone through by the women in having their heads made up, let alone the discomfort experienced in trying to rest in them at night. For "heads" were supposed to last for some days. The most revolting part, however, was the general lack of cleanliness of the various materials that went into the composition, making their heads itch and burn. There was time for a "head" to become infested, for it was kept intact for as much as three weeks. In magazines of the period, advertisements and recipes for formulas which will destroy the insects appear again and again.

Returning now to America, one may form some idea of the fashion of heads from the diary of Anna Green Winslow. In the year 1772 she writes:

> "I made my HEDDUS roll on, aunt Stoere said it ought to be made less, Aunt Deming said it ought not to be made at all. It makes my head itch, & ache, & burn like anything Mamma. This famous roll is not made wholly of a red Cow Tail, but it is a mixture of that, and horsehair (very course) & a little human hair of yellow hue, that I suppose was taken out of the back part of an old wig. But D—— made it (our head) all carded together and twisted up. When it first came home, aunt put it on, & my cap on it, she then took up her apron & mesur'd me, & from the roots of my hair on my forehead to the top of my notions, I mesur'd above an inch longer that I did downwards from the roots of my hair to the end of my chin. Nothing renders a young person more amiable than virtue & modesty without the help of fals hair, red Cow Tail, or D—— (the barber)."

An incident chronicled in "The Boston Gazette" of May 1771, tells of a young woman out driving in her carriage. The horses became startled and she was thrown from her equipage into the street, damaging her great headdress, the greater part of it in fact being torn off. The inside of the head proved a revelation, for it was filled with tow, yarn, curled hair, and hay.

A good example of a colonial headdress of about 1775 is seen in Figure 63 A. The hair is arranged for full dress and is carried over a framework of wire or rolled over a high cushion and powdered. It was usual to arrange a twisted muslin headdress in the form of a small turban on top of the "creation." Arranged on the left side of the turban might be a bunch of artificial flowers. In this round type of headdress two curls might hang from the back, over the shoulders.

The hair, instead of being built up in this rounded form, might be brushed up in a severe manner from the sides of the face and from the back and front of the head, its severe lines softened only by a few curls or puffs over the ears (Fig. 63 B C). The hair would then be plastered with pomades or powder washes to the foundation already referred to. If there was not sufficient natural hair to accomplish this, false hair would be added. In the top of this coiffure might be placed feathers or plumes that gently swayed back and forth in the breeze. Marie Antoinette is accredited for the fashion of plumes not only in France but throughout

Europe and even far distant America. The Queen, a leader in all fashions, in a spirit of play placed two peacock feathers and several ostrich plumes in her already elaborate coiffure. The King, Louis XVI, expressed his admiration for this new effect; he had never seen the Queen look so well. Marie Antoinette, pleased by the flattery of the King, appeared at court that evening with feathers and plumes waving from the top of her head-dress. Immediately, feathers came into fashion. On state occasions the great rooms of the palaces and chateaux looked like forests of waving plumes.

FIGURE 63

FIGURE 64

HEADGEAR.—Except for hoods (Plate 74) and kerchiefs (Plates 13, 14), the hair, as a rule, was left uncovered until after 1680. Then a new decoration appeared for the coiffure. At first it was called a *fontange;* toward 1700 the name became *commode-fontange*. To what extent this new headdress was worn in America, it is difficult to state. It does not, as far as one is aware, appear in any portraits painted of American women. It was, however, fashionable in England shortly after its intro-duction in France, and it seems only reasonable to assume that a style so

popular in England, where the fashions were set for the colonies, would
sooner or later have appeared in America. The new mode of dressing the
hair received its name from Mademoiselle de Fontange, one of the several
mistresses of Louis XIV.

The story goes that: one day when hunting with the King, the wind
disarranged her hair, which fell about her shoulders, upon which she
took off one of her garters and tied it up hastily with that. His Majesty
was so pleased with the effect, that he requested her to continue to wear
her hair dressed in that fashion.

This was only the beginning of the fashion. It was to be greatly
elaborated upon by the addition of a lace or lawn cap fitting over the
back of the head and trimmed with lace, frills, and ribbon; the most
characteristic feature being a series of graduating tiers of lawn and lace
rising in the front and inclining forward (Fig. 64 A B C). Streamers or
lappets could hang down the back (Fig. 64 C) or could be dispensed
with (Fig. 64 A). This new addition was known as the commode. When
in addition to the commode, the ribbon and bowknot of the fontange is
retained, the combination received the name of the "commode-fontange"
(Fig. 64 A). The Duchess of Portsmouth in an undress (Plate 74) wears
one.

Whether or not the commode-fontange was worn in all its grandeur
by American women is problematical, but it was worn by at least one
child (Plate 94 F). Yet, surely the small linen or lace cap appearing shortly
after 1700 upon the low-dressed heads and lasting until the hair began
to be dressed in a tower is a form of the commode without "the special
features" (Plates 54, 58 B). This small cap still retains the lappets or
streamers in the back, which could be worn either hanging down or
fastened up (Fig. 64 D). The hair was arranged close to the head and then
left plain (Plate 51), entwined with beads (Plate 56), partially covered
by the fashionable close cap (Plate 53 B), or simply relieved with a spray
of flowers fastened at the top a little to one side (Plate 55). It emphasized the fullness of the hooped skirts.

Toward 1770, however, when the hairdress was beginning to tower,
caps were made higher and wider (Plates 75, 76, 77, Fig. 61 A). These
large caps continued to be worn until the end of the century. One cap
rose to a high point in front, fitted close around the face and could be
tied under the chin (Fig. 65 A). The edge was usually made in a fine
full ruching. Another type of cap curved over the ears and was fitted
tightly around the back of the head by a drawstring (Fig. 65 C). As the
hair grew higher, the pointed type, which was originally a French night-
cap, no longer encircled the face, nor was it tied under the chin. It was
perched on top of the head like a gabled roof on a haystack and called
a "dormeuse" after its forerunner (Plate 75 B C). Elderly women throughout the eighteenth century wore linen or stiffened gauze caps that fitted
over the head and ears, usually tying them under the chin. A stiffened
edging frequently encircled the face (Plates 72, 78, 79). Personal inclina-

tion as well as age played some part in the selection of caps. In Plate 79 A, Mrs. Peck wears a cap of a style much older than her years demand, and Mrs. Winthrop, 79 B, wears a much younger looking one. Plate 52 shows portraits of sitters whose backgrounds range from Massachusetts to South Carolina and whose ages range from forty to sixty. These portraits were all painted in the middle years of the eighteenth century by varied artists. Whether the caps are plain or ornate, they all have a crisp, starchy look. Certainly by chance, all the women in this group are painted with direct, shrewd, and even calculating expressions. One is tempted to ponder upon possible relationships between the period, the middle years of the century, and the sitters' middle years, and the assured looks of both caps and faces. Plate 69 shows a group of women of a somewhat older average age whose portraits were painted earlier in the century. Their caps are rendered as soft and somewhat floppy in style. The faces within the caps seem tentative in expression. England had the same sequence of styles: the floppy cap in the earlier years of the century, the starchier and more ornate caps in the middle and later years. But the women of Queen Anne's day were painted as alert faced, under their soft caps. By the time of the Georges, many of the portrayed faces have a dreamy and sometimes simpering expression. How easy it would be to make an allegory of this; the women of the new land leading with strength; the women of the old world hiding weaknesses by wearing spirited headdresses. Enough of speculation and back to the recital of dress.

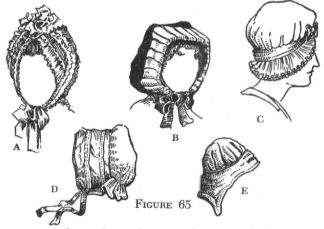

FIGURE 65

Hoods were worn throughout the period. Some of them enveloped the head, and the front edge was usually turned back revealing the lining, which was generally of a gay and contrasting color (Fig. 65 B). Such hoods were tied under the chin. For cold winter weather there were warm quilted hoods with stiffened brims extending around the face (Fig. 65 D). There were also small, quilted hoods, fitting the head very close, that were probably worn under lighter silk hoods in uncertain weather (Fig. 65 E).

As long as the hair was dressed close to the head, the hood was retained without any very noticeable change in its style. With the change to dressing the hair in towered forms, the style of the 1770's, the old hoods gradually lost favor. In their place came the calash, "a vast hood on hinged hoops which could be raised or lowered" over the high head-dresses without disturbing them (Fig. 60 D E). Planché, in describing the calash, says: "A hood made like that of the carriage, called in France calèche, to pull over the head, whence its name."

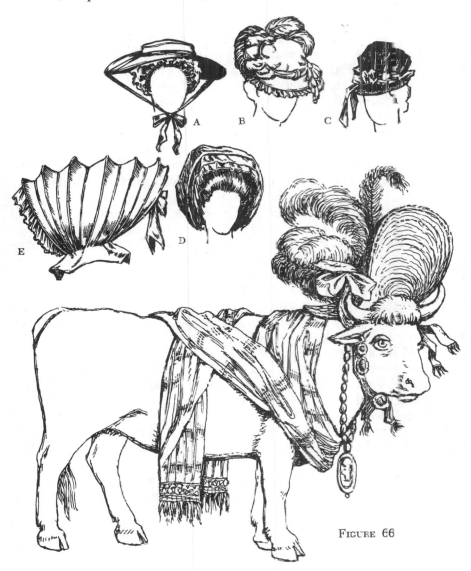

FIGURE 66

A French caricature about 1790.

Straw hats with broad brims and low crowns (Plates 80, 81, 82) had appeared shortly after 1730. They were inspired by the pastoral styles worn first in England, later in France. They were usually worn over the small linen cap edged with ruffles (Fig. 66 A). They were held in place by two long ribbon ties fastened to the ribbon that went around the crown, brought out over the brim, and tied beneath the chin.

From the 1770's on, hats were all the style and were of every shape and form. Hats were worn at every conceivable angle, either low on the head (Fig. 66 B C) or perched on top of the high coiffures. They were trimmed with artificial flowers and fruit, plumes and feathers, ribbons and laces. The two shown in the drawings (Fig. 66 B C) are but a suggestion of the great variety easily found in numerous drawings and fashion plates still extant (Plates 81, 82, 83).

SHOES.—High-heeled shoes with a round toe were fashionable until 1730, when shoes with pointed toes came into style from England. They retained the high "French" or "Louis" heel. Shoes for fashionable wear were expensive, being made from a rich selection of beautiful silks and damasks, plain or flowered. In 1750 a pair was described as being made of "white and russet bands closely stitched with wax threads." By 1760 heels began to be lowered. Both buckles and small rosettes were worn on the instep.

LINEN.—The chemise (Plates 53 B, 58 A B, 59) is seen as an edging to the line of the *décolletage*. From under the elbow sleeves of the bodice appear the ruffles of lace (Plates 53 A, 68). The shoulders and neck above the low-cut gown were often covered by a fine kerchief and scarfs (Plates 72, 77, 79). The ends were often tucked into the bosom, or the two ends were brought down the front over the stomacher and held in position by ribbon bows (Plate 52 A). Rich bands of lace edged the *décolletage* (Plates 65 B, 67, 70 B). Around the neck was worn a band of black ribbon (Plates 75 A B & C) which, in a way, compared to the solitaire worn by the men. Close fitting necklaces of pearls (Plates 52 C, 60 B, 72 A, 79 A B) were often worn instead of a black ribbon. Pearls were apparently an outstanding favorite. Very few jeweled necklaces are to be found (Plates 48 B, 53 B). In place of the jeweled pendant, a cameo or miniature is occasionally seen (Plates 65 A, 73 B). More frequently, in portraits of children a jeweled pendant (Plate 68, B) or a pearl necklace with an attached jewel (Plate 65 A) is found. Ostentation is rare (Plates 48 A & B, 68).

In place of either the ribbon or necklace one finds the attractive small ruffle of lace, which was worn fastened under the chin and secured at the back by a ribbon bow (Plates 53 A, 62, 70 B).

ACCESSORIES.—Long gloves of white, black, or purple silk, or kid were very fashionable. Many women wore silk or lace mittens that were fingerless gloves and took the place of the heavier glove in summer. These fingerless gloves were black, white, pink, blue, or yellow. Aprons were worn in no special size or style, but as fancy suggested. Parasols, called "quitasols," were extremely rare and do not appear in any of the advertisements of the eighteenth century. They were made of oiled muslin and were in various colors. The umbrella, known for centuries in Eastern countries, began to make an impact on Europe late in the seventeenth century. By the middle of the eighteenth century, it was in style in France, not only as a parasol, but as a "parapluie." Oddly enough, it did not get to England in a popular sense, until much later. Actually, the chance purchase of an oiled silk umbrella, made in India, from a ship's stores by a Philadelphia merchant in 1772 set off a wave of interest in this country eight years before London was upset by the sight of one. Umbrellas did not become popular until wigs disappeared and hat brims became smaller.

Every woman in evening dress wore a bunch of either real or artificial flowers at her bosom. If the flowers were real, in order to preserve them, the stems were placed in a small glass tube about four inches long, filled with water, known as a "bosom bottle." This was concealed in the stomacher of the gown. A small cluster of either real or artificial flowers was often worn in the hair. Muffs continued to be worn throughout the century and varied in size and material, from time to time as fashion dictated.

Paint, powder, and patches were generally used in fashionable circles, although not to the same extent here as in France. The French court ladies used so much paint and powder that their faces appeared like enamel. An English lady visiting Paris remarked that "their wooly white hair and fiery red faces make them look more like skinned sheep than human beings." Upon the painted and powdered cheeks of American ladies, patches were placed. Every woman of fashion carried a patchbox of enamel, brass, silver, china, or tortoise shell. The placing of the patch usually had significance. Politically, ladies who sympathized with the Whigs wore patches on the left side of their face. Those who preferred the Tories wore patches on the right side of their face. A patch near the corner of the eye was known as the "impassioned patch"; one on the middle of the cheek was called the "gallant." The coquette placed one on the lips. The patchbox and fan were to the lady of the eighteenth century what the snuffbox was to the gentleman. It is strange that while so many advertisements of "gummed patches" appeared in the New England papers, no lady appeared in any of the portraits of this period wearing the patch. The étui, or "ornamental case, hanging from the waist, intended to hold thimble, scissors and scent bottle," was worn by all ladies of fashion. The pomander, in the form of a silver box or ball with perforations, was used for holding perfume and was fashionable.

The planters' wives in Virginia were known to use the fan during the early seventeenth century. Later, in New England, about 1660, fans were at times brought from England. From 1730 on, they became increasingly popular. At this time, the making of fans was a well known industry in the colonies. Armorial fans and Chinese monogram fans were imported by the East India Company; they were highly decorative in design, bearing the family crest or monogram beautifully woven into the pattern.

Contemporary with these were the "minuet" fans, which also found favor in America. This fan was of ivory; upon unfolding it three oval medallions decorated by an artist of note were disclosed.

Various publications in the American colonies always advertised the fan. They were sold at both the stationers' and the jewelers' and at auction sales. Women of all classes now carried them; the wealthy women owning several. Fans were made of tortoise shell, vellum, satin, feathers, silver filigree, or ivory. The French fans were the most beautiful of those imported. During the time of Marie Antoinette, who favored the satin fan, exquisite ones were made. Fan makers in many of our cities copied the imported fans, often with great skill. These first years of the new Republic were the years of superb craftsmanship, not only in the manufacture of fans but also in the expanding area of luxuries.

CHAPTER VI

Pennsylvania and the Quakers

Vernier - Del.

*Guillaume Penn achetant la terre de Pennsylvanie : 1683
D'après une gravure de la fin du XVIII siècle*

Woodlands, Philadelphia, Pa.—1770.

CHAPTER VI

Pennsylvania and the Quakers

Early Pennsylvania was an ethnic and religious patchwork. A greater variety of nationalities and creeds found homes within its borders than in any other colony. Clinging together and settling in groups they were a curious pattern of self-sufficient communities. Each community attempted to preserve its own manners and ideals, and each resisted, but did not prevent, partial assimilation.

The flags of Holland and Sweden had flown over portions of the colony, and traders and settlers from both countries had appeared along the shores of the Delaware as early as 1632. Although the real history of Pennsylvania begins with the granting of the royal charter of 1681, the settlements previous to that date were not without significance. The little villages with Swedish, Dutch, English, and Finnish settlers scattered along the banks of the Delaware were quietly prosperous communities, pleasantly pastoral in character. They hugged the river and little attempt was made to use the resources of the forest skirting the shores. They had been content to cultivate the rich river bottoms, to fill the meadows with their red cattle, to cut ditches and dikes, and to plant orchards and gardens. They might have influenced the future of the colony, but their numbers were too scanty to resist the influx following the granting of the charter. They rapidly lost their identity and were absorbed by the waves of English, Welsh, Germans, and Scotch-Irish immigrants that swept into the colony.

The granting of the charter which gave William Penn almost sovereign power over the colony was the signal for the release of this great stream of migration. Penn, although a Quaker, opened his lands not only to the members of his own sect but to ". . . all who confess and acknowledge one Almighty and eternal God to be the creator, upholder and ruler of the world, and that hold themselves obliged to live peaceably and justly in civil society."

The development of the colony began late, but, once under way, its growth was astonishing. In 1681 there were perhaps six thousand inhabitants within its borders; the forest stretched unbroken from the river bank westward to beyond the Alleghenies. A century later, it was one of the richest, most populous, and important of the commonwealths. Its principal city, Philadelphia, had grown to be the largest on the continent; another of its cities, Pittsburgh, was the largest inland municipality. Pioneers were raising their cabins in the river valleys of the Great Basin.

When William Penn landed at New Castle in 1682 to the welcoming shouts of Dutch and Swedish settlers in woodland garb, the men in leather breeches and jerkins, the women in skin jackets and linsey petticoats, he found his young colony already established. There was very little Indian danger because of the Quaker philosophy of non-violence. The well-stocked farms of the Swedes and Dutch were a guarantee against famine, and the climate was temperate and healthful. To Penn, the new country seemed like "the best vales of England watered by brooks; the air, sweet; the heavens, serene like the south of France; the seasons, mild and temperate; vegetable production abundant, chestnut, walnut, plums, muscatel grapes; wheat and other grains; a variety of animals, elk, deer, squirrel and turkeys weighing forty or fifty pounds, water birds and fish of divers kinds, no want of horses, and flowers lovely for color, greatness, figure and variety. . ."

It is evident the early Pennsylvanians suffered little of the distress encountered by the founders of other colonies. They labored to such purpose that by the end of 1683 the newly laid out site of Philadelphia contained three hundred and fifty-seven dwellings, many of them of framed wood and some of red brick. Settlers continued to stream in, hungry for land. Almost overnight, Philadelphia became the principal port of entry in the colonies. The English Quakers continued to come in numbers, and newcomers of many faiths arrived with the increased migration—German Protestants of a dozen sects, Scotch-Irish Presbyterians, Moravians, Dutch Baptists, Welsh Quakers and Baptists, and some Irish Catholics.

There were almost no men of wealth in the ranks of the newcomers. They were recruited largely from the yeomen and peasant classes, men who wanted to make their way in the world, or who sought homesteads of a workable size. Their numbers, earnestness, and energy helped to establish Pennsylvania among the leaders of the colonies. However, the tendency of each nationality and faith to settle apart prevented the colony from becoming wholly unified in thought and action.

Philadelphia attracted numbers from each group. Nevertheless, it was essentially a Quaker town, with a strong English representation. The counties adjacent to the city were also controlled by the Quakers. The next band of counties, Lancaster, Berks, Lehigh, and parts of Montgomery and Bucks were occupied by the Germans. Beyond, along the Susquehanna and in the Cumberland Valley, were the Scotch-Irish settlements. A fourth group were the Welsh, who settled themselves on the "Welsh Barony," about the towns of Merion, Haverford, and Radnor, just west of Philadelphia. These national enclaves were a serious obstacle to unity. However, even in its beginning days, the colony achieved a marked individuality, developing an atmosphere singularly simple and tolerant.

During the early years both Quakers and German Pietists made no separation between their religious and secular lives. They practised their creed in every aspect of their daily life. The sobriety and earnestness of this way of life enabled both the Quakers and Pietists to resist the influence of surrounding economic pressures and the new ways of later immigrants. Quaker ideals and manners were, for a long time, the most potent factors in its growth.

When the Quakers first appeared in Pennsylvania, their faith was still a new one, and many of its forms were far from being crystallized. In the matter of dress—and it was important in the precepts of their church—they had been merely admonished to clothe themselves in a plain and sober manner and to avoid all appearance of vanity or luxury. They did not consciously bring to these shores a planned form of dress. Their garments were cut like those following the general vogue in the England they had left. Their own contribution was the elimination of the mostly useless decoration—the braid, ornate buttons, ribbons, plumes, and laces. The so-called Quaker dress was not new and different. Though it avoided conspicuous color and shiny surfaces, it was often remarked that it was made of the finest quality materials. Once plainness and sobriety had been achieved, the tendency was to retain this form in spite of the influence of passing fashions. Thus, in a few decades, the Quaker was well behind the mode. Reluctantly and sparingly, they borrowed from the changing dress about them and followed at the distance of a generation or two the curious fashions of the outside world.

As the colony grew and amassed material benefits, the old, familiar cleavage between town and country life appeared. The cleavage expressed itself as eloquently in dress as in other ways. The country folk, secure from worldly contacts, kept their gray and brown simplicity almost untouched; but those of the city who had felt the quickening touch of prosperity and were in contact with outside influences usually found some compromise advisable. Philadelphia, through the expanding years of the eighteenth century, grew into the first city of the land. The ships of the world dropped anchor in the Delaware. The city's warehouses were piled high with goods gathered from the markets of East and West; the back country added its supplies of foodstuffs as well as iron, lumber, glass, and paper. The luxuries of the early days became the necessities of the later century. Carpets, India prints, chintz hangings, handblocked wallpapers, and complete silver services were commonplace. All the new and strange products from the workshops of the world found their way to the counters of the new city. Philadelphia, young, lusty, and greedy for fine things, quickly purchased them for her homes and institutions. The eighteenth century had effaced the last lingering touch of the medieval in art. The dignity of the Georgian architecture had replaced the broader, sturdier architecture of the previous century. The graceful designs of Chippendale and Adam had replaced the heavier lines of the Jacobean and William and Mary styles. It was an age in which an art of great refinement and sophistication reached fruition, and with it grew up a society of equal refinement and sophistication. In all the continent of North America there was no center more receptive to this art and society than Philadelphia. By the time of the Revolution, the luxury and extravagance of the city had reached its peak. Its culmination was the great "Mischianza," that Georgian version of medieval pageantry and tournament.

Exposed to the color and attraction of this setting, it was inevitable many of the Quakers actively engaged in worldly affairs should find the color and variety of new fashions irresistible. In the gay Philadelphia society of the eighteenth century, which adopted the latest London vogue as quickly as fast sailing ships could bring it, it would have been impossible to pick out the wealthier and more worldly Quakers through any difference in their dress. There were others who, although affected by the fashion of the day, did not copy its excesses, and who worked out a compromise between the Quaker and the worldly ideal.

The Quaker tendency to show a sense of cohesion by their manner of dress is more evident in the clothing of Quaker women than of the men. Many Quaker women clung to quiet grays and browns and to styles of an earlier generation (Plate 84 A B). In a general way, the same principles influencing the dress of the Quakers can be applied to that of the various sects of German Pietists. They, too, were "plain people," frowning upon anything that smacked of ostentation. Yet, although they all worked toward an ideal of simplicity, each sect had its own restrictions and prohibitions and differed from the others in minor ways. Mennonites, Schwenkfelders, Amish, Dunkards, Seventh Day Baptists, United Brethren, and others all worked out the problems of plain dressing in their own way. If the general result was the same, there were minor variations which will be discussed in a forthcoming volume. Once these groups found a type of dress expressing their ideal of plainness, they held to it tenaciously, allowing few changes to be made. This was all the more possible, since, living in a district of their own, they were isolated from the rest of the colony. Some of these groups have maintained their integrity to this day.

Other national groups brought certain distinctive articles of dress that gradually disappeared under the restrictions of a new life, as in the case of the high, conical-shaped hats of the Welsh women and the wooden shoes of some of the redemptioners of German peasant origin. When individual tastes were not guided by religious convictions, usually the tendency was to drop the ways of the homeland and to adopt the habits of the new. In the Pennsylvania of the eighteenth century all the color and glitter were concentrated in Philadelphia. Quaker gray and Pietist drab surrounded the city; beyond these settlements were the characteristic tans and yellows of homespun and buckskin worn by the pioneers of the border country. The city's only rivals were the western hills of the state clad in the glorious colors of autumn. Spectacular today, but imagine what they must have been before man's encroachments!

I. DRESS OF THE QUAKERS: MEN

The male dress of the Quakers who came to America shortly after the signing of the charter was the fashion worn during the latter part of the reign of Charles II. A comparison between the dress of a man of fashion with the dress of a Quaker gentleman in America during these years will illustrate the differences that existed. Among the gaily dressed men of the world, the Quaker was markedly conspicuous, not because what he wore was different in cut and style, but for the lack of the popular extravagances which had become such an important part of the fashionable dress of the time.

The Quaker had not adopted a distinctive type of dress at this period, but from the very beginning a note of neatness, plainness, and simplicity pervaded their attire. Quaker simplicity and plainness, however, did not mean cheapness. The material possessions of the Quakers were of the best. Their houses were furnished with the best walnut and mahogany furniture, although restrained in carving and decoration. The most costly silver and china, and the finest of imported rugs went into their homes, and the best materials into their clothing

COATS AND WAISTCOATS.—If Figure 43 B is compared with Figure 67 A, it will be noticed that the cut of the two coats is identical. In both cases the coats reach to the knees and extend several inches beyond the long waistcoats. The sleeves have the great turned back cuffs from the middle of the forearm to beyond the elbow. It will be noticed, however, that there is a staidness and plainness in the Quaker garment, a lack of figured materials in the waistcoat, not found in those of the fashionably dressed man. Furthermore, there is a noticeable lack of embroidery and braid around the edges of the coat and waistcoat in the Quaker garment.

By comparing Figure 46 A with Figure 68 A it will be noticed that, though both men are dressed in the style each wore previous to and during the Revolution, the Quaker had not as yet accepted the newer coat and waistcoat but still wore the dress of about 1750 (See Fig. 45 A). The Quaker's coat and waistcoat were still unadorned and noticeably free of embroidery, braids, and edging.

BREECHES.—Breeches are about the same, although the Quakers never seem to have worn the full exaggerated breeches worn during these early years by the more fashionably dressed men.

LINEN.—While the linen worn by the Quakers was splendid in quality and often edged with lace, it never became as rich and extravagant as that worn by others. In Figure 67 A, can be seen the neck cloth that was worn about 1660. It was passed around the neck and tied under the chin with short spreading ends; while in Figure 43 B, the ends of the neck cloth were brought together and fastened at the throat with a ribbon bow. In Figure 68 A, the Quaker gentleman is wearing the cravat fashionable in the 1680's, a time when the tie was lengthened and fell over the neckband and freely down the front in two long ends. In 46 A, we see the more fashionable frill of lace, known as the jabot, appearing under the neck band. The solitaire was worn in combination with the bag-wig and the jabot.

FOOTGEAR.—In comparing the shoes worn in 67 A with 43 B, the Quaker still wears the shoe roses, although as a general fashion they are rarely worn. The newer fashion was the high-heeled shoe, with the tongue rising high over the instep. In place of the shoe rose, the shoe would be fastened by a buckle. Later, when the tongue was much reduced in size (46 A) the Quaker still wore the older fashion (68 A).

HAIR.—While gentlemen following the latest modes wore their long periwigs, powdered or black as their tastes dictated, the Quaker was apt to wear his own hair falling over his shoulders. If he did wear a wig, as many Quakers did, it was less voluminous and "dandyfied."

HATS.—The Quaker hat in 1680 was practically the same as that worn by other men. However, instead of cocking the brim at various angles, he usually preferred to wear his hat with a natural wide brim uncocked (Fig. 67 A). Among the Quakers, the hat was kept on the head much of the time, whether indoors or out. He refused to lift it in the form of a salute; to the Quaker mind, this was an affectation. Later on, the cocked hat, as well as the broad-brimmed hat, was worn. In 68 A the Quaker hat with the brim rolled up at the sides at quite an angle is seen, but it never rivaled the exaggerated cock of the Kevenhuller hat worn by the gentlemen in Figure 46 A.

II. DRESS OF THE QUAKERS: WOMEN

BODICE AND SKIRT.—The gown of the Quaker woman of about 1682 is seen in Figure 67 B, and represents the general style of Quaker dress for many years to come. The opening at the neck is filled in with a fine linen or lawn kerchief, the ends drawn down under the lacings of the open bodice. The same material seen in the kerchief appears from under the elbow length sleeves of the bodice. The full skirt is gathered into full pleats where it is joined to the bodice. Over the silk gown the apron is worn. A comparison of this costume with the costume seen in Figure 55 A shows the low cut bodice of the latter and the full-looped skirt over a satin petticoat. The petticoat is edged along the lower border with two flounces of lace. The looped up skirt is probably held in place

FIGURE 67

FIGURE 68

by ribbon ties which match those of the bodice. These graduated ribbon bows are known as "échelles." Instead of the plain undersleeves of the Quaker dress, we find sleeves of fine lawn or lace, puffed at the elbow and finished with lace ruffles.

The clothing of a Quaker lady on the eve of the Revolution is shown in Plate 52 B, Fig. 68 B, though the fashion is that from 1735 to 1740. The modish dress of this time (1775) was the robe "à la française" (Fig. 57) or the polonaise (Fig. 59). The bodice (Fig. 68 B) is laced over a white stomacher, the sleeves of elbow length. Edging the slight décolletage, appears the ruffle of a lawn undergarment turned over the neck like a falling band. The open skirt was worn over hoops, exposing the petticoat. However, the petticoat is not nearly as distended as those worn by women of fashion. Plates 84 C and 85 A are of Quaker dresses worn at the close of the century.

THE QUAKER CAP.—The cap must not be confused with the bonnet, which, tradition says, was not introduced to the Republic until 1798 and barely comes into the scope of this volume (Plate 85 A). The cap was a snug and simple lawn or linen headcovering which was tied under the chin. This cap was worn in the middle of the century; at that time it had no connection with the Society of Friends. Called the "Joan," the cap probably came from the English countryside to London. It was admired and was stylish for about the decade beginning with 1755. At this time, it was worn by Quaker women who continued to wear it for well over a century after its fashionable heyday. By the later years of the century, the "Joan" cap was generally known as the Quaker cap (Plate 85 B).

* George Fox—"From the engraving by Holmes after a portrait painted in 1654 by the Dutch painter, Honhorst."

* The only Honhorst to be in England was Gerrit, who left there in 1630, when Fox was six years old. Willem Honhorst, another Dutch painter who did not come to England, was a possibility. However, Fox does not seem to have been in Holland until 1677, ten years after Willem's death. Gerrit had been dead for twenty years. The selection of this portrait as that of Fox was probably dictated by the hat and hair. Though the portrait may be apocryphal, the hat and hair are as Fox may have worn them. The cravat above the doublet and the brandenburg worn over the doublet date this portrait about 1670 to 1675.

George Fox.

CHAPTER VII

The Revolution And The New Republic

House on Queen St., Alexandria, Virginia about 1800.

CHAPTER VII

The Revolution And The New Republic

The successful rebellion against the armed forces of England left the newly freed colonies exhausted and a little bewildered. The formerly loosely related colonies were impelled, during the armed conflict, to move toward closer political unity. At the end of the rebellion, the nature of the future ties between the former colonies, and the entire political framework of the central government had to be formulated. There was considerable diversity of view among the leaders, but those who advocated a strong central government, and a system that would incorporate the spirit of the then current democratic social doctrines, were, in the main, victorious. Thus, the conflict which had started as a rebellion ended as a political revolution, with the revolutionary spirit embodied in the Constitution. The young republic was free to launch its hopes and experiments in more enlightened and democratic channels.

Seven years of war had left its scars from Vermont to Georgia. The death of many young men, fire and pillage, the disruption of commerce and industry, the departure of large bodies of loyalists with their wealth and chattels, the debasement of the currency, and the wastage of material had left the country weakened. Fortunately, America's frontier-like civilization had weathered the storm of war better than had been the case in the more complicated and centralized communities of Europe. The new nation was still one of small, self-sufficient units—farm households in which almost everything necessary for maintaining existence could be produced. Although these households felt the pinch of war conditions, there was no essential change in their mode of living from that of pre-Revolutionary times.

The greatest change occurred in the cities and towns. During the British occupation, the larger cities, like Philadelphia, New York, Boston, and Charleston had been centers of gaiety and fashionable life. Much of the color and brilliance departed with the British armies. Little was left to take its place. Those families of wealth and station still remaining were either more soberly inclined or restrained from displaying ostentation by the new democratic slogans in the air. The phrases of the Declaration were in circulation, and none cared to risk the epithet of "aristocrat."

The growing restraint in dress was also due partly to the lack of imported materials. Commerce with England had been cut off during the war, and contact with other countries was hazardous because of the British blockade. This meant greater use of the materials at hand, homespun of undyed yarn with its grayish hue, leather with its dull brown, and the last remnants of faded finery. The Spanish south, unscarred by the war, was able to sell in northern markets. Goods that came into the new "states" from the Spanish Colonies were characterized by the military nature of the Spanish occupation. Clothing styles would soon show the influences of the shorter coat and the trimmer waistline that was Spain's contribution to style at the end of the eighteenth century. With the signing of the peace treaty of 1783, new life began to stir on the deserted wharves of the seaport cities. America was now free to trade with the world, unhampered by navigation acts or trade restrictions. The country's young strength asserted itself, and in a remarkably short space of time she had repaired the ravages of the conflict and was winning a place in the world's commercial and industrial spheres. The hatred toward England was still intense, and many did not want anything English—either art or industry. With independence, some had hoped for a new, democratic art. However, most still looked for their models among the older nations of Europe. Of these nations, France was the chosen country. She was popular because of her aid during the Revolution; numbers of her émigrés had found homes in the United States, bringing with them French culture and a taste for French art. France was in a new phase of the classic revival which, some two decades later, when it crystallized into the Empire style, was to leave its mark on the art of all western Europe and America.

During the last quarter of the century, French influence on American dress and on art was evident. But it is interesting to note that even when dislike of things English was common, and conscious efforts to eliminate all English characteristics were made, under the newly acquired French veneer, the English foundation was always visible. It was impossible for the new Republic to disavow, much less to hide, its ancestry.

The upheavals of the late eighteenth century finally reached the field of dress. The weight, expanse, and cumbersomeness of the dress worn had attained such dimensions that nothing short of a reaction could suffice. High headdresses, hoops, voluminous skirts, powder and patches, high-heeled shoes, and large broad-brimmed hats were discarded. In their place, evolving through the closing years of the century, came the grace and simplicity of a new style—lower coiffures, straight, clinging lines of the gowns, low-heeled shoes and sandals, the turban headdresses, and use of thin, semi-transparent materials. For the women the new fashion was just another swing of the pendulum. A half-century later they would go back to hoops, full skirts, and tight bodices. The men committed themselves, however, to a type of dress that leads in a direct line to the dress worn today. Their trousers had reached the middle of the calf on their downward trend. Wigs had vanished and with them a certain flamboyance which had characterized the eighteenth century.

I. DRESS OF THE MEN
1775–1800

One is apt to suppose that during the years just previous to the Revolution, and the actual years of fighting that followed, men would have had little chance to think of dress. Probably for a time military dress was given more special attention than the cut of a coat. Men in civilian life could not dress in the finest materials. (Yet, their dress still had the nicety of detail seen previously.) Thus, greater severity appeared and lasted for at least a decade. Compare Plate 86, A & B with the earlier Plates 44 and 48 A. Charles Willson Peale's portrait of Mr. de Haas (Plate 33) is the very epitome of the well-dressed man shortly before the Revolution.

BODY GARMENTS AND BREECHES.—The coat, waistcoat, and breeches as described in Chapter V, Section I (Plates 32 A, 33; Fig. 46) were still the dress of a man during the period of the Revolution, and until 1800. Thus, the coat worn for dress occasions still remained about the same. The sleeves were still worn quite tight, with a small cuff at the wrist, and the front of the coat sloping away to the back in two narrow coattails. The pockets with small flaps were placed upon the hips. However, the side pleats, set more to the back and pressed flat, were much smaller in size than formerly. The waistcoat had a short skirt. The knee breeches were gathered to a tight waistband, although they were still made full in the seat. The legs of the breeches fitted well down over the calves, with buttons and buckles at the sides of the legs, and the leg bands fastened over the silk stockings (Plates 28, 33, 86 A).

In 1780 a new fashion in coats for ordinary wear made its appearance. The new coat gradually grew in favor, until in the early 1790's it was worn for all occasions. The new coat (Fig. 69 A) was made in a high-waisted, double-breasted style. The skirt was now cut away in front to a little above the waistline and curved back over the hips, leaving the back part of the original skirt as a tail. A characteristic detail in the 1790's was the high "stand-fall cape," or collar. It was cut in one piece and could lie flat (Plate 87). The English prototype had a somewhat shawl-like cut (Plate 87 A). At the beginning of the 1790's the collar rose from the lapel notch; lapels were generally quite wide and sharply triangular. Then, the collar began to be cut back and the lapels were rounded. After 1796 the gap between the collar and the lapel became wide and had a square look (Plate 90 A & B).

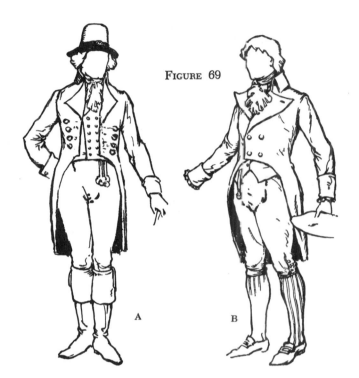

FIGURE 69

A   B

The sleeves were close, and extended to the wrist with a small cuff. Small lace ruffles might (Fig. 69 B) or might not (Fig. 69 A) appear at the wrist. Waistcoats, which had been quite short, were cut still higher in a straight line across the front. They were double-breasted and might or might not have large lapels. When the waistcoat was cut still higher, it conformed to the shortened cutaway coat, although three inches or so of it still showed from under the buttoned coat (Fig. 69 A B).

From the middle of the 1780's when the double-breasted waistcoat had large lapels, it became fashionable to wear the lapel of the waistcoat turned out over the lapel of the coat (Plate 88; Fig. 70 A). The smart Newmarket vest shown in Plate 88 had become high fashion in London only months before Earl completed the portrait. If there had been a list of the ten best-dressed men in America of 1790, Colonel Taylor would have joined the ranks, in a manner of speaking.

From the beginning of the period, skin-tight, buckskin riding-breeches were seen (Fig. 70 A). From the 1790's on, all fashionable breeches were tailored to fit tight to the thighs and were not supposed to show any wrinkles or creases.

OVERCOATS.—Overcoats in the style of the earlier period were still worn. They were usually termed riding-coats, but were generally worn for coaching, traveling, or even walking. The coat in Fig. 70 B is a double-breasted riding-coat, probably made out of serge or kersey, with

FIGURE 70

two rows of buttons down the front. The coat is long, almost covering the legs and without much shape. The large revers, or lapels, lie over the chest. Around the neck is the triple cape.

In the 1780's the overcoat (Fig. 70 c) was a little more fitted at the waistline. It was left open, and the revers were buttoned back. The skirts of the coat were full and long. The sleeves were closed at the wrists and had small cuffs. Two small capes encircled the neck.

In the 1790's the riding-coat with an extremely smart cut was seen (Fig. 70 A). The collar was worn up around the neck. When buttoned, the riding-coat was made to fit slightly at the waist, the skirts hanging a little full from the waist down. Another overcoat specifically designed for riding was the "Spencer," a very short-waisted jacket without tails, which was worn over the coat. It had a stand-fall collar and cuffs on long sleeves (Plate 95 H). Women wore Spencers too, with a flat collar and often cuffless sleeves.

Banyans and morning gowns were fashionable to the end of the century (Plates 34, 35).

LINEN.—Ruffles of lawn or lace still appeared from under the coat sleeve at the wrist (Plate 91 B). Gradually they were seen less, and by the 1790's they had generally disappeared (Plate 91 c; Fig. 69 A). Throughout the period, the plain folded stock, which buckled in the back, was worn with the "jabot." The jabot was a frill of lawn or lace which filled the opening of the waistcoat at the throat (Plate 91 c). At times, the jabot was quite small and almost hidden by the waistcoat, which was buttoned almost to the top (Plate 49 B). From the beginning of the period there was a new form of the cravat. A "muslin neckerchief" was tied at the throat in a large bow, the long ends of the bow spreading out over the waistcoat front (Plate 91 A).

COIFFURES.—The wig was worn in all the different forms of the queue dealt with in detail in Chapter V, Section I. It continued to be worn by many in that style until near the close of the century, when it went out of fashion. Toward 1770, however, it became quite customary for the men who were not bald, or whose hair had not been ruined by wig wearing, to cease shaving their heads. When the hair was of sufficient length they discarded the wig. The natural hair was now dressed in imitation of wigs. When powdered, it is exceedingly difficult to determine in portraits whether the man was wearing his own hair or a wig (Plates 87 A, 91 A).

An engraving by Matthew Darly in 1773.

The natural hair, dressed up in the back in a queue, was often left unpowdered. In fact, powder for everyday wear was usually omitted as early as 1760 and went out of fashion in the 1790's (Plates 87 B, 88).

From the 1780's the hair was occasionally dressed with studied negligence, in what was termed a "disheveled crop" (Plate 90 A). A curl or puff was sometimes carried over the top of the head from ear to ear, a fashion that came in during the eighties. The back hair was done in a pigtail queue (Fig. 71 D); or a small puff was placed at each side of the head over the ear, the hair brushed back from the forehead, and the back hair likewise made into a queue (Fig. 71 C). This could be varied by dressing the hair in a puff over the top of the head, and in place of puffs at the side of the head, the hair would be frizzed over the ears (Fig. 71 A). One of the plainest methods of dressing the hair was to brush it smoothly back from the brow without its being puffed, curled, or frizzed (Fig. 71 F). If the hair was thick, it might be brushed straight back from the forehead (Fig. 71 E). While the pigtail queue was the more usual way of fastening the back hair, at times it was brought into a simple tie or thrust into the bag. In the full length portrait of Washington painted by Gilbert Stuart, in the costume worn by the President at the time of his second inauguration in Philadelphia the ribbons of the bow fastening the bag can be seen over his left shoulder. See Plate 50 for Darly's view, 1776.

FIGURE 71

HEADGEAR.—The cocked hats worn by gentlemen retained their popularity more or less throughout the period. However, they varied in size, angle, and style of the cocked brims. From about the mid-1770's the greatest variety prevailed (Plate 50), and had it not been for some curtailment due to the fighting, the parade of hats might have seemed like an invasion of another sort. The more military kind of hat with a high front (Fig. 72 A) was generally worn. In 1765 the "Nivernois," or, as the London Magazine dubbed it, "the never-enough, made its appearance. It was a large umbrella-like hat. The decline of the cocked hat was signalled by "a Beaver the size of a cockelshell" (Fig. 72 C).

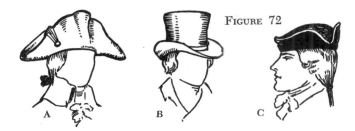

Figure 72

A   B   C

A favorite hat from the beginning of the 1770's was the uncocked, broad-brimmed felt or beaver called the Quaker hat. The Quaker hat, because of the influence of sharply cocked hats, would sometimes be worn partially tied up in the back and sometimes tied on the sides as well. The sides were not pulled too tightly to the crown and left a wide opening in the front, known as an "open cock." Crowns varied from high to round, with a general compromise as in Fig. 70 A C. Occasionally the brim was rolled up on one side. This hat was much worn for traveling, riding, hunting, and undress, that is, informal clothing.

From the 1780's a new fashion, hats with flat or narrow brims and high, tapering crowns were seen (Fig. 69 A). In the next ten years, beginning with 1790, the top hat, with varying contours to the sides of the crown and the roll of the brim, was popular (Fig. 72 B).

STOCKINGS.—Silk stockings, usually clocked, were worn under the leg-band of the breeches generally throughout the period. Striped stockings came in in the late 1790's (Fig. 69 B).

FOOTGEAR.—The low shoes were of ordinary shape, with rounded toe and low heels, the short tongue coming over the instep and fastened by a large square buckle. After about 1794, the shoes were fastened by ties (Plates 90 A, 91 B; Fig. 69 B, 70 C). Leggings of leather, spatter-dashes, and top boots, referred to at length in Chapter V, Section I, were worn throughout this period, especially in the country. Top boots became extremely fashionable for general wear from the 1790's on (Fig. 69 A). The lower part of the top boot, made of black leather and highly polished, fitted tight over the calf of the leg, while the upper part of the boot made of brown leather came some inches below the knees. For hunting and riding, top boots were worn with skin tight buckskin breeches.

ACCESSORIES.—Swords were hardly ever worn now, except on state occasions. In their place men carried sword-canes. Canes were generally carried throughout these years (Plates 88, 91 B). A little before 1800 heavy sticks became fashionable. The snuff box was still indispensable to a gentleman.

II. DRESS OF THE WOMEN
1775–1800

During the fighting with England, extremes of rich and plain attire in women's dress were most marked. In the large cities, especially in those occupied from time to time by the British, balls, dinners, dances, and parties kept women preoccupied with fashion. However, throughout the country districts, the majority of women dressed as plainly as possible, wearing domestic materials and curtailing expenses wherever possible in order to send help to their men who were fighting.

BODY GARMENTS.—Bodices remained similar in shape and style as described; this trend continued until about 1780. They retained their long-waisted shape and were styled to be worn closed, or open enough to show a laced-in stomacher. The low-necked gown remained in fashion, with sleeves usually of elbow length, although a sleeve close to the wrist became fashionable early in the 1770's and was to become more and more popular. The sacque, the robe *à la française* (Plate 70 A), or the polonaise (Fig. 59), lasted until the 1780's. In the sacque the box pleats were sewn tighter to the body, and the full pleat from the shoulder down the front went out. From 1777 on, hoops and panniers were worn less and less, except on dress occasions. In place of the hooped skirt, toward 1780, the skirt was attached to the bodice around the waist with small drawn gathers which were either bunched, reefed, or looped over a quilted petticoat (Fig. 73 A). The low-cut bodice was retained until the 1790's, though there was an increase on the use of fichus.

The fashion for sacques which had the character of jackets continued during the 1780's. The Pet-en-lair (Fig. 73 B), which had inaugurated the style, was going out of fashion. In its place was a shaped jacket, with no seam at the waist, called a caraco (Fig. 73 C). The polonaise, a fitted sacque, with a shortened overskirt worn in three festoon-like sections, was extremely popular during the decade. It was worn over a petticoat of the same name (Fig. 73 A).

Many women tended to follow a masculine mode of dress as the year 1790 approached. The jacket and vest or coat was fashionable. The coats were made with lapels fastened across the front with buttons and loops (Fig. 73 D E).

FIGURE 73

About 1780, the prevalence of panniers and hoops marked a change in the style of women's dress. The bodice, though it retained a low décolletage, became shorter in the waist and with less point in the front. There were, in a variant fashion, some bodices cut on Van Dyke lines (Fig. 8 B) but with the fashionable low décolletage. The sleeves followed the seventeenth century mode also and were fitted tightly from shoulder to wrist, but they lacked the wings at the shoulder seam. Above the corsage the décolletage was filled in with a fichu below which was worn a "zone," a false front shaped somewhat like an upside down stomacher. This gave the illusion of the closed bodice or jacket (Fig. 74 A). With the gradual disuse of the hoops or panniers, the full-gathered skirt attached to the bodice was held out in the back by a bustle. This was worn all through the 1780's (Fig. 73 C).

There was also a simple dress consisting of a low-cut bodice with either short full sleeves, edged with a ruffle, or long tight sleeves. A medium flowing skirt was gathered around the waist without the bustle. Around the waist, a wide scarf or sash was worn tied in a bow, either in the back or at the side (Fig. 74 B).

It was in the middle 1780's that women fancied themselves as pouter pigeons. To achieve this desired effect the kerchief of gauze or fine linen called a "buffont," was arranged to give an exaggerated bosom (Plate 75 C; Fig. 74 B).

FIGURE 74

A   B

Another change occurred in women's dress about 1790, when the waistline was again raised, and the neck bared in a deep, full décolletage, edged on the under side with a full lace ruffle. Above the corsage, the décolletage was filled with a fine gauze fichu, called a "tippet," as a variation from the buffont (Plate 92).

Between 1795 and 1797, a decided change may be noted in women's dress. Hoops and panniers, full skirts of heavy brocades and silks went out of fashion. The "Classical Revival," which was one of the aftermaths of the French Revolution, swept away all of the last vestiges of corseting, boning, and padding that had created the women's figure of the earlier 1790's. Even before that, the powder and patches, the high-dressed hair, and the high heels of the shoes had gone. From then on, fashions changed with great rapidity, a multiplicity of styles coming in with the dawn of the nineteenth century. The new gown was made with a short bodice, accentuating the high waistline now in fashion (Fig. 75 A B). The narrow skirts were made of soft clinging materials. The décolletage, still low, was either round (Fig. 75 A) or square (Fig. 75 B) and no longer covered by a tippet or kerchief. For out-of-doors, long scarfs (Fig. 75 A) were thrown around the shoulders, the ends almost reaching the ground.

FIGURE 75

A   B

RIDING HABITS.—(Continued from Chapter V, Section II.) During the 1760's the rather long-skirted riding habit was used in England. It was called a "Joseph," and it had to be green—any green was permissible, from forest to pea. Although there is no evidence that the pattern was followed in the colonies, it probably was. In the middle of the 1780's, the Joseph became old-fashioned and a short, narrow-tailed jacket, anticipating men's styles by a decade, came into style. It had a collar and large triangular lapels and was firmly fitted to a tightly laced figure with ruffled frills at the neck and long, tight sleeves. With it, a wide-brimmed hat in the pattern of the period was worn. A hat of this type would be unsuitable for a journey of any distance. So a riding hood was probably substituted for it (Fig. 76 A).

During the 1790's, the long riding-coat (Fig. 76 B), which buttoned down the front and had revers or lapels, was seen. It had several small capes over the shoulders in imitation of the box coats worn by the stagecoach drivers. The front between the turned down lapels could be filled-in with a buffont, or with a rich frill of lace. With this coat, it was fashionable to wear a tall-crowned, flat-brimmed hat of felt or beaver, which was decorated with bands, bunches of ribbon, and buckles. A dress

FIGURE 76

B

A

FIGURE 77

made like the coat seems to have been exceedingly popular habit, and while primarily designed for sporting wear, it was the garment most worn "when travelling by coach, or carriage, or walking, and even in the house." It was generally made out of heavy cloth, or of a velvet of a bright color, scarlet or red predominating. The dress and the hat *à l'anglaise* are illustrated in Plate 83.

With the general change of dress that took place after 1797, the masculine riding-habit of previous years gave way to a garment more in accord with the feminine fashions of the day (Fig. 77). Coats, waistcoats, and cocked hats were discarded. In their place was substituted a tight, short-waisted bodice with revers or lapels. The bodice was open at the throat with a small ruching, or lace frill, at the edge of the opening. The sleeves were tight from the shoulders to the wrists. The long skirt was not made very full. In place of the impractical and extravagant styles in hats, a close-fitting, brimless, black velvet cap was worn.

COIFFURES.—There was very little change in the manner of dressing the hair from that of the last period. After 1775, however, there was a tendency to widen and flatten the high-dressed coiffures at the top. In one such style the front hair, gathered from the forehead, was pressed in a forward curve over a high pad, with one to three curls at the sides, and one at the shoulder, the back hair being arranged in a loose loop curled on the top and set with a large bow at the back (Plate 89). The hair was often covered with a white powder. Powder had reached the height of its popularity just preceding and during the early years of the Revolution. It went out of favor in the 1790's Extravagance in headdresses in America never reached the absurd flights of fancy indulged in by the French. They were generally not popular, except for full dress or for special occasions. One reads more about them in the diaries and letters of fashionable young ladies, who loved to relate how they were tortured and tormented by having their "heads" made up. However, from such actual evidence as portraits painted during those years, this "torture" did not occur often. About 1781 the "high towers" for dress occasions were greatly lowered. At the same time the hair for everyday wear and general occasions was dressed in a new style, with curls clustered over the head and long, flowing hair in the back. A curl often hung over one shoulder (Plate 92 A; Fig. 78 A). The hair was either powdered or left its natural color.

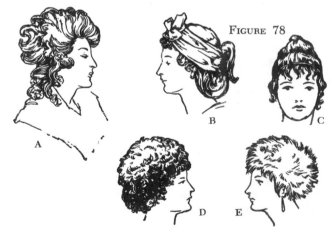

FIGURE 78

From the earlier 1790's to 1797 another fashion for dressing the hair was introduced, as evidenced in many pictures and miniatures of that date. Curls were worn over the forehead and at the side of the face. The long back hair was folded into a flat chignon at the nape of the neck, then brought up to the crown of the head, where it was secured by a comb or a ribbon; the free end was then allowed to fall back in a loose curl (Plate 92 B; Fig. 78 B).

Coming into fashion with the high-waisted French gowns of 1797, was a style wherein the hair was dressed in a most disheveled mode. The back hair was brought up on the crown of the head in a mass of curls or in a twisted knot. From the center of the head, brought forward over the brow and cheeks, was a long, straggling bang, or lock, of hair (Fig. 78 C). Many women, however, did not follow this absurd mode. They simply dressed their hair high in a knot, parting it in the center, and waving it back off the brow and to the sides. Among the many exotic fashions of the Directoire period in France, was a style of dressing the hair "à la victime." From good evidence, it was followed by women of the United States. This entailed the sacrifice of having the hair cut off quite close to the scalp. It was then brushed out from the head to make it stand stiff and perpendicular, a few straggling locks being brought forward into the eyes (Fig. 78 E). This style of dressing the hair may have come as a relief to many women of fashion, whose hair had been broken, scorched, and worn out in following the various modes of the tower headdress. The new mode was further supplemented by many women who wore wigs of short, curly hair over their closely cropped heads—surely a temporary relief from all they had gone through at the hands of the hairdressers in following Dame Fashion (Fig. 78 D).

HATS AND CAPS.—The tremendous increase in the variety and style of hats during the 1770's has already been noted (Plate 81). Fashion in hats was even more varied than it was during the period from the 1780's to the middle of the 1790's. Hats of all sizes and materials, from small hats, caps, and close shapes, to large enveloping bonnets and great, broad-brimmed hats, were worn in such fabrics as straw, beaver, felt, silk, and gauze. Through the introduction of a black lace called "grenacine" from Chantilly, a great stimulus was given to millinery during the years from 1775 to the close of the century. Many of these lace and gauze hats, made either with or without a crown and in a variety of shapes, were such huge affairs that they fairly overbalanced the figure (Fig. 79 A B). In the course of two years, or from 1784 to 1786, the style of hats changed some seventeen times in the Paris fashion books, and the ladies in America who could afford to keep up with these fleeting fashions did so by importing many of their hats from abroad. A few of these styles are shown in Figures 79 A B C D. Note Plate 89.

With the advent of the style of short-waisted gowns in 1795 which lasted for two decades, the vogue of the large hat passed. However, the fashion of hats changed so rapidly that it is impossible to treat the subject of hats comprehensively here. It is only necessary to add that turban-like bonnets imported from France were particularly popular (Fig. 80 A).

Caps for morning and for house wear were still generally worn. About 1780, the large mobcap made of gauze or net became fashionable. It was full about the head, with a big bow in the front (Plates 75 B C, 76 A B; Fig. 80 D).

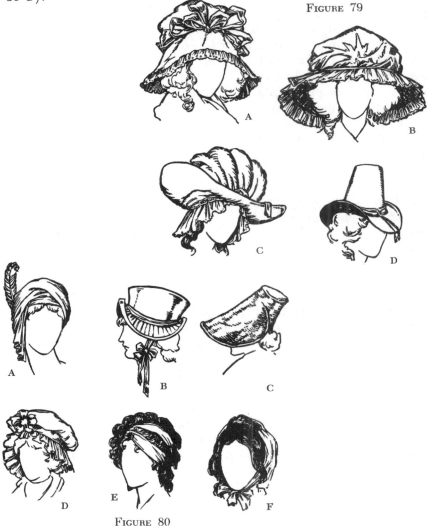

FIGURE 79

FIGURE 80

From about 1797 on, a favorite fashion was to dress the hair with scarfs of gauze, bands of crepe and silk, either plain or with a fringed edge, and with silk tasseled cords. Scarfs were braided and looped into the back hair (Fig. 80 F). Silk scarfs, kerchiefs, and broad silk sashes were twisted around the head in the form of a turban. Fillets were worn in the classic manner around the head, holding the hair in place, while in the back, loops of hair, called a chignon, were confined in silk nets.

Pieces of ribbon were wrapped around, and tucked into, the hair. The hair was pulled through where the ribbon did not overlap (Fig. 80 E).

SHOES.—Shoes with high heels continued to be worn, but by 1775, heels, especially for everyday wear, began to be lowered. The toe was rounded. Until 1785, wide latchets were buckled over the instep. Then, both latchets and buckles went out of style, and the pointed toe gave way to a rounded front. The heels were also considerably lowered. By 1790 the heel was a mere suggestion, and during that decade it practically vanished. With the disappearance of heels, buckles, and latchets, the French fashion of fastening the shoes with ribbons about the ankles in the manner of sandals came in.

ACCESSORIES.—Gloves, fans, parasols, muffs, scarfs, and jewels were all part of the fashionable attire of this period.

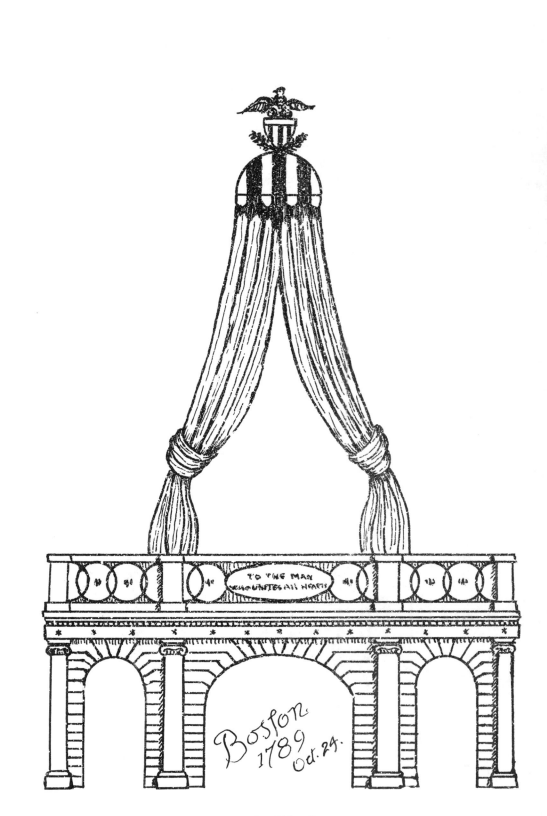

TO THE MAN
WHO UNITES ALL HEARTS

Boston
1789
Oct. 24.

CHAPTER VIII

Children In North America

1585-1790

New York (New Amsterdam). Nursery furniture of about 1675.

CHAPTER VIII

Children In North America
1585-1790

In 1585 Sir Richard Grenville commanded an expedition to Roanoke Island, off the coast of Virginia, to determine its suitability as the location for the first English settlement upon the North American Hemisphere. Among the members of the expedition was the scientist, Thomas Hariot, and the artist John White whose task it was to graphically record the terrain, fauna and flora, and the indigenous inhabitants. The expedition returned to London in 1586, and there White rendered his scores of drawings into watercolors. These watercolors constitute the first full pictorial representation of life along that coast; their rendition of Indians is exceptionally honest, and quite skilled. Unlike similar later illustrations, mostly free adaptations from White—altered to suit the prevailing European taste and morality—White's drawings conform to contemporary travellers' reports, the Indians' own oral history, and today's anthropological findings. It was White who gave us our first authentic glance at North American Indian children and their (un)dress [Fig. 31]. He was to return to Roanoke in 1587, this time in an attempt to establish a permanent settlement.

White's drawings are a rich historical heritage, whose importance was underlined by the publication of THE AMERICAN DRAWINGS OF JOHN WHITE (two sumptuous folio volumes, with scores of plates, Oxford University Press, 1964). Thanks to the many scholars associated with that project, we now know a great deal more about those drawings, some additional facts about the artist, and many pertinent matters about the expedition and the "Lost" Roanoke colony.

There were seventeen women, eighty-four men, and eleven children* on board the ship that brought the first settlers to Roanoke in 1587. John White, who had been appointed Governor, had been joined by his pregnant daughter, Eleanor, and her husband, Ananias Dare. That same year, Eleanor gave birth to a daughter to be named Virginia, the first such

---

* These figures, contradicting most current books, are reported in the Oxford John White volumes. Based upon the evidence presented by W. Sturtevant, C. Raven, R. Skelton, R. Wright, and others associated with this undertaking, we have accepted their conclusions on this, and other points.

recorded birth of a European settler upon these shores. It seems possible, and even likely, that White made sketches of the colony, its children and his granddaughter. If he did, they were left behind when he departed for England in November of 1587. Upon his return to Roanoke on August 18, 1590, he found the colony burned down, its settlers disappeared without a trace, and his paintings destroyed. We will never know whether White had drawings showing the dress of the first American children. He went back to England but, after a short time, even he, like the colony he helped found, was lost to history; a victim of a name so common that we cannot trace him in the records of the period inundated by his namesakes.

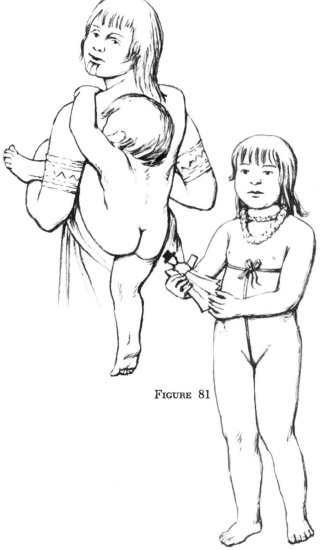

FIGURE 81

Indian Mother and Children, a watercolor by John White—1585.

Not until 1670 do we have an extant contemporary painting of a child in America, and that painting (Plate 13) has none of the charm, insight, and "unvarnished truth" of White's Indian children. Until well into the eighteenth century, there are so few portraits depicting children, and still fewer portraits whose attributions and dating can be trusted, that the problem of reconstructing children's dress in colonial America is a severe one. This is compounded by the dearth of detailed reports and the almost complete lack of artifacts.

In reconstructing children's clothing, we must therefore rely in great measure upon European prototypes, and common sense. (The latter generally useful). We must assume, for example, that the first children arrived on these shores dressed in a manner similar to that of the home country (Fig. 82). Certain adaptations may have been made to accommodate to sea climates and the 6-12 weeks' journey across a frequently hostile ocean in boats no larger than some of the private yachts of today. What specific changes in clothing were made by the Roanoke colonists during their brief stay, is a matter of pure speculation.

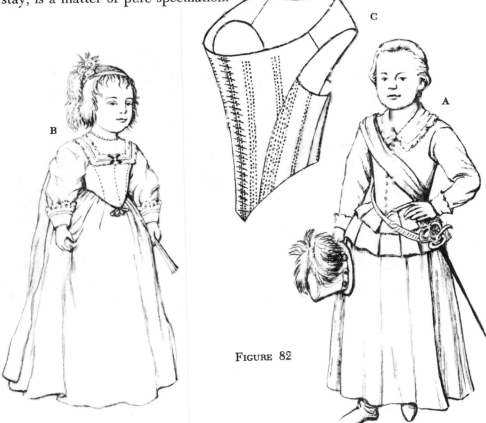

FIGURE 82

A From a painting by Marcus Gheevaerts, England, 1596.
B From an engraving by Jacob Van Langeren, England about 1635.
C Typical corset (drafting) English, 1650.

The thirty-four children who came to Plymouth Rock on the May-flower must have set a pattern for those who were born there or came shortly thereafter as immigrants. The first settlers were Pilgrims, and again allowing for some improvisations and adaptations (probably furs and skins), they must have dressed very much like their brethren in England and Holland (Fig. 83 A D).

A From a painting in the hall of Boughton House, Kettering, England, about 1650.
B From an engraving by William Marshall, England, 1630.
C From a painting by Alonzo Coello, Spain, 1577.
D From a painting by Pieter de Hooch, Holland, about 1650.
E From the portrait of Mrs. Freake and Baby Mary, America, about 1670.
F From a drawing by Watteau, France, 1720.

FIGURE 83

In June of 1609 the first permanent settlers in the Southern regions had arrived in Virginia, to be followed by a thousand more in August of that year. Both groups included children. The composition of that colony is discussed elsewhere. We suppose that these children were dressed in a manner acceptable to their British cousins and nieces. About fifty years later, when two generations had been born and new immigrants continued to swell the ranks, the population growth had been such that the loss of more than three hundred settlers had no lasting effect upon the colony as a whole. With growth and prosperity, a more stable family life was possible, permanent dwellings were constructed, and greater attention paid to fashions in clothing. By this time, the dress of the southern colony was a little richer and more elegant than their New England counterpart, and tighter and even slimmer than that of New Amsterdam. Although the clothing of infants and very young children was affected only slightly by the vicissitudes of these three colonies, changes in the general welfare of the colonies undoubtedly had some effect upon the clothing of the older children.

The manner of dressing infants and younger children changes very slowly, evolving over the course of centuries at a snail's pace. National and even class differences in this age group are far less pronounced than among adults, where we can generally spot a Dutchman, Scot, and Frenchman "a mile away." Throughout the West in the temperate zone north of the equator, infants were swaddled or bound for the first few months. This was supposed to encourage strong backs and straight legs. Although it did neither, it must have developed good lungs, and a skin impervious to urine. (Swaddling persists throughout recorded history until today.) As soon as the crawling age came, the child was relieved of clothing. In the warmer climates and in warm rooms, he was naked. A precautionary napkin was sometimes wrapped around the child when it was held on the lap. There is mention of a "baby clout" which we can imagine as similar to that worn by women during menstruation, but such a clout does not show in any drawing or painting. In colder climates, in and out of doors, children wore a shift or shirt. This garment has as long a history as the loincloth and was worn over a much wider geographical range. Originally the shift was a tunic, and then a shirt. When it became an undergarment, in the times of the Vikings, the shirt was called a "shift," a Norse word which means "divide." The shift's use as a major garment for children continued until the nineteenth century Boys in the lower estate wore this garment until they reached their "teens."

The shift was cut in many different ways. For the infant, it was often very long or very short. For the walking child it was knee or thigh length; and for the more active and older child, it was slit up the side, or in front of each thigh. For ceremonial occasions, such as baptisms, it was often very elaborately embroidered. To add warmth, or for stylish reasons, a short vest or jacket was worn over it. The noteworthy point is that nothing was worn under the shift until the child was at least an adolescent.

Other than the "saffron shirt" of the Scottish Picts, shifts seem to have been of natural linen or cotton, but later they were also of bleached muslins and lawns. To this day most male underwear is white.

From the ages of standing and walking until about four years old, little difference was made in dressing boys and girls. The wealthier children were dressed to exemplify their station. Their garments aped adult clothes in many particulars. Small boys, who were still in the "women's domain," wore long skirted dresses and caps that were almost like their sisters. Even the boys' hair was dressed like the girls'. But, from the first year on certain stylistic differences mark the boys' clothes from those of the girls. The upper part of the dress of the boy was cut with a suggestion of a doublet. The waistline was frequently finished off with points, though they served only a decorative purpose. The short sleeves ended in cuffs, a man's style, only later appropriated by the women. By the age of three or four, miniature swords hanging from baldrics were worn by the boys.

The medieval style of "hanging sleeves" persisted in children's dresses until well into the eighteenth century. By the sixteenth century the hanging sleeves were already used on children's clothes as "leading strings" or reins. When the hanging sleeves were no longer in style on children's dresses, they were soon replaced by bridles and reins which to this day serve the same purpose. These hanging strips not only served in many useful ways, such as supports for baby's first steps, restraints, ties to keep the youngster from falling out of chairs, but they were worn also as a mark of girlhood long after boys were considered old enough to do without them. The hanging sleeves seem to have been most consistently worn. If they do not show in portraits, it is likely that they are there nevertheless, for it was the custom to knot them together behind the back when they were no longer needed. Or, if they were in actual sleeve form, which had become rare by the seventeenth century, the cuff buttons and buttonholes of the two sleeves might be buttoned together [Fig. 93 F].

All young children wore close caps and these seem to have been worn in layers. There is no clue to a reason for the layers other than style. Over these double caps, little girls wore bonnet-like caps or bonnet scarfs. Little boys never seem to have had any addition in the form of a cap or scarf, but when they were still in the tumbling stage, they wore buffers as did their sisters. In the Southern colonies children past infancy do not seem to have worn caps. This may have been due to the influence of their Spanish neighbors, for in Spain children past infancy did not wear caps. This was understandable, for caps, as the rest of Europe knew them, were rarely worn by Spanish women. Small hats, large hats and head scarfs were occasionally worn by the Spanish women, but children, boys and very young men seem to have been bareheaded.

Aprons were worn by small children throughout the whole Colonial period. Those for small boys seem to have been simple and efficient as a protection to the dress. Instead of a bib or "pinner" in the front, frequently seen on adult aprons, the upper part of the apron seems to have gone over the head, or around the neck. There was a piece of the apron hanging down the back, though it appears to have been just short of reaching the ties which fasten the apron around the waist. As the children got a little older, the girl's apron became very elaborate, and little boys no longer wore aprons

At the age of three and four, girls were dressed completely as mimics of their elders, even to such accessories as fans. Small boys, however, had a special outfit at that age. It was an underdress with ankle length skirts over which was worn a fitted coat with skirts reaching nearly to the ground. This coat was sometimes tied in at the waist with a handsome sash in the early years of the eighteenth century. The coat mimicked the original Persian vest in every way; on occasion buttonholes and pockets were merely outlined in braid so that, though quite useless, the effect was that of an adult coat. To the end of the eighteenth century, young boys were wearing coats that copied the styles of a hundred years before. To this day there is a tendency for parents to dress children in the "antique mode." School uniforms seem to make a point of this, particularly in England for "Board School" youngsters. Could this device be a means of warding off the evil moments of adulthood?

Girls were put into "stays" from about four years on. Some were the more flexible "packthread" variety, but many were stiffened with wooden busks to assure an erect carriage. At school age the girls spent part of each day strapped to a "backboard" so that they should stand and walk erect. Their feet were in stocks, thus training the girls to keep them at right angles when walking. This gave women an elegant and erect but flatchested look which is often apparent in the portraits. This corseted look is portrayed all the way up the social scale; from peasant women to the merchants' ladies to the countesses. In rendering the corseted servants, we may be confronted by an artist's convention, but this is somewhat belied by the drawings and caricatures of the periods which show people at menial work, but with the corseted look. It is safe to assume that even young, indentured serving girls were well laced into their bodices.

Children's hairdressing followed adult fashions through all the earlier part of the Colonial period. But there were certain concessions to youth: when adult hair was well hidden under a cap, little girls were allowed to show a few curls. When wigs for men became popular, boys began to wear their hair in imitation of the wig: or sometimes, when the parents could afford it, the boys had wigs of their own. This was the usual practice until near the end of the eighteenth century. Very little girls escaped the drudgery of the great wigs worn by their mothers. Mobcaps and dormeuses were very smart, as were close caps with bonnets and even large straw hats. Many paintings show little girls wearing elaborate caps; and, in some, they are otherwise quite naked——a charming and airy effect (Fig. 88). A whimsical fad of the late eighteenth century? No, the next century will carry on this tradition, but with an approach characteristic of the nineteenth century——the photograph of the desexed child on the bear-skin rug.

Although seventeenth century children were often engulfed in ponderous replicas of their parents' clothes, their little necks were spared the great ruffs which were in style as the century began. At most, a multiple collar of soft material, which suggested a ruff, was worn by small children. Falling bands and simple collars were common. For a very dressed effect, both boys and girls wore gollilas. These were usually of moderate size; for state occasions they were sometimes enlarged until they were very nearly the size of the piccadils worn by Queen Elizabeth [the First]. As the falling bands developed into lace collars, the children's collars followed suit, becoming very elaborate and sometimes many layered; but they never seem to have become as exaggerated as those worn by their elders. Once this sort of collar became well established as a children's style it persisted right through the changes of style that opened the eighteenth century. As the various styles in cravats became popular, the lace began to disappear from the children's collars and they became a muslin or lawn ruffle. The effect was often very untidy, and as the stock got higher the combined stock and ruffle tended to swallow up the boy's neck. In reaction, the smaller boys were relieved of the stock, and the ruffle-edged neckband of the shirt was allowed to fall open. There was no fastening of any kind for the shirt and it was cut to be open to about the navel. The amount of bare chest that was exposed depended on how high the vest or coat was buttoned. By the third quarter of the eighteenth century this style had been adopted by boys well into their "teens" and was worn with an increasing degree of exposure. This may have been a matter of season, for if no vest was worn, the shirt would fly open.

A type of shirt that we call a "jersey" today was worn by workers. This was striped, had a round neckline and no opening over the chest; it had long sleeves and a body long enough to come over the waistband of the breeches to about mid-buttock. These jerseys are one evidence of the type of knitted garments which had been known in France since at least the tenth century, and in England since the eleventh century. They seem to have come to England with William in 1066. Knitted wear was in common use in the reign of Henry VII, for at that time price controls were put on knitted caps. Although there is no evidence from portraits, the importance of such materials in the American colonies made knitted goods, especially stockings, the major industry of Germantown, Pennsylvania by 1683. We should not rule out knitted garments for children, despite the lack of pictorial evidence. All little girls were taught to knit, and many of the fancier mitts, as well as the more commonplace stockings, were their work. With all the knitting it is easy to imagine that the pastime of "knitting tiny garments" was already commonplace.

Artifacts bear out the evidence of portraits that very many tiny articles of dress and their accessories were patterned after adult models. Shoes were made for little girls out of delicate leathers and silks, and with the same type of high heels as their mothers wore. It is not surprising to learn from diaries and letters that little girls did not run about and play, but sat primly for hours, probably one way of solving their juvenile delinquency problem. Rigidly corseted in stays that often had iron sections, and dressed in voluminous skirts and high-heeled shoes, the youngster of those days must have sat against her backboard and dreamed of an early marriage and the relief that pregnancy would permit. And if she did have a few minutes to run outdoors, there was always the danger of getting a touch of sun on the skin. To avoid such a disaster the sunbonnet was sewn around the youngster's head so that it could not be taken off except by the adult. She wore a facemask and long muslin gloves. There is some evidence that very small boys also wore corsets. All boys shoes were as carefully made as their fathers' and probably were heavier in proportion to size.

Shoes were made for wear, not display. A great many of fancier men's shoes from the seventeenth and eighteenth centuries have survived, nearly all silk and frequently embroidered and beaded. The adult leather shoes—the only type used for daily wear—did not survive, and neither did boys' leather shoes. If boys had fancy shoes, made of silks and embroidered, some artifacts would have survived. None did. No boys' shoes have survived and the supposition is that their shoes were worn until they had to be replaced. Children when they were not being "little ladies and gentlemen" were commonly barefoot (and that's most of the time). For "formal" occasions liveried boys and serving wenches were supplied with shoes. Children's shoes were equipped with buckles. These may have been of a somewhat smaller size than those affected by their elders. This would add to the confusion in dating buckles. During the middle years of the eighteenth century there were several major shifts in the size and shape of buckles, and every male adult and child possessed at least two pair. In the last decades of the century the use of buckles came to an almost complete end. One wonders what happened to the thousands upon thousands of buckles that were produced in those years.

A man may have worn as many as six buckles at a time. In addition to those at the knees and on the shoes, one buckle was used to fasten the stock at the back of the neck and another to close the back vent of the breeches. The young lad did not use the stock buckle as generally as did the man, but the vent at the back of boys' breeches, which was about four inches deep, was closed by a buckle. For the first third of the century, the back vent had been closed by lacing. During this same period the front of the waistband of the boys' breeches was fastened by laces or buttons. This was probably the only fastening used on boys' breeches until the front fall came in style shortly after 1730. There is no pictorial evidence of any fly fastening on boys' breeches as there is for the older and heavier adult. From the evidence of drawings, the use of buttons to close the fly grew in direct proportion to the adult "paunch." The slim, figure is usually drawn without any visible means of fastening the fly. The mature, mesomorphic man often shows three or four buttons on a flap about midway up the fly opening. The heavy man (and he was much in evidence throughout the earlier eighteenth century) had a whole row of buttons which barely fulfilled their mission. Based on this pattern we can assume that no one saw a need for buttons to close a boy's fly. The breeches were hardly visible during the boy's normal round of schooling or church-going for the vest was fairly long and was very generally worn (Fig. 84). Smaller boys, when they did not wear a vest, wore a sash about the waist to hold in the very full shirt. Occasionally an adult would do the same. When boys played, they took off the long coats, and sometimes the vests. In very active play, judging by contemporary drawings, they loosened the tight waistbands beyond what we would consider a convenient tolerance. This allowed the not too long shirttails, the only other covering, to fly loose. With shirttails flying, breeches and stockings falling down, the youngster of the day presented a very different picture than that of the studio portrait.

FIGURE 84

From an engraving by Augustin de Saint-Aubin, France, about 1750.

Trousers, the rather full ones worn by boys, were a style for young-sters before the 1780's were over. Small boys were dressed in colorful calico outfits with straight long trousers and without a fall front. As they grew older, cloth trousers with a fall front, and a related coat which was stylishly short became very general. It is interesting that it was two decades before similar trousers were stylish for men. By the end of the eighteenth century boys of about five were smartly and distinctively dressed in very full silk shirts with frilled and very open necklines and long satin trousers. At this same time, girls of about the same age group were wearing full, rather long muslin dresses which were girdled in just under the breast line. The high waist had also anticipated the style that their mothers were to wear a few years later. By now the children were fully in possession of a style of their own, and the aping of adult styles in children's clothes was only to reappear sporadically, and then as a fad. This fad exercises a hold over parents' imagination to this day. Another fad, current to this day, is the dressing of children in "cute" period clothing. An example of this is Thomas Alexander Fermor-Hesketh, the third Baron Hesketh, and all of seven years old, photographed in just such a late eighteenth century outfit in April of 1958. The Baron looks supremely sure of himself (Fig. 87).

FIGURE 85

FIGURE 86

FIGURE 87

From a painting by an unknown American artist.

From a portrait by Sir Joshua Reynolds—1781.

In almost every portrait of a boy, he carries a hat, or one is at hand on display nearby. All of these hats are replicas of adult ones. "Genre" painters frequently show small boys in action and in those paintings a different hat story is told. In these paintings small boys are hatless except for school, church, and "state" occasions. In their daily life the older boys wore, or at least had with them caps and hats, though again far more informal than the ones seen in officially posed paintings. The caps have that kind of eccentricity which we frequently see to this day in improvised headgear. Perhaps it was made out of the high crown of his father's old hat. This he would shorten to his head size by a crease all around it, or with the bottom edge turned up in an irregular band. Some boys' hats were low-crowned with broad brims and made of felt. Others were made of straw with a round crown and with a broad, curling brim. And still others were miniature three-cornered cocked hats. In the last decade of the century felt hats were varied by higher and somewhat conical crowns. When this hat was worn with the frilled, open-necked shirt and the long satin trousers, the effect of a small sized Italian "Pulcinello" is marked

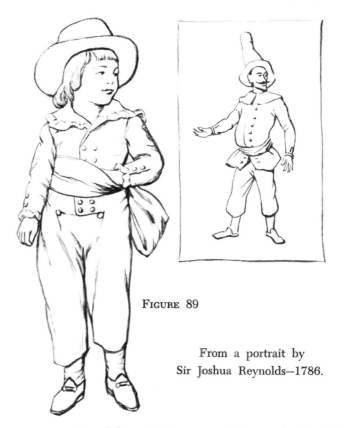

FIGURE 89

From a portrait by
Sir Joshua Reynolds—1786.

(Fig. 89). The younger Tiepolo's paintings were being acquired by collectors throughout Europe and his "Pulcinelli" were amusing many by 1791. The low crowned hat remained in style also. Perhaps because of another resemblance, this time to the sailors' dress, the hat became even lower in the crown and ribbon streamers hung from the band down over the brim. This "sailor hat" had been evolving throughout the century and was by now in the form which was to be retained by the child's sailor hat to this day. The actual sailor's hat changed with the new century to a stiffer form.

As the eighteenth century drew to a close, small girls continued to wear caps, some of which were very elaborate in form and others surmounted by large hats. The older girls had a variety of hats, but the ones most depicted are broadbrimmed, low crowned straw hats, usually trimmed with wreaths of flowers. Straw was a favorite material for young people's hats and it was used to make every shape of hat. Some of these shapes are still made, such as an untrimmed jockey cap of woven straw [Fig. 90]. But trimming could go to extravagant lengths on the hats for girls of all ages; sometimes yards and yards of wide ribbon were used. Other hats seemed to be made of puffs of lawn-like material. The later years of the eighteenth century were a milliners' heyday that has not been reached again.

FIGURE 90

From an engraving of 1761. The hat, from an engraving of 1730.

The expression: out of sight, out of mind, can, in the case of under-clothing, be extended to out of sight, out of record. There is a tiny bit of record of adult underclothing; none of children's underwear. There is report of women's drawers in eighteenth century France, but no trace in word or artifact of any in England in that century. It is unlikely that young girls wore drawers; their skirts were as long and voluminous as their mothers'. There is considerable listing of men's drawers in the contempo-rary records, and a handful of artifacts. A fair percentage of surviving men's undergarments come from a highly suspect source, the costumes put on effigies used in state funeral processions. These effigies, made of wood, often dressed in real clothing, were carried through the streets. Many have survived and are in museums and cathedrals. The underdress of an effigy is done for effect, not authenticity; for bulk, not gender.

Although drawers appear on many lists, they may have been some-what different from our contemporary concept of underwear. When Frank-lin writes of taking his ease in hot weather in long drawers, he is using the very words that the Portuguese used when they described the Hindoo paë-jamas or pyjamas that they had introduced to world trade over a century before. These pyjamas were lounging garments, not underwear. Certainly such lounging garments would have been thought quite unneces-sary for a young boy. For the adult, the need for undergarments was in direct relation to their occupation, pastimes and the type of material used in their outer clothing. This was all reflected in their social class and morality (or lack thereof) which was the basis for their mode of life.

The social distinctions between the upper and lower classes in the late seventeenth and eighteenth centuries created certain recogniz-able characteristics. The upper class was supposed to have inborn a certain strength which they liked to call moral fibre. This was the certainty that what they thought was right, was right. And the person of lower rank had better not tread upon this moral ground—or try to dress according to this high station—lest they run afoul of many sumptuary laws. Oddly enough, with the upper class' moral toughness went a soft dermal fibre. They were physically thin-skinned: hard physical labor, and exposure to all kinds of weather, was not part of their lives. (The lower class had a tough hide which was able to cast off dirt, cold, disease and beatings, and of course without complaint.) Thin skin was easily irritated: the upper class refers constantly to doctoring for rashes.

The rough materials that were used for country or hunting clothes could be uncomfortable. The shirt amply protected the upper body from the doublet, vest or coat. In the earlier days its very long tails had been a protection from the hose and heavy breeches. But now the breeches were getting tighter and tighter, and there was no longer room under them for bulky shirttails. The shirts became shorter until many were half-shirts that did not reach far below the waistband. When rough materials were worn, therefore, a sort of lining was needed to protect the delicate skin from the breeches, and thin linen or cotton drawers, frequently very tight, served as easily laundered linings. Breeches for house and city wear did not need this protection for they were of sleek materials such as silk or satin. That no needlessly encumbering materials were worn by the adult is made abundantly clear in eighteenth century diaries, for entry after entry bears witness to the instant availability of the sexual apparatus. It would be safe to assume that the lad no more wore drawers than did the father. However, according to the Cunningtons, basing themselves upon an artifact found on an effigy, there were drawers for men without opening in the front. If their interpretation is right, and this is indeed a pair of drawers for a male, we can only report that this is, to the best of our knowledge, a unique exemplar. A more likely explanation is that effigies, by their very nature, are a less than reliable source for underclothing: the topclothes, seen in public displays, are in almost every respect true to historical fact, but the undergarments served frequently as nothing more than convenient padding to build up the crude sculptural forms. Also, because an effigy's top garments had, from time to time, to be replaced, cleaned, or otherwise tampered with, the date or the style of clothing found on them, especially the undergarments, is often suspect.

From the clothing of the effigy of Charles II

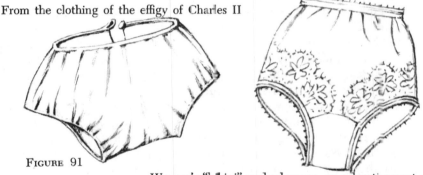

FIGURE 91

Woman's "bikini" underdrawers—an advertisement of 1965

If the aforementioned early seventeenth-century effigy had been refurbished in the later eighteenth century, replete with eighteenth century male drawers (sans opening), we'd still be confronted with the uniqueness of it all. But here a historical fact comes to the rescue, and gives us license to indulge in conjecture and build up a theory. For it was in 1760 that Dr. Tissot's violent polemic against masturbation was issued. Written in French, and translated into many languages, including English, it was widely circulated. From the panic it produced, many repressive measures were instituted. Possibly such male underclothing without an opening was made for young boys—one of Dr. Tissot's accomplishments. Why Tissot's invention (if it ever was) should be placed on a wooden effigy is still another story, on which we will not conjecture. Suffice it to say, that we can find no convincing textual or pictorial evidence, or artifacts for that matter, to prove that there were anything like such undergarments for boys or men in the American Colonies.

DRESS OF BOYS

1585–1790

AMERICAN INDIANS.—There is no reference to boys in early narratives. This leads to the conclusion that they were naked, a condition that the sixteenth century explorers found unremarkable.

SETTLERS AND IMMIGRANTS to the early settlements.—European boys' clothes from the point of emigration were worn without adaptation to the climate, which must have been a hardship in the south. All infants were swaddled (Fig. 92 A). Up to the crawling age boys were naked indoors (Plates 94 A, 93 C) and were wrapped in blankets when carried outdoors in cold weather. From one to five years old the usual daily dress was a shift (Plates 70 B, 95 F, 93 D; Fig. 92 B C F). If the weather was colder a jerkin was worn (Fig. 92 E). Another garment was like a coverall that was open at the crotch but closed again about each leg. The open crotch of this garment was covered by the tails of the shift. (Fig. 92 D). In cold climates, when social position demanded and for other "dress up" occasions, the dress of boys was a strange hybrid. The upper part was a miniature doublet and the lower part was a full skirt which was worn until the boy was adequately house-broken. For the youngest the skirted doublet hung straight (Plate 11 A; Fig. 93 A) but when an apron which went over the head and hung in front to the hemline was worn, the whole was belted in at the waist (Fig. 93 E, 92 G, 83 A B, 93 D). At its most formal level the doublet was a perfect miniature and the skirt was treated as though it were a gown (Fig. 83 C). The useful hanging sleeves (Figs. 93 E, 92 G, 83 A) continued to be attached to the younger boys dresses until the eighteenth century. As they became vestigial, they were

FIGURE 95

kept out of the way (Fig. 93 F). Older boys in the middle colonies probably wore a type of buff coat (Fig. 94). Some of them wore sailor's skilts for informal occasions (Fig. 90). The dress-like coat for the younger boys continued into the third quarter of the eighteenth century (Plates 26, 93 B, 95 A). When the boys reached the age of breeches, the long coats continued as a style, lasting until they were wearing trousers (Plates 95 J D G C, 96 B). The coat was still long in 1789 in the country, (Fig. 95) but was already short in the more stylish south (Plate 93 D).

From a fractur of 1789 at Winterthur.

By the very end of this period trousers had become common for boys of the five to ten year group and the coats were shortening to create a style (Plates 83, 94 G; Fig. 85). From the middle of the century to the end of the period the young boys had very open-necked collar arrangements (Plates 93 B, 95 G, 31 A, 95 A, 40 C, 93 E, 75 B, 93 D, 94 B, 89, 95 H, 83, 94 G).* The somewhat older boys went to the other extreme (the "cover up" period is very marked in boys of eight or nine years) with tightly closed necklines topped with a ruffle and ribbon tie (Plates 96 B, 95 C). In the later seventeenth century and until about the middle of the eighteenth century all boys, from those just old enough to walk to boys in their "teens" wore adult cravats (Plates 11 A, 95 J, 26 B) or plain neckband and frills on their shirts (Plates 26, 95 D, 43 B, 93 B) as well as all adult accessories (Fig. 96). Towards the end of the third quarter of the century some of the "smart" older boys wore the military black stock (Plates 95 B, 96 A). There is no evidence that boys wore the tremendously high stocks and neckcloths that came into style in the last quarter of the century, but they did wear the tied neckcloth (Plate 90 A).

---

* Plate and figure numbers are listed by chronological, not numerical order.

FIGURE 96

FIGURE 94

From a painting by an unknown artist in the National Gallery of Art

From Diedrick Lemkus— late 17th century.

FIGURE 93

A From the so-called Duff-Ogilvy portrait, England, 1567-68.
B From a painting by Cornelius de Vos, Flamand, 1625.
C From a painting by Abraham Bosse, France, 1650.
D From a painting by Velazquez, Spain, 1630.
E From a painting by Marcus Gheevaerts, England, 1596.
F From a French engraving, about 1635.

FIGURE 92

A From a painting by George de La Tour, France, 1650.
B From a drawing by Stephen Lochner, Germany, 1440.
C From a painting by Jacob Jordaens, Holland, 1630.
D From a painting by Carvaggio, Italy, 1600.
E From a painting by Bartolommeo Schedoni, Italy, 1611.
F From a painting by Annibale Caracci, Italy, 1760.
G From a painting by Jan Steen, Holland, 1650.

Hair styles for boys were modeled on those of adult wigs, or they wore wigs (Fig. 96) until late in the eighteenth century (Plates 11 A, 26, 24 B, 43 B, 40 C, 95 B, 31 C, 93 D) when the disheveled styles of the end of the century were preceeded by a style with trim bangs (Plates 89, 83).

From a portrait by
Sir Joshua Reynolds—1788

FIGURE 98

When the boy of about twelve left home, to attend an Academy, we know how he was dressed (Fig. 98). Academies, sometimes referred to as "colleges," were good schools (Boston schools, for instance, were the finest in the Western World). The young man from a well-to-do home did not, unlike a great many poorer lads, study for a specific trade. In the Academy he learned Latin, Greek, French, Mathematicks (Algebra, Geometry, Doctrine of Triangles, Projection of Spheres, Surveying, Navigation, Accompting—including some double-entry after the Italian method), the manner of Writing in the English and German styles of lettering, and also in the Court, Roman, Secretary, and Italian Hands. Shorthand was generally part of the curriculum, as was Vocal Musick.

This might seem a heavy program by today's standards, but when one remembers that the Academy schoolday was at least nine hours long and that there were five and a half days each week, with very few holidays from school, it is easier to understand the undertaking. But how much of all this was truly mastered? After all, even the graduation age from such advanced colleges as Harvard and Princeton was, on the average, a mere eighteen or nineteen. As a college graduate he was undoubtedly fully cognizant of what he had studied, and had mastered.

Each student had to recite his lesson at the master's desk. This was the method used from the very lowest grades after the "dame school" level. The students sat around the room on benches and advanced to the teacher either as he called upon them for examination or when they volunteered. From all reports, the rooms were dirty and cold and frequently dark as well. In the New England states, almost from the very outset, schooling was compulsory for all, so that even the poorest attended. These latter were there by public support. Warm workaday clothes certainly must have been the garb for the children in the lower forms. Figures 83 D and F, 84, and 94 probably give a very good idea of how the children were dressed for school, or looked shortly after they arrived there. Later, in the eighteenth century, the boy attending the more expensive Academy was dressed much like the schoolboy in Figure 85, and so were most boys for about another forty years. Even the rather dandified clothing of young men attending the more expensive schools (Fig. 98) would be changed to trousers by the end of the century, for by that time trousers were no longer identified with small boys' clothing. It is possible that even during the late eighteenth century the young man nearing graduation did not wear the academic gown that was worn on English campuses, for the resentment of things English was at its strongest. When Paul Revere engraved his view of Harvard in 1767, he depicted gowns here and there. But in the varied views near the end of the century, such as the Houdin-Dorgement one of 1795, no gowns are in evidence, and they do not appear in the prints again until the end of the first quarter of the next century. The gown was worn in the Academic Procession of Graduation Day, but perhaps the growing democratization of the Republic discouraged its daily use about the campus.

DRESS OF GIRLS
1585–1790

AMERICAN INDIANS.—A girl of the age of 8 or 10 years in John White's drawing wears a necklace and a cord tied around under the breasts and from it a cord which goes down through the crotch (Fig. 81). There are some later variations of this drawing such as by deBry and Vander Aa, which will be interpreted in detail in the volume on the American Indian. The interest shown in such a detail as the string indicates that a naked girl child is more remarkable to European eyes than is a naked boy. In the sixteenth and throughout the seventeenth centuries painters had made the very masculine and naked "putto" (a cupid-like figure) almost a trademark of the craft. Although there is no dearth of older female nudes in European paintings of the period, it is rare to find a very young one. Such a nude is no less fascinating to paint, so the lack of them would indicate a prejudice against a little girl naked.

FIGURE 88

"The Mob Cap" by Sir Joshua Reynolds—1781-82.

EARLY SETTLERS AND IMMIGRANTS.—Little girls among the early settlers, on the basis of the reasoning above and pictorial evidence from their countries of origin, were more consistently clothed than the boys. Regardless of the climate or their activity they had several layers of cloth on them. Infants in arms had long dresses (Fig. 97; Plate 94 B) and little jackets or vests (Plates 11 A, 93 E). Caps were popular for infants (Plates 11 A, 94 B) and even hats (Plate 94 E). Between one and three years old some little girls had the advantage of running around in shifts (Plate 95 E) but most of them were dressed in the adult style with the addition of hanging sleeves which by this period had become vestigial and were straps attached to the upper back quadrant of the armscye (Fig. 93 E B C 83 D E and Plate 13, Fig. 83 F, Plate 96 D). The hanging sleeves do not appear after 1740. In a few earlier paintings, though the dress probably had them, they do not show (Plates 65 A, 93 A B C, 63, 94 L, 93 E, 32 B, 94 H, 95 C, 84 A).

FIGURE 97

From a watercolor by Francis Cotes, England, 1766.

The dress of "Baby Mary" in the portrait with her mother, "Mrs. Freake" (Plate 13) presents a problem to the dress historian. The child that is shown is the size of at least a year-old boy. An error in scale is common in primitive painting, but the painter of this figure worked over it quite a bit and had an opportunity at least to gauge sizes. The dress is not that of an infant except for its length. The doublet cut of the upper part, the chemise sleeves, the falling band and the hanging sleeves are all typical of the dress of a child old enough to walk. Figure 83 E is redrawn to show this dress on a standing child. The cuffs on the short sleeves, though not exclusively masculine, were most frequently used on boys' doublets at an age when the sex is indicated by such accessories as swords and plumed hats. Gabriel Metsu painted just such a dress on a child about 1650 with the same style of cuffs. The child, who is perhaps a little younger, appears to be a boy.

When we reach the end of the seventeenth century, possibly the one headdress that appealed most to European mothers and their daughters alike was the fontange (Plate 94 F). There is no evidence that women wore the style in this country, though they may have admired it enough to put it on their daughters. There may have been a very utilitarian reason for not wearing such a high headdress. The earliest houses built in this country had low ceilings and very low door lintels. Early in the century this had effectively discouraged the women from wearing the tall, conical-shaped crowns on their wide brimmed hats which were so popular in England at the time. The architectural mode had not changed during the vogue of the fontange. Little girls could, of course, readily go about the house without having to stoop or dismantle an elaborately built headdress. Without the fontange, and after its vogue, girls wore their hair parted and rolled back on the sides into a sort of bun at the back, or combed straight back, fastened with a ribbon or combs and then formed into the bun. A curl might be brought over the shoulder or the bun might be dropped into a chignon by older girls (Plates 65 A, 93 A, 96 D, 93 B, 63, 93 C, 94 D). When the women's hair styles began to get higher and higher, architecture was forced to accommodate its planning and rooms and doors grew higher too. Oddly enough, little girls did not follow suit and now wore their hair very close to the head, with bangs over the forehead, and sometimes with curls (Plates 93 E, 32 B, 94 H, 96 C, 84 A). Their older sisters did follow the style enthusiastically (Fig. 63).

Children's hats showed a regard for gender at a younger age than any other part of the garment. Caps were much the same for both sexes as long as they were worn, but a hat might be worn over the cap and then it would be a girl's hat, or a boy's, if that were the case. The boy's hats seemed to be literal copies of their fathers', the girls' were marked by whimsey (Plates 32 B, 94 E) or copies of adult styles (Plate 96 C). Occasionally a hat reflects the headdress of the child's parents' homeland (Plate 96 A).

Corsets, although not worn only by females, were part of a woman's life from about four years to death, and were used in almost the same form from the eleventh century on. The very youngest girls had a sort of corseting, which was built into the bodice, and was confining. For somewhat older girls the corset was a small version of the adult one somewhat simplified (Fig. 82).

Once a girl was past infancy, there was little except size to distinguish her dress from that of a woman. The girl of twelve, at the beginning of the eighteenth century, had not only the appearance of her elders, but much of the discipline "fitting to a woman." Mothers were still carrying on the age-old tradition of seeming to accept the Old Testament stigmas while consolidating their position by indirect means. They were at pains to pass on this attitude to their daughters. The poor contented themselves with admonitions and laments; the well-to-do sent their daughters to boarding school. It is interesting to note that a girls' boarding school was a "Finishing School" in contrast to the boys' Academy, which was a "Preparatory School." To finish means to come to an end, and that end of course was matrimony. But no matter how much preliminary contract work had gone into it, no marriage deal could be closed easily unless the girl involved would give the illusion of acceptance. So the girl to be finished must be supplied with deal-closing dresses, and taught how to show them off properly.

> *"Tell me how you improve in your work,"* wrote Alice Shippen to her daughter Nancy: *"Needle work is a most important branch of female education, & tell me how you improve in holding your head and shoulders, in making a curtsy, in going out or coming into a room, in giving & receiving, holding your knife and fork, walking & seting. . . . These are absolutely necessary to make you shine, but above all let me know how you improve in* humility, patience & love, *these will make my dear Girl shine to all eternity. These are the inheritance that fadeth not away. I was pleased with your last & only letter I received since I left you. I say it pleased me because it informed me your good Mrs. Rogers (the headmistress of the school) has found out a way of encourageing you in your work & by way of joining her in encourageing you to be* industrious, *which makes so great a part of a female character."*

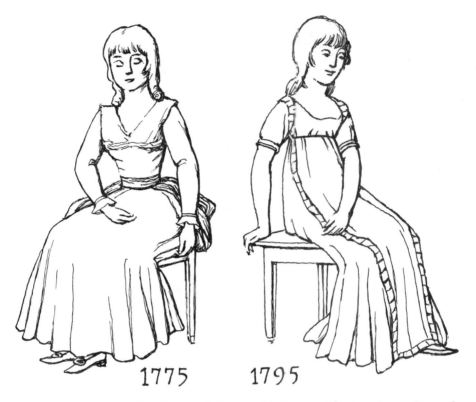

1775   1795

Nancy went to school in a Colony which was fighting for independence from England but she, like her classmates, still dressed in the restrictive corsets and hoops of the time. Had she gone to that school twenty years later she would have been dressed in loosely flowing muslin without benefit of corset, and had she stayed in New Jersey, she would have been able to vote upon graduation.

True to eighteenth century concepts of freedom and duty, Dr. Shippen, Nancy's father, fought for liberty from England and, having helped to win that battle, he came home and forced Nancy into an advantageous, though unhappy, marriage. By the time the French Revolution afforded a glimpse of freedom for women, politically and sartorially, Nancy was suing for divorce from a vindictive husband. The American battles had brought about a revolution in political thinking, the French one was to plant the seed for revolutions in human relationships.

> "I tell thee, no longer can it be said,
> That Book'ry, Cook'ry, Thimble, Needle, Thread,
> Are all she needs, nor that the pritty Fool,
> Shall just jigg her Crupper at Dancing School."

(with apologies to an unheralded author)

SHOES OF BOYS AND GIRLS.—The first walking shoes put on children had no gender nor did they have foot differentiation. At no age, until early in this century, was there a marked right and left last for common shoes. During the early centuries the foot fit the shoe, not the shoe the foot. The distinction between boys' and girls' shoes was occasionally made, but at other style periods the difference was hardly noticeable. The simplest way to clarify these shifts in style and gender is the following chart.

1620   1640   1660 G.   1660 B.

1720 B.   1720 G.   1775 G.   1775 B.

Children's shoes.   1790 B.   1795 G.

As a rule, shoes outlast style. They continued to be worn by the owners, after styles of clothing had changed and if still serviceable they were handed down to the younger children. The boys' shoes in the early years of the eighteenth century were sturdy and usually of heavy leather. The girls' shoes were frequently elaborate; made of finer leathers, brocades, embroidered silks. They could not be used for formal wear for as long a period as the boys' stronger and simpler ones. Later in the eighteenth century the boys' shoes were also made of fine leathers, which made them less durable, despite the greater care they demanded.

Adult's and children's shoes shown at the end of the chart were alike except for size. One cannot fail to note the contrast between this almost slipper-like eighteenth century footgear and the so-called "practical" very heavy boots and shoes worn by the first adventurers to these shores. At first thought it seems ironic that just as the largest migration on foot that this country has known—the great westward trek—was under way, fashion should dictate such light footwear. Although fashion is a most haphazard performer, this time it seems to have landed on its feet, for it was on just such footgear that the trek west proceeded and succeeded. True, the

Indian moccasin was made of a bit heavier leather, but in principle, the slippers and the moccasins were alike. Both conformed closely to the contours of the foot, thus serving as protection without hampering the foot's action. Military design of footgear to the contrary, greater distances have been travelled on foot in light gear than were ever slogged out in heavy boots or shoes. It was lightly shod that the pioneers of the new nation headed west into the wilderness.

✳ FORT HARMAR.

CHAPTER IX

Frontier Life

CHAPTER IX

Frontier Life

The earliest settlements along the seaboard had hardly come into being before the more venturesome pioneers were making their way into the wilderness which confronted them. Groups of fur traders and lone hunters went first, working westward by the more accessible routes, the navigable rivers, along the level valleys and through the gaps of the wooded mountains. The topography of the country favored this western advance. The great Atlantic coastal plain, almost entirely covered with dense forest and intersected only by faint Indian trails, was penetrated most easily by way of the rivers which originated in the Appalachian watershed. These rivers cut across the plain and afforded dozens of routes for the pioneers to push their way into the foothills. The mountains were their most serious obstacle. They rose ridge after ridge across their path, forcing them to seek out the infrequent passes through the mountains. Beyond, these hardy families found pleasant valleys running from north to south between the ridges. They were fertile and well watered, inviting those who had come in search of permanent homesteads. But the more adventurous pushed their way over the last chain and descended into the wide basin of the Mississippi.

The early hunters and trappers were tough men, crafty, tenacious, and self-reliant to an unusual degree. They learned the lore of the wilderness from the best of all possible teachers, the Indian. They learned from the Indians the use of the bark canoe which was light enough to float in a few inches of water and be portaged around rapids and waterfalls. They borrowed from the Indian his way of dress and shelter, adapted many of his foods and ways of cooking them and copied his elusive methods of fighting.

In addition to absorbing all the red man had learned through centuries of outdoor life, the white man possessed mechanical knowledge. He had mastered two efficient tools of prime importance in subduing the wilderness: the ax and the rifle. With his steel axes he blazed trails, cut wood for fires, fashioned shelters, built rude furniture, and performed a thousand and one necessary tasks. Had it not been for the Indian defending his family, home, and land against the intruders, perhaps the white man could have tamed the wilderness with this single tool—the ax.

Against the Indian, and as a means of providing meat for rude meals, the long rifle was indispensable. It was an unusually long weapon, heavy in the barrel, short and light in the stock (Fig. 99). Daniel Boone's own rifle was five feet three and a half inches long and eleven pounds in weight. This might seem unnecessarily long and heavy for a weapon used in the close confines of the forest lanes and carried for so many hundreds of miles; yet, it was a weapon developed by experience and necessity. It had been given this shape to insure greater accuracy. The barrel was heavy so that it might vibrate less and have less tendency to "whip" the bullet from its mark. It was long to increase the distance between the front and rear sights and, therefore, to lessen the margin of error in sighting quarry. Such a barrel gave more accurate results when light charges of powder were used; and because the hunter's activities carried him far from all sources of supply, it was imperative that he use no more powder in a charge than the occasion demanded. The stocks had deeply scooped butt-places, and on the right side a trap holding patches and grease was hollowed out and covered with a hinged brass plate. The flintlocks were set with the finest French flints and equipped with delicate, adjustable "set triggers." When compelled to by necessity, the hunter used the home-made, colonial gunpowder, but for dependable shooting, he preferred the fine black French powder.

These men often took their families with them deep into the tree country. On some pleasant hillock near a convenient spring, they would hack a space in the forest wall and build a log shelter. The logs of the little home were notched and grooved so deftly with the ax that, without nails or metal supports of any kind, their cabins stood the stress of the severest weather. The chinks between the logs were plastered tightly with clay and moss, and the roofs were covered with bark and wooden slabs. Small windows, or loopholes, were often covered with greased paper and provided with shutters. The doors were sturdy enough to resist assault. The cabins, exposed as they were to constant attacks, were built to withstand them.

Within, the furnishings were simple. The furniture, fashioned and shaped with an ax, was strong, if rude. Skins and fir boughs, mattresses of pine needles, and dried moss made the beds comfortable. By the stone fireplace would be a few pots and cooking utensils brought from the older settlements. The floors were earthen, although occasionally they were made of logs split in half with the flat side turned up.

Around the cabins, as the trees were cleared away, fields of corn, and patches of potatoes, beans, cabbages, and turnips were planted. In the autumn the scanty crops were harvested and stored in outhouses, or buried in leaves, dried grass, and earth, to be used during the winter. Nuts, berries, and wild fruits were added to the larder during the summer and autumn months. Meat, of course, formed the bulk of their diet, for deer, bear, elk, buffalo, quail, and turkey ran wild in the forestways, and the streams were abundant with fish. Wild animals furnished them with clothing. The pioneers learned the Indians' way of curing and tanning: stretching the skins in the sun, and soaking and kneading them under water until they were as soft and pliable as fine woven woolen cloth. They followed the Indian fashion of cutting and sewing their hunting smocks and leggings, and copied his way of making moccasins. Imitating Indian ways, the pioneer paid a sincere tribute to the natives' ingenuity, and learned in this way the ability to cope with the wilderness.

Behind the advance guard of hunters, traders, and trappers was a constantly pressing army of newcomers seeking homes. They were mostly new arrivals from Europe, with few material goods but hardy and ambitious. The early hunters, many of whom were resentful of this invasion, gathered together their families and chattels and moved westward. These newcomers who had pre-empted the hunting land were tillers of soil and builders in search of permanent homesteads. They cleared all the available land and built larger and more comfortable houses. They constructed and erected bridges to link them with the teeming life of the seaboard. They cleared and fenced their fields for the cattle and sheep they had brought with them, and they planted orchards.

It was all part of the extraordinary process that quickly transformed the harshness and discomfort of the frontier into the orderly world of snug homesteads and cultivated acres.

Spinning wheels and looms were brought in, and buckskin slowly gave way to linen and homespun. Peddlers and merchants came over the new roads with pack trains loaded with crockery and gewgaws of all sorts. Artisans and professional men arrived and soon schools and churches were built, and a regular machinery of government began to function. These settlements were the meeting place of the hitherto divaricate cultures of the Indian and the white man. From this confrontation was induced the most colorful, picturesque, if shameful, phase of our national life. It made a strange blend of the rude, elemental existence with some of the graces of the cultivated life of larger cities and of the foreign countries from which many of the settlers had come.

The Frontier extended from Canada to Spanish Florida, its boundaries moving steadily westward as successive waves of migration swept up from the eastern seaboard. In these geographically changing frontier zones, a type of dress developed which owed almost nothing to the fashion current in the "civilized" circles of the day. The frontier dress is a supreme example of clothing shaped by the conditions from which it had sprung, and it is a dress truly and uniquely American.

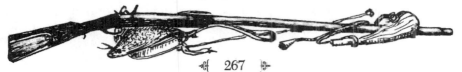

I. DRESS OF THE FRONTIER
THE MEN

FIGURE 99

HUNTING SHIRTS.—The principal garment of the border fighter was the hunting shirt, or hunting smock (a "wamus," as it was sometimes called). It was not a coat in any sense, but a loose tunic that was slipped over the head. Close fitting sleeves were attached to it, and it was usually slit open for a little distance down the chest and laced together with buckskin thongs. It was cut to varying lengths, according to the caprice of the wearer. Usually, however, it reached to just above the knees (Fig. 99). Almost all these wamuses were made with broad capes or collars attached to the garment (Fig. 99 A). The seams of the sleeve and the bottom edges of the shirt and the cape were usually decorated by fringing the leather. Sometimes the shirt and cape were edged with fur, as in the familiar portraits of Daniel Morgan and Sam Houston. Most of these garments were made of buckskin, carefully tanned. This was a material which was not only readily available, but it was light and warm and resisted both water and wind. The finest hunting smocks were made of elkskin, manipulated and kneaded until it was "soft and white as milk." These white elk shirts were apt to be more richly decorated than the ordinary ones, and must have been what the frontiersman considered his

"Sunday best." Some hunting shirts were made of homespuns or linsey-woolsey, in which case they were usually dyed blue and sewn with yellow fringe. It was this type of smock that most of Morgan's riflemen wore—from Quebec to Cowpens. The wamus hung loosely from the shoulders without any effort to shape it to the body and was confined at the waist by a broad leather belt.

LEGGINGS.—The leggings were much like those of the Indian (Fig. 99 B). They were often gartered or tied in below the knee to prevent dragging and hampering the movements of the wearer. As in the case of the hunting shirt, the outer seams were lined with fringe. At the bottom of the leggings the seam was opened a bit to permit the easy passage of the foot. They were of leather or sometimes of fur, made up with the hair inside for warmth.

FOOTWEAR.—The type of hunter who spent his days hunting in the dense forest wore the Indian moccasin. It fitted his foot snugly but not tightly. In winter he stuffed it with buffalo hair or moss for warmth. Sometimes the moccasins were sewn to his long leggings, and often they were ornately patterned and stitched.

HEADGEAR.—In the dense forest a close fitting head covering was necessary. Caps of coonskin, fox, bear, or squirrel were worn. Sometimes they were provided with flaps that folded back in warmer weather. A coon or fox tail was often sewn to the cap, hanging down behind (Fig. 99 A). In open country, free from clutching branches and exposed to the sun, a flapping felt hat was worn, sometimes decorated with wampum or the bushy tail of some small wild animal (Fig. 99 B).

UNDERGARMENTS.—If any undergarment was worn, it was usually a breechclout, as was worn by some of the Indians.

OTHER GARMENTS.—The hunter on the border always carried as little, and dressed as lightly, as possible. In cold or stormy weather he would use a blanket, skin, or fur robe as a cloak. He would wrap these about the body, held in place with a belt or with buckskin thongs

ACCESSORIES.—The rifles were long and heavy in the barrel, with short stocks that "dropped" sharply (Fig. 99). These were described in the early part of the chapter. The leather belts were often worn with the buckles at the back to conceal the glitter and to avoid catching in the underbrush. A long hunting knife in its leathern scabbard hung from the belt on the left side, and at the right side the tomahawk was slung. The bullet pouch hung at the right side from a strap that passed over the left shoulder (Fig. 99 A). Just above it hung the powder horn, made from a cow or buffalo horn. It was scraped almost to a paper-like thinness, so that it was translucent. The black powder could be seen through its walls. Sometimes a small amount of food, a blanket, and an extra supply of powder and shot were carried in a pack strapped to the back.

HAIR.—The hair was worn long and carelessly. It was seldom given any attention, except to cut it when it became too long, or to tie it behind in a rude pigtail.

II. DRESS OF THE FRONTIER

THE WOMEN

FIGURE 100

There were fewer frontier women than men. Their dress had neither the picturesqueness nor the individuality of masculine attire. As with the men, leather was the most important material, supplemented by crude homespuns and such cloth as infrequently came up from the towns.

BODICE.—The bodice was of fustian, linsey-woolsey, or leather cut loosely to the body and sometimes laced in front. Under it was worn a coarse linen or cotton chemise (Fig. 100). Collars were seldom worn; a small shawl or kerchief made of soft material might be thrown over the shoulders and around the neck.

SKIRTS.—The skirts were cut full, but without an excessive amount of material. They fell in rather straight folds from under the bodice and hung to the ankles. They were shorter than those worn in the settled districts because of the more active life the frontier women led.

HEADGEAR.—The women of the frontier seldom wore hats. In inclement weather, a hood or shawl was thrown over the head.

FOOTGEAR.—Stout, square-toed shoes or moccasins were worn, but often in warm weather the women went barefooted.

HAIR.—No attempt was made to achieve the formal and elaborate coiffures of the town ladies. The hair was worn long, gathered into plaits, or coiled in a knot at the back of the head.

ACCESSORIES.—Coarse linen aprons were worn frequently. Woolen stockings were worn in cold weather. Such aids to feminine adornment as jewelry, fans, patches, or ribbons were practically unknown. At best, they might display a few strings of "trade" beads or a carefully hoarded ribbon or two.

The pioneer movement westward has a history going back to the early eighteenth century. The pattern had been established: first the lone explorers, trappers and hunters, then the more hardy permanent settlers, still few in numbers, and finally a more massive influx. But still, the westward movement was limited in scope and size: its targets were more or less limited to the Appalachian mountain ranges. Not until the very end of the eighteenth century were the sights set to the vast and fertile plains of the Mississippi River lands. The impetus for this new westward flow was the treaty of 1783. That treaty was a confirmation of the faith of the Continental Congress of 1780, and had as a matter of the greatest practical importance, more than doubled the land holdings of the original states. The domain of the recent united states now encompassed almost a million square miles, a territory equal to that of Western Europe and the British Isles. With these new lands officially incorporated into the United States of America, the stimulus for westward migrations became irresistible for the tens of thousands who sought land and fortunes. That movement was to change the way of life of the new nation, and was to have a significant impact upon its dress. For the first time in our history, we had a way of clothing which might truly be called American.

The birth of the American nation had been slow, and at times seemingly in vain. Settlements were wiped out because of lack of preparation for the realities of the New World. Still, the potential rewards were too great to deter the adventurers for long, and by 1620 a handful of people had secured four hundred miles of coast. By 1675 that area had been extended to one thousand miles, with tentacles anchored far from the shoreline. From a handful of pioneers, the New England colonials had grown to close to one hundred thousand, and those in the middle colonies numbered about forty thousand. Although no absolute and reliable figures exist for the southern population of that period, we know that here too the numbers were considerable. In the southern colonies the large proportion of Negro slaves have already been noted, with those in South Carolina outnumbering the whites. The first official population-wide census was taken in 1790, the terminal period of this volume in the HISTORY OF AMERICAN DRESS. There were nearly four million inhabitants then, including about three quarter of a million slaves. The new nation emerging from the ravages of war, and the internal dissension which came upon the heels of the successful rebellion, faced a new century, and a new world. The problems were manifold, some plaguing us to this very day. But the possibilities for a freer and more rewarding life for significant sections of the population were immeasurably increased with the founding of the New Republic. There was hope and anticipation for new land, new opportunity, and greater freedom.

Introduction To The Plates

WITH NOTES ON THE ARTISTS

Those acquainted with the course of early American painting will appreciate the difficulty of finding representative portraits to present an orderly chronological progression. There are major gaps in time and place, especially prior to the mid-eighteenth century. Another problem, and one that applies to the whole period of Colonial America, is the difficulty of locating full-length portraits, one of the better records of the total effect of clothing and especially the effect of motion upon garments. One reason for this scarcity is made clear when we realize that the cost of a painting was determined by its size and what was included. When a client paid for a half-length portrait, he got a painting of his head and torso. He paid an extra fee for each hand that was added, and additional amounts for legs and feet. (I wonder what the charge was for dogs. They seem to have been a favorite supplement.) The American colonists had not reached, by nearly mid-eighteenth century, that state of affluence which caused so many Englishmen to commission full-length portraits.

Of the early American full-length portraits that are known, there are fewer examples of women posed standing than there are of men in similar poses. For this reason we must turn to European portraits and fashion plates to see how skirts, overskirts and petticoats hung at this period. One of the clues to fashion dating is the hemline: does it touch the floor all around; does it dip in the rear; does it show the shoes?

Another favorite clue for dating styles of clothing is the portrait painting to which a definite execution date can be assigned. But that date of execution is by no means always the same as the date of the style of dress depicted in the painting. Until well into the eighteenth century, accurately dated American paintings are so rare, that this problem seems almost academic. Even given all the essentials for the proper dating of such paintings—provenance, donors, dates of purchase, and other such data—we can then generally measure accuracy of dates for early American portraits by the decade only. And even when completely accurate, the date of the painting is only one more clue to be used in dating the styles of dress.

II

Although American paintings are usually unsigned they are a spirited and helpful record. Much of the painting was untutored, but it is not lacking in strength and honesty.

The first known drawings of America made on this soil were executed in 1564 by Jacques LeMoyne. He was one of the few survivors of the

St. John's River massacre the following year, and fled these shores, never to return. John White, the governor of the "Lost Colony," made some studies of Indian life on a visit in 1585 to survey the site of the colony. If he made any paintings during his residence as governor in 1587 they were lost with the colony.

A scene of New Amsterdam harbor, tentatively dated 1650, was done by a Dutch artist, Laurens Block. No other American work of his is known. In New England Thomas Smith—reputedly a former sea captain—had painted after 1660 a self-portrait and two or three other portraits of great competence. In 1680 he was paid a fee by Harvard College for a portrait, and this is the last known reference to Captain Smith.

In the New York area, about 1666, there was the so-called "Stuyvesant limner" who painted several members of this family. Any portrait that corresponds to the style of the Stuyvesant portraits is attributed to that limner. (For the sake of convenience, we identify other anonymous artists of the period by the name of the family they painted.)

The somewhat esoteric term "limner" appears again and again throughout this section because that contemporary term best describes the work of painters of the period. They so advertised themselves: "Limner—coach and carpet painting, signs, walls and likenesses . . ."

The date of 1670 is assigned to the first woodcut made in America. Its creator, a New Englander, John Foster, taught school, did decorative designing and may have done some portrait painting. There is an undated and unsigned portrait of Richard Mather. Shortly after Mather's death in 1669, Foster did the woodcut, probably from the portrait; the similarity between the two portraits is marked. During these years several portraits that have an important place in dress history were painted. A primitively painstaking craftsman with an appealing style painted the Freakes, husband, wife, and child perhaps sometime after 1670. The same limner may or may not have done the likenesses of the Gibbs children some years before. From the same period there are portraits of the Mason children, which have stylistic similarities, but a noticeable difference in the brush technique of the craftsman. Other names, this time of artists, are mentioned throughout these years. The work of Thomas Child is approvingly referred to in several notes and so is that of Lawrence Brown, but there are no known paintings of theirs.

In the earliest years of the eighteenth century we find a similar confusion: painters without identified works; paintings done by still unnamed hands. In New York the Duyckincks (grandfather Evert, son Gerrit, and his sons Evert and Gerardus) are reported to have done several portraits. But which portrait was done by which Duyckinck, if by any of them, we do not know. Many paintings by J. Cooper and dating from 1714 to 1718 have been found here but there is doubt that Cooper ever left his native England. In Boston, we have Nathaniel Emmons, born in that city in 1704 and working there until he died in 1740. He is the first native-born artist known to us, self-trained, and appreciated during his lifetime.

III

There were no recognized teachers and no galleries in which to see paintings by others. A chance view of some portrait or subject painting seems to have inspired many of the beginners. Then they had to cast about for some clues to more experienced practitioners' methods. A great deal of the beginner's knowledge was drawn from available engravings and mezzotints. These were almost all of European origin and from them painters and students unhesitatingly copied poses, surrounding "props," draperies and landscape backgrounds. Occasionally, they copied the dress and its accessories too.

Although engravings could be made in color, the work was a network of lines which could only approximate the gradations of hue and texture in the original work. The mezzotint, a new method of reproducing a painting which was developed at just this time, brought to the eager American student some idea of the continental use of color and the English manner of painting flesh.

The mezzotint is unlike a line-engraving and etching. In the latter, lines are engraved, or burned, by means of acid, into the metal. The plate is inked, then wiped clean—with the ink remaining in the channels of the lines. These "inked channels," when pressed against paper, will print black. In the mezzotint, the process is changed. The entire metal plate, by means of a "rocker," is covered by myriads of tiny lines which cross in every direction, giving the plate a very fine and even, but nonetheless, rough surface. If ink were applied at this stage, the impression would be completely black. By smoothing out sections of the plate various shades of whiteness (or light) can be obtained, for the ink will not adhere to the smoother surfaces. The reversed image of the painting is then rendered on the plate by varying the degree of smoothing on the roughened surface. The net effect is one of softness and delicate shading, almost like a painting in ink. The process did not at first have any practitioners in colonial America, but many were imported from Britain and the mezzotint was immensely popular on these shores, and a rich source for native artists.

The first half of the eighteenth century was a busy one, artistically, in the colonies of the Atlantic coast. In Massachusetts about 1721 the Ann Pollard limner did that very memorable portrait; a few years later, Peter Pelham set up as a mezzotintist.

At about the same time, we have a limner, perhaps a team of limners working in the Hudson Valley, who inscribed the legend "Aetatis Suae" (meaning "of the age of") on the canvas, together with date of the sitter seen on the canvas. The style of these paintings is so distinctive that they have been attributed to one painter, unfortunately anonymous. Because many are dated, these paintings are of major importance to the dress historian [See Plate 45]. Pieter Vanderlyn, a sailor, was ashore for a few years and in that time painted one portrait that can certainly be attributed to him, and perhaps several more that bear traces of the same handiwork, but have not yet been certified. Justus Englehardt Kühn came to Maryland in 1708 and painted many competent portraits before his death a decade later (Plate 94 F). A well-trained artist, Gustave Hesselius came from Sweden in 1712 and roamed and worked throughout the Philadelphia area. His portraits of the Indian delegates are among the most convincing portraits that we have of Indians of the period. He trained his son, John, who became a successful portrait painter. A Scotsman, John Watson, painted with a fair amount of competence in New Jersey and New York.

Far to the south, in Charleston, Henrietta Johnston, though ailing, eked out the meager funds of the "Bishop of London's Commissary" and the Rectory of St. Philip's by doing some very unique, very feminine portraits in pastel. Mrs. Johnston probably had a few lessons in her native Ireland. As an observer of dress, she is not our most helpful guide. An exception is her "Thomas Moore." Another English artist, no longer young, spent a few years in Virginia. Charles Bridges painted in a very traditional but charming manner and used color in his painting with great skill. At about this time, nearing the middle of the century, Jeremiah Theüs arrived from Switzerland and joined the active, rarely mentioned, colony of artists in Charleston. Portrait painting was now in demand and he must have had a busy life, for many portraits by Theüs, or attributed to him, are hanging in homes along the littoral from Charleston to Savannah. In addition there must be hundreds of portraits buried in attics throughout the south which were painted during these busy years by artists of every degree of skill. By the time these portraits are brought to light they will be in every imaginable state of decay.

IV

The colonies were by now the promised land to the English artist who was competent, but not talented enough to compete in an England already monopolized by Kneller and his growing school. John Smibert, who came in 1729, brought a comparatively advanced skill to this country. William Williams, John Wollaston and Joseph Blackburn were others who not only brought their varied talents to these shores, but they served to help and direct native-born, gifted artists who were to leave their mark on the century and on the future of American art. Robert Feke in a decade of work left a group of skillful portraits painted with all the charm and dishonesty typical of the English-cum-German school. John Greenwood, who went the opposite way with an uncompromisingly honest style, and Joseph Badger, who had a countryman's shrewd ability to read character and an artist's ability to render it, come close to establishing an "American school" of portraiture.

Four painters were to be critically and popularly accepted as great before the end of the century. Two of them, Benjamin West and John Singleton Copley, were actively studying their craft shortly after the middle of the century. Although both were born on these shores, they preferred England and it was there that they rose to the heights of their painting fame. They are by courtesy "American" artists. The other two artists were Charles Willson Peale and Gilbert Stuart. Both were born here, studied abroad and returned to this country to secure their fame and to finish their lives on this soil. Peale returned to this country in 1769 after studying abroad—with West, of course—and becoming disgusted with the European scene. Like Franklin and Jefferson, the Renaissance men of their time, Peale was vitally concerned and involved with many facets of life: he fought for independence, grew into a skillful and perceptive painter and, because he was at heart a palaeologist, opened one of the first museums in this country. Gilbert Stuart was a lifelong portrait painter. He began when quite young and was quickly recognized as a promising painter. Knowing that he needed to study with a good teacher, Stuart sought out Cosmo Alexander who was on a visit to this country. When Alexander returned to Scotland, Stuart went with him to continue his studies. In 1773, Alexander died and Stuart returned to this country. Within two years, disturbed by the imminence of war, he went to London where he joined West. After a brief period of study, Stuart became West's assistant and soon, his competitor. A popular portrait painter, Stuart outspent his fees and was quickly in debt. Despite many influential friends, he had to flee his debtors and so painted his way back home via Ireland. Here he continued to paint in a drunken but brilliant and psychologically shrewd way until his death.

V

In compiling the following alphabetical list of some of the painters whose work I have selected for illustration, the usual biographical data was brushed aside. Instead, there is comment on the fashion, or dress "sense" of the artists. If these artists were alive today, and saw this list, they would rightly be offended, for the critical comments are at the level of "fashion artists." Painting values, skill in composition, subtlety of shadow and all other paraphernalia of the critical faculty are ignored. My obvious intention is to focus the readers' attention on the dress, not the painting. Each artist seen this way, contributes to a fuller knowledge of clothing, which is the aim of these studies.

(AETATIS SUAE and other similar inscriptions)—There were a host of limners doing portraits during the latter part of the seventeenth century and the early part of the eighteenth century. They probably *mass painted* the dresses and coats seen on the canvases before they had any notion of who the sitters would be. In this way they spared them many hours, for sitters had to pose only for the faces. As a result, all the dresses are just right for going to church or the church bazaar. The men were always clothed as if they wanted to demonstrate their fitness for political office.

JOSEPH BADGER—1708-1765. Although self-taught and provincial, he endowed his merchant-class sitters, regardless of age, with style. The clothes are never above the apparent social station of the sitter and have a rightness which is "smart." In addition he has painted these garments in a way that we can trust as "right" for clothes worn at that time.

JOSEPH BLACKBURN—There is a sense of elegance in his paintings done in New England during the 1750's. The student of dress, however, cannot be sure if the sitter really dressed as painted. The social class of the sitters is unsure, as though they had been up-graded. One wonders if they paid a premium for such an effortless upward step.

CHARLES BRIDGES—An artist with a sophisticated, European elegance, he painted in Virginia during the late 1730's. Perhaps the Virginia ladies had a London insouciance. Whether they did or not, Bridges gives them this quality in his portrait. He probably painted very few portraits personally. However, he was imitated. His few works and its imitations are the only visual report we have of the style worn in Virginia.

WINTHROP CHANDLER (1747-1790)—Chandler was a painter who depicted what he saw as accurately as did the camera of the early nineteenth century itinerant photographer. He may have suggested improvements in the dress of his sitters, for they are obviously "dressed up." But whatever changes of dress were made, they were made by the sitters, and were not inventions of the artist.

JOHN SINGLETON COPLEY (1738-1815)—A dressmaker at heart, he revelled in materials and decorative details. Nearly all his sitters are handsomely overdressed. He ordered dresses from abroad so that his sitters would have a "London smartness." There is a great deal of the entrepreneur in all his painting. Oddly enough, though the materials are rich and the details meticulously rendered, the total effect lacks "chic." In a period of new, self-made wealth, Copley was just the painter to have been popular because he made the clothes he painted appear quite expensive.

JOHN DURANT (1774-1832)—Durant was an artist with that rare talent—the ability to render "good taste" in clothes. The sitters are dressed as they should be; never above nor below their social station. Because the clothes are "right" they are "chic" even though they may not be in high fashion. Although the sitters seem to be country cousins, they will never embarrass their city hosts.

RALPH EARL (1751-1801)—This painter should be the "Sweetheart" of the costume designer. A very accurate renderer, he had the knack of giving a sense of style to even a dull outfit. Although the sitter is always believable, nevertheless one is always aware of his self-conscious pose and his very fitting clothes. Earl was a native and self-taught artist. He had barely enough skill to paint battlefield scenes during the Revolution. His early portraits are of the "clubroom genre," but after he went to England and studied briefly with West, his style improved and his portraits had greater insight into character and the rendering became more fluent.

ROBERT FEKE (active in 1740's)—Feke was the prototype of the portrait painter who has flourished for the last two and a half centuries. He was satisfied as long as his sitters looked younger, smart, or elegant. The men were appropriately sophisticated, the women modest, yet appealing. He was not concerned with depicting the latest fashions, but rather the tasteful attire. He would copy the same dress or coat from portrait to portrait.

JOHN GREENWOOD (1727-1792)—He seems to have painted what he saw, although he was aware of the duty of the artist to reveal the best characteristics of his sitters. The clothes are believable and can be studied with confidence.

JOHN HESSELIUS (1728-1778)—The son of Gustavus, an artist of considerable talent, John was a painter who seemingly did not delve into the personality of his sitter to achieve the desired effect. He probably did not hesitate to embellish the sitter or his attire nor to suppress whatever did not make a good picture. He may be classified as a "society painter."

CHARLES WILLSON PEALE (1741-1827)—Peale was a painter almost as photographic as Chandler, with a talent for preciseness. He would have loved a camera and forsaken the brush for it. He fussed over details and added or suppressed at will. But when the "exposure" was made it was as honest as the camera. Indeed, his paintings can be used as if they were camera studies.

CHARLES PEALE POLK (1767-1822)—Polk's paintings looked as if they were the result of a close-up done with a pin-hole camera. Not everything "comes into focus." However, what he does depict is painted in a straightforward manner.

MATTHEW PRATT (1734-1805)—Pratt is another "photographic" painter. Very honest, he depicts the style and taste of his sitters as they are, but keeps all under perfect control. Although little seems to have been included to make his painting dramatic, selective planning is evident.

JOHN SMIBERT (1688-1751)—Smibert was a painter with a good eye and a facile brush. The final effect was important to him; his major interest was the face. Very conservative about dress and, although he subordinated its importance, what he depicted is honest.

THOMAS SMITH—Smith was reported to have been a seaman. He had an artist's eye and a surprising sense of contemporary style. The two, perhaps three, canvases we have are most believable. (Late 17th century)

GILBERT STUART (1755-1828)—He disliked painting full-length portraits and rarely did any but half-length paintings. He concentrated on the personality of his sitters with rare insight. If a sitter's clothes failed to reveal him properly Stuart would surely have sent him to change or painted him as he saw fit. There is always a definite connection between the character of the sitter as portrayed and the garment he was wearing.

JEREMIAH THEÜS (1719-1774)—Theüs was a shrewd judge of social position, or at least what social position he thought the sitter would like to be. The clothes he painted were used to convey character rather than illustrate fashion and these clothes were borrowed from other portraits or even invented to suit the painter's particular needs.

BENJAMIN WEST (1738-1820)—The painting of dress was a painful necessity to West. Although it was noted and recorded with honesty, there was no attempt to attach independent importance to the dress of the sitter.

WILLIAM WILLIAMS—Once a theater man, always one. Williams had been at one time a scenepainter, and the technique of the scenepainter is always evident. He had a designer's eye for total effect and used this talent to good effect in his paintings. He is almost the only painter of the 1760's who has given us any idea of how a dress is worn and looks in motion.

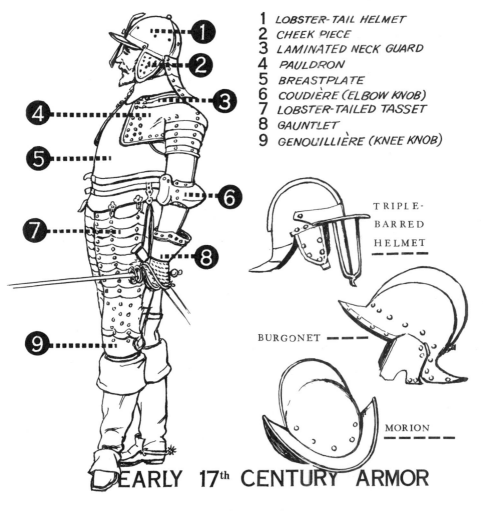

1 LOBSTER-TAIL HELMET
2 CHEEK PIECE
3 LAMINATED NECK GUARD
4 PAULDRON
5 BREASTPLATE
6 COUDIÈRE (ELBOW KNOB)
7 LOBSTER-TAILED TASSET
8 GAUNTLET
9 GENOUILLIÈRE (KNEE KNOB)

TRIPLE-BARRED HELMET

BURGONET

MORION

EARLY 17th CENTURY ARMOR

List of Plates

WITH ATTRIBUTIONS, SOURCES,
AND OCCASIONAL COMMENTS

The criterion for the selection of the following illustrations was that they directly reflect the styles of dress seen in the Colonies and the States. Most of these portraits are by American artists. A few, however, are by Europeans who, during visits to those shores, painted Americans in "American" clothing of the period. In some cases no adequate portraits or paintings exist to illustrate a style or article of clothing. In such cases I have selected for reproduction European engravings or drawings which show dresses described or mentioned by name in contemporary American documents. (Plates 2, 4, 7, 8, 11, 16, 17, 20, 50, 61, 64, 71, 74, 80, 81, 82 from my collection.)

Except for those noted, the portraits are nearly all in American public collections, although they are not necessarily on public display. The plates are solely for dress reference and may have been cropped of material which was not pertinent to that use. Therefore, some may not do justice to the artist's sense of composition.

Plate 1A Portrait of a Man of the Bowdoin Family. Painted by an unknown artist of the French school in 1647. The ruff which is of a type which began to go out of style in 1620-25, would be a very late version of this fashion trend. Or, this painting may be a copy of an earlier portrait. Courtesy of the Bowdoin College Museum of Art. Bequest of James Bowdoin III in 1813.

Plate 1B Governor John Winthrop (1587-1649). Painted by an unknown English artist possibly in 1629. Courtesy of the American Antiquarian Society.

Plate 2A King Charles I of England and his Family, about 1620. Engraved by Willem van de Passe.

Plate 2B John Paulet, Marquis of Winchester, about 1630. Drawing by George Tobin after a miniature by Peter Oliver.

Plate 2C Drawing by Anthony Van Dyke of Hendrik Van Balen, his teacher. Undated.

Plate 2D George Villiers, Duke of Buckingham. Engraved by Martin Droeshout, possibly in 1648.

Plate 3 John Leverett (1616-1679). Painted by an unknown artist (said to be Peter Lely). This may have been painted in 1650 just before Leverett returned to the colonies. Lely was beginning to paint in London at that time. Courtesy of the Essex Institute.

Plate 4A Tobias Venner, M. D., 1660

Plate 4B Turner (probably James. An execution broadside of 1664).

Plate 4C Anthony Sparrow, Theo. D, 1640

Plate 4D Sir William Curtius, Ph. D., undated

Plate 4E Richard Kilvert, L.L.D. 1644

Plate 4F Moll Cut-Purse (Mary Frith), about 1612. Heroine of Middleton & Decker's *The Roaring Girl.* All (4 A-F) from James Granger—"Biographical History of England—adopted to a Methodical Catalogue of Engraved British Heads"—1769, 1779. Continued by Mark Noble—1806.

Plate 5 Governor Josiah Winslow, 1651. The portrait was painted when he was with his wife, Penelope (Plate 21) in England. Painted by an unknown artist, probably, English. Courtesy of Pilgrim Hall.

Plate 6A Governor Edward Winslow (1595-1655). Painted by an unknown artist, thought to be Robert Walker, a painter who was active and popular in the early Commonwealth. Portrait date 1651, with age given as 57. Winslow was in England from 1646 to 1654. He died at sea of a fever during the course of an unsuccessful expedition against the Spaniards in the West Indies. Courtesy of Pilgrim Hall.

Plate 6B   Governor John Endecott (1589-1665). Copy by T. Mitchell of the portrait of Governor John Endecott in the Council Chamber, Boston. The style of his collar is of 1655. Endecott, because he was not serving as the Governor of Massachusetts at this time, 1654-1655, might have been in England. This copy looks like Dutch painting. Courtesy of the Essex Institute.

Plate 7A   Sir Hugh Cartwright, said to have been in command of Fort Albany. From Granger.

Plate 7B   George Alsop lived in Maryland during the years 1658-62. During this time he did a survey of the state and a report on the "Susquehanoke" Indians which was published in this year—1666. From Granger.

Plate 8A   Charles II. Engraving by Pierre François Basan after Sir Peter Lely. This looks like the "exile-type" portraits, and may be a later head by the Lely Studio—perhaps the armor would date 1655, the head and the lace, after 1660. From L'Europe Illustré, duRadier, 1755.

Plate 8B   John Barefoot. From Granger.

Plate 9   Self-portrait of Thomas Smith. The engagement shown was very probably de Ruyter's naval operation of 1662. This was concluded by a treaty with the pirates of Algiers. An engraving of this appears in Ogilby's "Africa," 1670. The dress actually dates somewhat earlier. The painting was probably done after Smith saw Ogilby's "Africa," when the book actually appeared in 1671. See Plate 19. Courtesy of Worcester Art Museum.

Plate 10   Sir George Downing. Painted by an unknown artist, perhaps painted in the Hague. Downing, who was the second graduate of Harvard, became a baronet in 1663. He was in the Netherlands in 1670-71. A Harvard University Portrait. Courtesy of the Fogg Art Museum.

Plate 11A   The Barclay Children. Painted by an unknown artist, perhaps in Switzerland. From the collection of TenEyck Bronck Powell, Esq., with his permission and through the courtesy of the Frick Art Reference Library.

Plate 11B   Two large figures from the Nobility of Lorraine, etched by Jacques Callot in 1624. Group of five small figures by an unknown hand, from a Broadside of 1630.

Plate 12   George Corwin (1610-1685). Painted by an unknown artist, probably in 1675. By documentation which traces the portrait to its restoration in the early years of the nineteenth century we know that the area with the head, outlined in the reproduction, is real. The area with the head was then cut from an almost totally ruined painting, mounted on another canvas and the whole leveled off with the canvas of an old portrait. The joining is clearly visible. The major repainting was done by Hannah Crowninshield about 1819. The baldric and cane were still in possession of the family at the time of the restoration and are probably faithfully rendered. The embroidery on the cuff and pocket looks like nineteenth century embroidery. The cravat line has been raised on the neck, but the rest of the cravat is original. It was retouched again in 1864 by Hawarth. Courtesy of the Essex Institute.

Plate 13   Mrs. Elizabeth Freake and baby Mary. Painted by an unknown artist active in Boston in the 1670's. There is a Dutch influence in the work. The baby is wearing a Dutch cap and clothing usually worn by a year old boy. The tippet and collar arrangement worn by Mrs. Freake are Dutch. The fashions date from the 1650's, perhaps the time of the artist's schooling. Courtesy of the Worcester Art Museum. Gift of Mr. and Mrs.

Albert W. Rice in 1963. (There is some discussion of the gender of the baby in the chapter on children's dress.)

Plate 14　Elizabeth Paddy Wensley (1596-1675). Painted by an unknown artist, probably before 1660. This is apparently a wedding portrait, and the clothes therefore are relatively stylish. Courtesy of Pilgrim Hall.

Plate 15A　Deacon Samuel Chapin (1596-1675). A sculpture by Augustus Saint-Gaudens. A careful synthesis of the seventeenth century country costume done two hundred years after the death of the subject. The statue stands in a public square in Springfield, Massachusetts. A photograph by Woodward, Springfield.

Plate 15B　Captain (Sir John) Hotham. An anonymous engraving of 1642. From Granger.

Plate 16A　An eighteenth century student (1750). A German drawing

Plate 16B　Thomas Rowlandson. A drawing done about 1785

Plate 16C　Daniel Chodowiecki. An engraving done in 1781.

Plate 17A　John Pordage, Theo. D., about 1670. From Granger.

Plate 17B　Valentine Greatrakes, Ireland, about 1670. From Granger

Plate 17C　Robert, Viscount Yarmouth, about 1665. From Granger.

Plate 17A　John Pordage, Theo. D., about 1670

Plate 17B　Valentine Greatrakes, Ireland, about 1670.

Plate 17C　Robert, Viscount Yarmouth, about 1665.

Plate 18　Mr. John Freake. Painted by an unknown artist, active in Boston during the 1670's. The same odd reflection of Dutch taste appears here in the collar, a rare style. Few examples are to be found in portraits, and those found are undated. The more conventional style, seen in Plate 19, was current in the early 1660's in England and the Netherlands. Courtesy of the Worcester Art Museum. Purchased through the Sarah C. Garfer Fund.

Plate 19　Major Thomas Savage, shortly after 1370. Tentatively ascribed to Thomas Smith (See Plate 9). Courtesy of the Worcester Art Museum. With the permission of Henry L. Shattuck.

Plate 20A　Sir Edmund Andros. At the time of the restoration of Charles II, 1660 to 1665, before his varied colonial governorships.

Plate 20B　Thomas Wriothesley, Fourth Earl of Southampton This was about 1642 when he became Privy Counselor to Charles I.

Plate 20C　Wilhelm Brog, Colonel General, Scotland, 1635.

Plate 20D　Robert Earl of Warwick. This was done in the period 1635 to 1640 when he was active in the foundation of New England colonies. Engraving by Wenceslas Hollar. B & D from Granger.

Plate 21　Mrs. Josiah Winslow (1630-1703). This was probably painted in England in 1651. Although the artist is said to be unknown, it appears to be Robert Walker. This fashion is seen in portraits as late as 1665. Courtesy of Pilgrim Hall.

Plate 22A　Mrs. James Bowdoin II, 1748. Painted by Robert Feke, working from a mezzotint of the 1680's after a painting by Willem Wissing.

Plate 22B　Mrs. William Bowdoin, 1748. Painted by Robert Feke. This time a mezzotint of a portrait by Jonathan Richardson, Sr. of Ann Oldfield was used, both for the pose and the type of dress worn. 22 A and B Courtesy of the Bowdoin College Museum of Art. A bequest of Mrs. Sarah Bowdoin Dearborn.

Plate 23　Pieter Schuyler, about 1695. Painted by an unknown artist called the Patroon Painter. Courtesy of the Frick Reference Library. From the collection of the City of Albany, New York.

Plate 24A　Moses Levy (1665-1728) who was active in 1695 as a trader in New York. Painted by an unknown artist. Courtesy of the Museum of the City of New York.

Plate 24B   Adam Winne, named and dated 1730. Painted by an unknown artist. Courtesy of the Henry Francis duPont Winterthur Museum. A Gilbert Ask photograph.

Plate 25   The Trustees of Georgia. Painted by Willem Verelst in England in 1734-35. A detail of a larger canvas. This shows well the close adherence to a fashion by men of the same class. Dare we call it "conformity"? Courtesy of the Henry Francis duPont Winterthur Museum.

Plate 26   DePeyster Boy with Deer. Painted by an unknown artist. The background, deer and pose of the boy was from a mezzotint made in 1695 after a painting by Godfrey Kneller. The likeness of the boy and his garments are accurate to our knowledge. Courtesy of the New York Historical Society, New York City.

Plate 27   Theodore Atkinson, Jr. Painted by John Singleton Copley. The pose was an adaptation of one copied from a contemporary mezzotint of a portrait of Joshua Winslow. Courtesy of the Museum of Art, Rhode Island School of Design.

Plate 28   Samuel Mifflin (1724-1781). Painted by Charles Willson Peale in 1777. Courtesy of the Metropolitan Museum of Art. The Egleston Fund, 1922.

Plate 29   Governor Moses Gill (1733-1800). Painted by John Singleton Copley, perhaps in 1766. The Governor was a thrifty young man. This can be judged by the coat, which had gone out of style in 1760, as well as the vest buttoned to the neck. Courtesy of the Museum of Art, Rhode Island School of Design.

Plate 30A   Mann Page II (1713-1778) is labeled on the frame, although there is some question if the name is accurate. The style of dress is of the period 1725-1730. If Mann Page II is pictured, he would have been seventeen in 1730. A-C. Courtesy of the College of William and Mary.

Plate 30B   Alice Grymes (1723-1746). The first wife of Mann Page II, with son John born 1744. The portrait must have been painted about 1745 or 1746.

Plate 30C   Hon. John Page (1720-1774) is said to have been painted by John Wollaston, which dates the painting to the early 1750's. The frame bears the legend "Died 1780—Aged 60."

Plate 30D   Col. Matthew Page, as labeled on the frame (1769-1803). This painting has been attributed to John Wollaston and Charles Bridges. The style of dress is later than the 1740's. Courtesy of the College of William and Mary. Williams Photograph.

Plate 31A   Mann Page I, as labeled on the frame. He died in 1730 at thirty-nine years of age. Courtesy of the College of William and Mary.

Plate 31B   Judith Carter, second wife of Mann Page I. The artist is said to be John Wollaston. The sitter is wearing Wollaston's favorite dress of 1750. Courtesy of the College of William and Mary. Williams Photograph.

Plate 31C   John Page (1744-1808) as a boy. Painted by John Wollaston. Courtesy of the Virginia Museum. This portrait is on loan from the College of William and Mary. Photograph by Burris.

Plate 32A   Dr. Alexander Shearer. Painted by Matthew Pratt. Courtesy Amherst College Museum of Art.

Plate 32B   Mrs. Alexander Shearer and child. Companion portrait by Matthew Pratt. Courtesy of the Amherst College Museum of Art. Photographs by Jakstas.

Plate 33   John Philip de Haas (©1735-1786). Painted by Charles Willson Peale in 1772. Courtesy of the National Gallery of Art. The Andrew Mellon Collection.

Plate 34A   Edward Bromfield (1723-1746). This painting has been attributed to both John Smibert and John Greenwood. A Harvard University Portrait. Courtesy of the Fogg Art ·Museum.

Plate 34B   Ezekial Hersey (1708-1770). Painted by Edward Savage. A Harvard University Portrait. Courtesy of the Fogg Art Museum.

Plate 35A   Nicolas Boylston (1716-1771), 1767.

Plate 35B   Thomas Boylston (1721-1798). Both paintings by John Singleton Copley. Harvard University Portraits. Courtesy of the Fogg Art Museum.

Plate 36   Col. Jonathan Warner (1726-1814). Painted by Joseph Blackburn in 1761. Courtesy of the Museum of Fine Arts, Boston.

Plate 37   Col. Nathaniel Sparhawk (1715-1776). Painted by John Singleton Copley in 1764. Courtesy of the Museum of Fine Arts, Boston.

Plate 38   Jeremiah Lee. Painted by John Singleton Copley in 1769. Courtesy of the Wadsworth Atheneum.

Plate 39   General Samuel Waldo. Painted by Robert Feke, in the period from 1748 to 1750. Courtesy of the Bowdoin College Museum of Art. Acquired in 1855 through a bequest of Mrs. Lucy Flucker Thatcher

Plate 40A   The American School. Painted by Matthew Pratt in 1765. Courtesy of the Metropolitan Museum of Art. A gift of Samuel P. Avery in 1897.

Plate 40B   Daniel Hubbard. Painted by John Singleton Copley in 1764. Courtesy of the Art Institute of Chicago.

Plate 40C   Benjamin Badger. Painted by Joseph Badger. Courtesy of the Henry Francis duPont Winterthur Museum.

Plate 40 D & E   Pastels by an unknown artist in the Owens-Thomas House, Savannah. Courtesy of the Telfair Academy of Arts and Sciences.

Plate 41   Peter Faneuil (1700-1743). Painted by John Smibert. Courtesy of the Massachusetts Historical Society.

Plate 42   A Member of the Willson Family. Painted by an unknown artist and dated 1720. Courtesy of the National Gallery of Art. A gift of Edgar William and Bernice Chrysler Garbisch.

Plate 43A   Tench Francis (Sr.) (17? -1758). Painted by Robert Feke in 1746. Courtesy of the Metropolitan Museum of Art through the Marian deWitt Jesup Fund.

Plate 43B   Gov. James Bowdoin (1727-1790) as a boy. Painted about 1740 by John Smibert. Courtesy of the Bowdoin College Museum of Art. A bequest of Mrs. Sarah Bowdoin Dearborn, 1826.

Plate 44   William Bowdoin (1713-1773). Painted by Robert Feke in 1748, which was a busy year for him. Courtesy of the Bowdoin College Museum of Art. Bequest of Mrs. Sarah Bowdoin Dearborn, 1826.

Plate 45   Thomas Van Alstyne (1688-1765). Painted by an unknown artist of the Hudson Valley in 1721. Courtesy of New York Historical Society, New York City.

Plate 46A   David Provoost (©1630-?). Painted by an unknown New York artist. Courtesy of the New York Historical Society, New York City.

Plate 46B   Nathaniel Byfield (1635-1733). Painted by John Smibert in 1730. Courtesy, Metropolitan Museum of Art. A bequest of Charles Allen Munn.

Plate 47   Francis Brinley (1690-1765). Painted by John Smibert 1730. Courtesy of the Metropolitan Museum of Art. A bequest from the Roger's Fund.

Plate 48A   Bernard Elliott. (See 48B)

Plate 48B   Mrs. Bernard Elliott. Painted by Jeremiah Theüs. Courtesy of the Gibbs Art Gallery and the Carolina Art Association.

Plate 49A   William (?) Beekman. Painted by an unknown artist about 1750. Courtesy of the New York Historical Society, New York City.

Plate 49B   Dr. James Skirving. Painted by Jeremiah Theüs. Courtesy of the Gibbes Art Gallery and the Carolina Art Association.

Plate 49C   Mr. Motte. Painted by Jeremiah Theüs. Courtesy of the National Gallery of Art. From the Andrew Mellon Collection, 1947.

Plate 49D   James Peale (1749-1831). Painted by Charles Willson Peale. Courtesy of the Amherst College Museum of Art.

Plate 49E   Asa Benjamin. Painted by W. M. Jennys. Courtesy of the National Gallery of Art. A gift of Edgar William and Bernice Chrysler Garbisch.

Plate 50A   Hats, 1774.

Plate 50B   Wigs, 1773. Engravings by Matthew Darley.

Plate 51   Mrs. Margaret Sylvester Chesebrough. Painted by Joseph Blackburn in 1754. Courtesy of the Metropolitan Museum of Art. A gift of Sylvester Dering in 1916.

Plate 52A   Mrs. Isaac Foster. Painted by Joseph Badger in 1755. Courtesy of the National Gallery of Art. A gift of Edgar William and Bernice Chrysler Garbisch.

Plate 52B   Mrs. Richard Galloway (1697-1781). Painted by John Hesselius in 1764. Courtesy of the Metropolitan Museum of Art. Marie deWitt Jesup Fund, 1922.

Plate 52C   Mrs. Sarah Vinson. Painted by Jeremiah Theüs. Courtesy of the Gibbes Art Gallery and the Carolina Art Association.

Plate 52D   Mrs. Gabriel Manigault (1705-1782). Painted by Jeremiah Theüs, 1757. Courtesy of the Metropolitan Museum of Art. The Fletcher Fund, 1928.

Plate 53A   Deborah Hall (See Plate 96B). Painted by William Williams in 1766. Courtesy of the Brooklyn Museum.

Plate 53B   Mrs. John Sherburne (1725-?). Painted by John Greenwood. Courtesy of the Frick Art Reference Library. From the Collection of Mrs. John A. Reidy.

Plate 54   Mrs. Wynant Van Zandt (1692-1772). Painted by an unknown artist. Courtesy of the New York Historical Society, New York City. The style dating, 1735-45, refers to the Petenlair. Absence of any examples in later paintings indicate that the Petenlair did not catch on.

Plate 55   Mrs. Benjamin Blackstone, Jr. Painted by John Singleton Copley (in his early technique). Courtesy of the Amherst College Museum of Art.

Plate 56   Mrs. Jonathan Simpson. Painted by Joseph Blackburn in 1758. Courtesy of the Museum of Fine Arts, Boston.

Plate 57   Mrs. Theodore Atkinson, Jr. (1746-1813). Painted by John Singleton Copley in 1765. Courtesy, Lenox Library, the New York Public Library.

Plate 58A   "Pamela Andrews" heroine of Samuel Richardson's "Pamela, or Virtue Rewarded" 1741. Painted by Robert Feke. Courtesy of the Museum of Art, Rhode Island School of Design.

Plate 58B   Mrs. Jan Jansen Bleecker. Painted by an unknown artist. Courtesy of the Frick Art Reference Library. From the collection of Mrs. Delavan B. Downer.

Plate 59   Mrs. Benjamin Austin. This portrait was believed to have been painted by John Greenwood. Courtesy of the Henry Francis duPont Winterthur Museum.

Plate 60A   Mary Otis Gray. Painted by John Singleton Copley. Courtesy of the Massachusetts Historical Society.

Plate 60B   Sarah Prince Gill. Painted by John Singleton Copley. Courtesy of the Museum of Art, Rhode Island School of Design.

Plate 61A   The Review—an English satirical engraving of 1750.

Plate 61B   A cartoon of 1785 by Johann Hieronymus Loeschenkohl in Austria.

Plate 62   Mrs. Daniel Hubbard. Painted by John Singleton Copley, 1764. Courtesy of the Art Institute of Chicago.

Plate 63   The Royall Sisters—Mary (1744-?) and Elizabeth (1747-?). Painted by John Singleton Copley. Courtesy of the Museum of Fine Arts, Boston.

Plate 64A   Engraving by S. F. deGoez in 1784.

Plate 75A   Gov. & Mrs. Thomas Mifflin. Painted by John Singleton Copley. Courtesy of the Historical Society of Pennsylvania.

Plate 75B   Mrs. James Duane (1738-1821). Thought to have been painted by Ralph Earl. If so, painted before he left for London in 1778. Courtesy of the New York Historical Society, New York City.

Plate 75C   Mrs. Moses Seymour and son, Epaphroditus (Josephus's friend or Nero's friend?) Painted by Ralph Earl in 1789. Courtesy of the City Art Museum of St. Louis.

Plate 76A   Chief Justice and Mrs. Olive Ellsworth. Painted by Ralph Earl in 1792. Courtesy of the Wadsworth Atheneum.

Plate 76B   Mrs. Richard Yates. Painted by Gilbert Stuart in 1792. Courtesy of the National Gallery of Art. Andrew Mellon Collection 1940.

Plate 77   Mrs. Samuel Chandler. Painted by Winthrop Chandler. Courtesy of the National Gallery of Art. From the Collection of Edgar William and Bernice Chrysler Garbisch.

Plate 78   Mrs. Thomas Boylston. Painted by John Singleton Copley in 1766. A Harvard University Portrait. Courtesy of the Fogg Art Museum.

Plate 79A   Mrs. Benjamin Peck. This may have been painted by John Durand. Courtesy of the Henry Francis duPont Winterthur Museum.

Plate 79B   Mrs. John Winthrop. Painted by John Singleton Copley in 1773. Courtesy of the Metropolitan Museum of Art. Morris Jesup Fund, 1931.

Plate 80A   Mrs. Thomas Dering (1725-1794). Painted by Joseph Blackburn. Courtesy of the Metropolitan Museum of Art. Gift of Sylvester Dering, 1916.

Plate 80B   A Detail. Painted by François-Hubert Drouais.

Plate 80C   A Doe Macaroni. Engraved by Matthew Darley, 1772.

Plate 81A   The Cat's Funeral. Engraved by Frederick George Bryan.

Plate 81B   The Hat Shop. Drawn by Thomas Rowlandson, 1786.

Plate 81C   The Village Assembly. Engraved by Matthew Darley, 1776.

Plate 82   "A Lady of Quality in an undress for a Morning Walk in the Country." Drawn by Pierre Thomas LeClerc.

Plate 83   Mrs. William Mosely and her son Charles. Painted by Ralph Earl in 1791. Courtesy of Yale University Art Gallery.

Plate 84A   Mrs. John Hart and daughter. Thought to have been painted by Charles Peale Polk. It would have been after 1791, for in that year "Robertson's India" was published.

Plate 84B   Portrait of a Gentleman. Thought to have been painted by Charles Peale Polk. Both courtesy of the National Gallery of Art. 84 A and B from the collection of Edgar William and Bernice Chrysler Garbisch.

Plate 84C   A Quaker Dress of Silk. Courtesy of the Philadelphia Museum of Art.

Plate 85A   A Quaker dress of about 1795. The type of bonnet shown was said to have been introduced to this country in 1798 by Martha Routh. Courtesy of the Philadelphia Museum of Art.

Plate 85B   Mrs. William Gibbons (1735-1790). Painted by an unknown artist. Courtesy of the Telfair Academy of Arts and Sciences.

Plate 86A   Peace Negotiations. Started by Benjamin West in 1782. John Jay, John Adams, Benjamin Franklin, William Temple Franklin and Henry Laurens. Courtesy of the Henry Francis duPont Winterthur Museum.

Plate 86B   Man's Silk Suit of about 1789. Courtesy of the Metropolitan Museum of Art. The Rogers Fund, 1942.

Plate 87A   Man in a Green Coat. Painted by Gilbert Stuart in England, about 1788. Courtesy of the Metropolitan Museum of Art. A bequest of Mary Stillman Harkness in 1950.

Plate 87B   Benjamin Harrison Jr. Painted by Charles Willson Peale. Courtesy of the National Gallery of Art.

Plate 87C   Lawrence Yates. Painted by Gilbert Stuart. Courtesy of the National Gallery of Art. Andrew Mellon Collection, 1940.

Plate 88   Col. William Taylor. Painted by Ralph Earl in 1790. Courtesy of the Albright-Knox Art Gallery. Charles Clifton Fund.

Plate 89   Mrs. William Taylor and Daniel Boardman Taylor. Painted by Ralph Earl in 1790. Courtesy of the Albright-Knox Art Gallery. Charles Clifton Fund.

Plate 90A   "Staircase Group." Painted by Charles Willson Peale as a "trompe l'oeil," framed as a doorway, with a false step protruding and on display in his museum. Washington, who apparently dropped in everywhere, is said to have tipped his hat to the boys as he walked by. Courtesy of the Philadelphia Museum of Art.

Plate 90B   William Kevin Constable. Painted by Gilbert Stuart in 1796. Courtesy of the Metropolitan Museum of Art. A bequest of Richard de Wolfe Brixley in 1943.

Plate 91A   William Loughton Constable. Painted by Gilbert Stuart. Courtesy of the Gibbes Art Gallery and the Carolina Art Association.

Plate 91B   Daniel Boardman. Painted by Ralph Earl in 1789. Courtesy of the National Gallery of Art. A gift of Mrs. W. Murry Crane in 1948.

Plate 91C   Rev. Nehemiah Strong. Painted by Ralph Earl in 1790. Courtesy of the Yale University Art Gallery.

Plate 92A   Hulda Bradley. Painted by Ralph Earl in 1794. Courtesy of the Museum of Fine Arts, Boston.

Plate 92B   Mrs. George Pollock. Painted by Gilbert Stuart in 1793. Courtesy of the National Gallery of Art. Andrew Mellon Collection, 1942.

Plate 93A   Isaac Royall and Family. Painted by Robert Feke, 1741 Courtesy of the Fogg Art Museum. Lent by Harvard University.

Plate 93B   The Gore Children. Painted by John Singleton Copley. Courtesy of the Henry Francis duPont Winterthur Museum.

Plate 93C   The Gordon Family. Painted by an unknown artist. Courtesy of the Mrs. Seton Henry and the Frick Art Reference Library.

Plate 93D   Alexander Spotswood Payne and his brother, John Robert Dandridge Payne, with their nurse. Painted by an unknown artist. Courtesy of the Virginia Museum. A gift of Miss Dorothy Payne, 1953.

Plate 93E   Mary Bryan Wylly and her children. Painted by Henry Benbridge. Courtesy of the Telfair Academy of Arts and Sciences. A Sossmar Photograph.

Plate 94A   Mrs. Francis Brinley and her son, Henry. Painted by John Smibert. Courtesy of the Metropolitan Museum of Art. Rogers Fund 1962.

Plate 94B   Mrs. Benjamin Tallmadge, her children Henry and Maria. Painted by Ralph Earl in 1790. Courtesy of the Litchfield Historical Society and Frick Art Reference Library.

Plate 94C   Mrs. Forman and child. Painted by Charles Willson Peale. Courtesy of the Brooklyn Museum.

Plate 94D   Rebecca Woodward (a detail). Painted by John Hesselius. Courtesy of the Henry Francis duPont Winterthur Museum.

Plate 94E   Mrs. John Nicholson and child. Painted by Charles Willson Peale, 1790. Courtesy of the Art Institute of Chicago. A gift of Mr. and Mrs. Carter H. Harrison.

Plate 94F   A Child in a Red Dress. It is believed to be painted by Justus Englehardt Kühn. Courtesy of the Henry Francis duPont Winterthur Museum.

Plate 94G   Col. Benjamin Tallmadge and son, William. Painted by Ralph Earl, 1790. Courtesy of the Litchfield Historical Society and the Frick Art Reference Library.

Plate 94H   Mrs. Samuel Mifflin and her granddaughter, Rebecca Mifflin Francis.

Painted by Charles Willson Peale. Courtesy of the Metropolitan Museum of Art. The Egleston Fund, 1922.

Plate 95A   James Badger (1757-1817). Painted by Joseph Badger in 1760. Courtesy of the Metropolitan Museum of Art. Rogers Fund 1929.

Plate 95B   Richard Ray (1753-1783).

Plate 95C   Robert Ray (1759-1782). B and C painted by John Durand. Courtesy of the Museum of the City of New York.

Plate 95D   Boy in Blue Coat. Painted by an unknown artist. Courtesy of the National Gallery of Art. Gift of Edgar William and Bernice Chrysler Garbisch.

Plate 95E   Ann Byrd. Painted by Charles Bridges. Courtesy of Colonial Williamsburg.

Plate 95F   Thomas Moore as a Child. Painted by Henrietta Johnston. Courtesy of the Virginia Museum of Art. Gift of a member of Grace and Holy Trinity Church.

Plate 95G   Maurice Keating. Painted by Jeremiah Theüs. Courtesy of the Gibbes Art Gallery and Carolina Art Association.

Plate 95H   Everard Benjamin. Painted by William M. Jennys. Courtesy of the National Gallery of Art. Gift of Edgar William and Bernice Chrysler Garbisch.

Plate 95I   Pierre VanCortland (1721-1814). Painted by an unknown artist. Courtesy of the Brooklyn Museum.

Plate 96A   A Fractur from Berks County, Pennsylvania. Drawn by George Stovel Herrold in 1771. Courtesy of the Henry Francis duPont Winterthur Museum.

Plate 96B   David Hall. (See Plate 53A.) Painted by William Williams in 1766. Courtesy of the Henry Francis duPont Winterthur Museum.

Plate 96C   Miss Dennison. Painted by an unknown artist. Courtesy of the National Gallery of Art. Gift of Edgar William and Bernice Chrysler Garbisch.

Plate 96D   Magdalena Douw. Painted by an unknown artist. Courtesy of the Henry Francis duPont Winterthur Museum.

L'INDISCRET. D'après une gravure anonyme du XVIIIᵉ siècle.

1 A—STYLE OF 1620-25

1 B—STYLE OF 1625-30

2 A

2 B

2 C

2 D

See "Introduction to the Plates."

3—STYLE OF 1650

See "Introduction to the Plates."

4 A

4 C

4 D

4 E

Pattent for Wine

4 B

4 F

Turner, foe famous for his shifting arts,
Pragmatick bustlings, turns, and Protean parts
Through City, Camp, and Country, to the State
Tooke his last turn from ij full swing of ffate.

MOLL CUT=PURSE.

5—STYLE OF 1650

6 A—STYLE OF 1650

6 B—STYLE OF 1655

Sᴿ HVGH   CARTWRIGHT
Chavelier   Anglois
Aage 50   An 1656

7 A

7 B

See "Introduction to the Plates."   GEORGE   ALSOP.

Anno Lo: 1665. Ætati Suæ 28.

8 A

CHARLES II

8 B

See "Introduction to the Plates."

IOHN BAREFOOT.

9—STYLE OF 1665

10—STYLE OF 1670

11 A—STYLE OF 1685

11 B—Styles in France, 1620-40

12—STYLE OF 1675

13—STYLE OF 1670-75

14—STYLE OF 1650-55

15 A—STYLE OF 1630-75

15 B—STYLE OF 1640

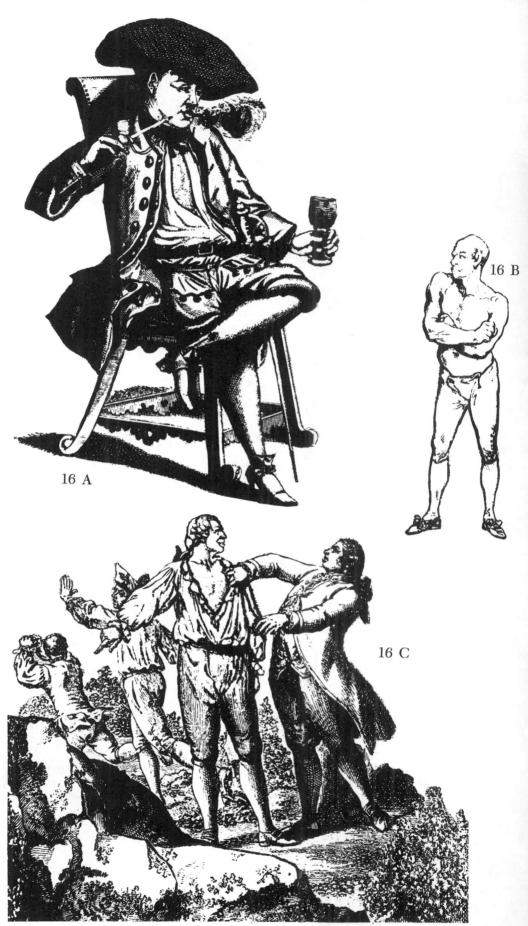

16 A

16 B

16 C

See "Introduction to the Plates."

17 A

17 C

See "Introduction to the Plates."

17 B

18—STYLE OF 1670-75

19—STYLE OF 1670

20 A

20 B

20 C

20 D

See "Introduction to the Plates."

21—STYLE OF 1640-50

22 B—STYLE OF 1745-50

22 A—STYLE OF 1745-50

23—STYLE OF 1690-95

24 A—STYLE OF 1715

24 B—STYLE OF 1730

25—STYLE OF 1730-35

26—STYLE OF 1725-30

27—STYLE OF 1755-60

28—STYLE OF 1775-80

29—STYLE OF 1755-60

30 A—STYLE OF 1725-30

30 B—STYLE OF 1745

30 C   STYLES OF 1745   30 D

31 A—STYLE
OF 1750-55

31 B—STYLE OF 1750

31 C—STYLE OF 1760-65

32 A

STYLES OF 1775-80

32 B

33—STYLE OF 1770-80

34 A—STYLE OF 1740-45

34 B—STYLE OF 1760-70

35 A—STYLE OF 1760-70

35 B—STYLE OF 1765-70

36—STYLE OF 1755-65

37—STYLE OF 1755-65

38—STYLE OF 1760-65

39—STYLE OF 1740-50

40 A

40 B

40 D

40 C

40 E

STYLES OF 1760-70

41—STYLE OF 1730-40

42—STYLE OF 1710-1720

43 A—STYLE OF 1740-50

43 B—STYLE OF 1735-45

44—STYLE OF 1745-55

45—STYLE OF 1700-35

46 A—STYLE OF 1690

46 B—STYLE OF 1730

47—STYLE OF 1720-30

48 A

STYLES OF 1760-65

48 B

49 A—STYLE OF 1700-30

49 B—STYLE OF 1760

49 C—STYLE OF 1760

49 D—STYLE OF 1790

49 E—STYLE
OF 1790

50 A

50 B

See "Introduction to the Plates."

51—STYLE OF 1740-55

52 A

52 B

52 C

52 D

STYLES OF 1750-65

53 A—STYLE OF 1760-65

53 E— STYLE OF 1745-50

54—STYLE OF 1735-45

55—STYLE OF 1750-55

56—STYLE OF 1755-60

57—STYLE OF 1760-65

58 A—STYLE OF 1745

58 B—STYLE OF 1715-30

59—STYLE OF 1750

60 B

STYLES OF 1765

60 A

A

See "Introduction to the Plates."

62—STYLE OF 1760-65

63—STYLE OF 1755-60

64 A

64 B

See "Introduction
to the Plates."

65 A—STYLE OF 1725-30

65 B—STYLE OF 1745-50

66 A

STYLES OF 1775

66 B

67—STYLE OF 1755

68 A—STYLE OF 1750-55

68 B—STYLE OF 1745

69 A—STYLE OF 1740-50   69 B—STYLE OF 1740-50

69 C—STYLE OF 1735-50   69 D—STYLE OF 1710-50

70 A

STYLES OF 1760-75

70 B

71 A—STYLE IN FRANCE 1730-45

71 B

STYLES IN FRANCE 1700-1720

71 C

71 D

72 A—Styles of 1760-65

72 B

73 A

STYLES OF 1790

73 B

74 A

SUSANNA PERWICH

See "Introduction to the Plates."

P. Rogerson Ad.

74 B—STYLE OF
1680-1710 IN FRANCE

75 A—STYLE OF 1770-75

75 C—STYLE OF 1785-90

75 B—STYLE OF 1770

76 A

STYLES OF 1790-95

76 B

77—STYLE OF 1780-90

78—STYLE OF 1745-1770

79 A—STYLE OF 1745-65

CUFFS 1745-55, AND AGAIN 1770-80

80 A

STYLE OF 1750-1755

80 B

80 C

81 A

81 B

81 C   See "Introduction to the Plates."

82 THE STYLE IN FRANCE 1765-75

83—STYLE OF 1790

84 A

84 B

84 C

STYLES IN THE CLOSING YEARS OF THE 18TH CENTURY

85 B—STYLE OF 1785-95

85 A—STYLE OF 1790-1800

86 A

STYLES OF 1780-85

86 B

87 B—STYLE OF 1775

87 C—STYLE OF 1795

87 A—STYLE OF 1785 IN ENGLAND

88—STYLE OF 1790

89—STYLE OF 1790

90 B

STYLES OF 1795

90 A

91 A

91 B

91 C

STYLES OF 1790-95

92 B

STYLES OF 1790-95

92 A

93 A—STYLE OF 1740

93 B—STYLE OF 1750

93 C—STYLE OF 1760

93 D—STYLE OF 1780

93 E—STYLE OF 1770

94 A—STYLE OF 1730   94 B—STYLE OF 1790   94 C—STYLE OF 1775-

94 D—STYLE OF 1765   94 E—STYLE OF 1790   94 F—STYLE OF 1700-10

94 G—STYLE OF 1790   94 H—STYLE OF 1780

A—STYLE OF 1760   95 B—STYLE OF 1770   95 C—STYLE OF 1770

D—STYLE OF 1730   95 E—STYLE OF 1735   95 F—STYLE OF 1700

5 G—STYLE OF 1750   95 H—STYLE OF 1790   95 J—STYLE OF 1725

96 A—STYLE OF 1770

96 B—STYLE OF 1765   96 C—STYLE OF 1785   96 D—STYLE OF 17

BIBLIOGRAPHY

COVERING THE PERIOD FROM THE FOUNDING
OF THE COLONIES TO THE UNITED STATES OF
1790.

No attempt has been made to include all, or even most of the books used in the compilation of this volume: the expert does not require it, and it is to spare the new reader just such detailed research that this book is written. For those, however, who would build beyond the confines of this book, the following annotated list is offered.

Books are tools, and the list below is planned to adequately stock a good workshop. There are a great many more books here than are vital to the knowledge of American dress, but none that will not enrich that knowledge. That some of the entries have major faults need not be stressed; their inclusion in this list indicates that they contained something of value to the subject under discussion or have been specifically referred to and quoted in the body of this book. The comments I have made will indicate those volumes whose special fitness merits a place right over the workbench.

We do not have a comprehensive record of American artists such as the *Klassiker der Kunst* (published in English as *Classics in Art*) which reproduces all the known works of an artist, whether or not the art is considered good, bad, or indifferent. Lacking this essential tool for the dress historian's workbench, we must use more fragmentary material.

One of the very best volumes in identifying dress, and one benefiting from modern scholarship, is Maurice Leloir's *Dictionnaire du Costume,* Paris, 1951. The language barrier may limit its usefulness, but it is so well illustrated that with a slight knowledge of French, it is of inestimable value. Ruth Klein's *Lexikon der Mode: Drei Jahrtausende Europäischer Kostümkunde* (439 pages and many drawings, Baden-Baden, 1950) may prove useful for those versed in German. Millia Davenport's *Book of Costume* (two volumes, 945 pages and 2778 illustrations, N.Y., 1948) benefits from that scholar's excellent text and selection of illustrations; it suffers greatly from the poor quality of printing which has made her exemplary selection of illustrations often useless to the dress historian and costume designer. The plates are frequently black, and many so reduced in size, that a great deal of vital detail is all but lost. The original edition also had some plates poor in color, which were eliminated in later printings; nothing was done to improve the quality of the half-tones. If this were not the case, and if the reproductions from original sources had been supplemented by line drawings based upon primary sources (the latter admittedly a huge task), this would have been the great dress history it deserves to be.

Five Centuries of American Costume by R. Turner Wilcox (200 pages, 107 of which consist of drawings, New York, 1963) has many of the problems discussed in the introduction to our book. The jacket bears the statement: ". . . one of the most comprehensive surveys ever attempted," and that is true enough. In a very sketchy way it touches upon the entire range of American dress, though strangely, women's dresses between the years 1835 and the 1870's are excluded, with the exception of that aberration of Amelia Bloomer's in 1851. Men's dress from 1861 to the 1870's is also omitted. Wilcox does make the only effort so far to record the entire panorama of military dress of this country, although once again, not in depth. The book makes many generalizations, and the drawings lack the necessary documentation essential for comparison with the original sources. One other tool that uses very generalized drawings, but has a short but more informative text than is reflected in the illustrations, is *Early California Costumes,* 1769-1850, by Margaret Gilbert Mackaye and Louise Pinkney Sooy (Stanford, California, 1932, 1949). *The Album of American History*, edited by James Truslow Adams, is a picture book with reproductions jumbled on the pages, and with a short but pointed text interspersed among them. Although, like the Davenport, its printing is crude, the reproductions in this case are good enough to be of use in determining sources, and choosing material for more careful perusal elsewhere. Volume one (411 pages, New York, 1944) covers the period to 1783. Care must be taken in using the Album to check the provenance of illustrations, for it is not made clear that many are not American. In the bibliography below is Davidson's *Life in America* which, published about seven years later, does a superb job of documentation and includes an exceptionally rich and carefully selected array of illustrations.

Excluded from this bibliography are the many entertaining and often colorful inventions called "American Costume" which will be found in earlier books on dress or travel. Libraries usually have a good collection of these volumes in their Rare Book Room, but they should be studied with great caution.

Tools work best when they are used. The good craftsman in dress history, as well as the designer of costumes, will soon know which of the tools presented in this bibliography will fit his needs, and then give them an honored place on his tool rack.

BIBLIOGRAPHIES

There are three major bibliographies of "Costume." Although two of them have been reprinted, no new general bibliography has appeared for twenty-five years. New, updated editions will be very welcome.

René Colas—*Bibliographie Générale du Costume et de la Mode*: Two volumes, 1411 pages, plus 69 p. "Table Méthodique,' Paris, 1933. (Reprinted, New York, 1963.) 3121 main entries, each with thorough bibliographical data, and frequently extensive and pertinent observations. Has no English language equivalent.

Hilaire and Meyer Hiler—*Bibliography of Costume: A Dictionary of About Eight Thousand Books and Periodicals*. xxxix-911 pages. New York, 1939. Elementary collations, and no critical and comparative commentary. Still, the most complete bibliography in the field.

Katalog der Freiherrlich von Lipperheide'schen Kostümbibliothek. Two volumes, xvi-645 pages, 310 illus.; xii-840 pages, 298 illus. Berlin, 1896-1905. (Reprinted, New York, 1963.) Over 5000 main entries, many even more thoroughly described and analyzed, some in even greater detail than in the Colas bibliography. Includes all manner of background volumes, such as travel, festivals, architecture, and so forth. Like Colas, indispensable to advanced study of dress. A new, and vastly expanded edition is now in advanced stage of preparation.

ENGLISH AND EUROPEAN COSTUME

Edwin T. Bechtel, *Jacques Callot*, 46 pp., 233 illus., New York, 1955. Valuable for a sense of the seventeenth century "Cavalier" in action.

R. B. Beckett, *Hogarth*, 80 pp., 200 illus., Boston, 1955. The epitome of the eighteenth century in all classes of English life.

Max von Boehn, *Modes and Manners*, trans. by Joan Joshua, 4 vols., profusely illus., Philadelphia, 1932-36. From the medieval period to the end of the eighteenth century. A difficult organization of material. The selection and reproductive quality of the illustrations are fine.

Dion Clayton Calthrop, *English Costume*, 463 pp., no index, 70 colored plates, 23 in black & white, more than 245 line drawings. London, 1907. A personal and very romantic account in both text and illustrations. A good group by Hollar and another by the Dightons are included.

Augustin Challamel, *The History of Fashion in France*, trans. by Hoey & Lillie, 293 pp., 21 color plates, London, 1882.

Cecil Willett & Phillis Cunnington, *The History of Underclothes,* 262 pp. & index, 119 illus., London, 1951. A very interesting and important study, almost unique in its field, with cogent comment on the psychology of underwear.

Cecil Willett & Phillis Cunnington, *Handbook of English Costume in the Seventeenth Century,* 213 pp., 100 illus., London, 1955. One of the most useful records—Redrawn figures from documents. Errors are rare.

Cecil Willett & Phillis Cunnington, *Handbook of English Costume in the Eighteenth Century,* 443 pp., 150 illus., London, 1957. (See above)

Cecil Willett & Phillis Cunnington, *A Dictionary of English Costume,* 218 pp., 203 illus., London, 1960.

Millia Davenport, *Book of Costume,* 2 vols., 945 pp., 2778 illus., NY 1948. (For comment, see above).

Frederick William Fairholt, *Costume in England: a history of dress to the end of the eighteenth century,* 2 vols., about 700 engravings, London, n.d.

Francis M. Kelly & Randolph Schwabe, *Historic Costume,* Second, revised edition. 305 pp., 71 plates; about 280 line drawings, New York, 1929. The classic modern study employing documentary illustrations and analytical drawings.

Francis M. Kelly & Randolph Schwabe, *A Short History of Costume & Armour, chiefly in England* (2 volumes bound as one). Vol. II 1485–1800, 86 pp., 36 plates, 52 line drawings. London, 1931. A short and very useful review of armor.

Ruth Klein, *Lexikon der Mode: Drei Jahrtausende Europäischer Kostümkunde.* 439 pp., many drawings, Baden-Baden, 1950. (For comment, see above)

James Laver (ed.) *Costume of the Western World.* Six profusely illustrated monographs on the dress of Spain, England, France, and Holland, 1485-1660. All plates are reproduced from contemporary sources, several in full color. London & New York, 1951.

James Laver, *Costume Illustrations: The Seventeenth and Eighteenth Centuries,* 116 pp., 96 illus., London, 1951

James Laver, *English Costume of the Eighteenth Century,* 86 pp., 40 pp. of illus. by Iris Brooke, London, 1931. Planned as "a general guide for those with slight knowledge" of dress, it is nonetheless useful for quick reference.

Maurice Leloir, *Dictionnaire du Costume,* posthumously completed by André Dupuis. 390 pp., thousands of drawings, Paris, 1951. (For comment, see above)

Maurice Leloir, *Histoire du Costume de l'Antiquité à 1914,* 5 vols., many illus., Paris, 1933-49. The five vols. cover 1610-1795 in great detail.

James Robinson Planché, *A Cyclopaedia of Costume,* Vol. I *The Dictionary,* 527 pp., 28 plates, many woodcuts. 1876. Vol. II *A General History of Costume in Europe,* 448 pp., 38 plates, many woodcuts. 1879. London, 1876-1879.

Emil Schaeffer, *Van Dyck, des Meisters Gemälde*, 559 pp., 490 reproductions, Stuttgart & Leipzig, 1909.

Daniel Ternois, *Jacques Callct: catalogue complet de son œuvre dessiné*, 613 pp., 1479 illus., Paris, 1961.

AMERICAN DRESS AND ITS BACKGROUND

Alice Morse Earle, *Child Life in Colonial Days*, 418 pp., New York, 1899. Reprinted 1957. Many illustrations, but poorly reproduced.

Alice Morse Earle, *Costume of Colonial Times*, 264 pp., several illustrations. New York, 1894.

Alice Morse Earle, *Two Centuries of Costume in America* 1620-1820, 2 vols., 140 illus., 807 pp. and index. New York, 1903. The first systematic survey, and a very entertaining example of early scholarship which still contains a vast amount of important data and critical commentary. The text, however, must be checked against later research. Many of the plates are European, or, if American, the attribution and dating may not be acceptable.

Douglas W. Gorseline, *What People Wore*, 266 pp., New York, 1932. Redrawings which in the later years are taken from actual daguerreotypes, etc., and not from fashion plates. This provides useful comparisons.

Rufus Wilmot Griswold, *The Republican Court*, 408 pp., 21 portraits, New York, 1860.

Amelia Mott Gummere, *The Quakers: A Study in Costume* 232 pp., 29 sepia plates with add. illus., Philadelphia, 1901.

W. C. Langdon, *Everyday Things in American Life*, vol. I, 340 pp., 145 illus., New York, 1941.

Margaret Gilbert Mackaye & Louise Pinkney Sooy, *Early California Costumes*, 1769-1850, 138 pp., Stanford, Calif., 1932, 1940. (For comment, see above).

Elisabeth McClellan, *Historic Dress in America: 1607-1800*, 2nd edition, 377 pp., a good glossary and index, 385 illustrations, Philadelphia, 1917. There are some useful tables. A serious attempt to survey the whole period. There are many entertaining and informative references in the text, though here and there errors, very similar to those in Mrs. Earle's work, have crept into this text. The redrawings by Sophie B. Steele, carefully identified in the titles of the plates, are presented without indicating the provenance in any way that is readily visible. The rapid viewer may too easily assume that all the examples are of American origin. (Reprinted by Tudor, New York, 1937, under new title: *History of American Costume, 1607-1870*.)

Paul McPharlin, *Life and Fashion in America: 1650-1900*, 40 pp., New York, 1946. This is an entertaining booklet and therefore makes an impression on the casual viewer which is often misleading.

Charles Lee Meyers, *Bibliography of Colonial Costume*, 36 pp., New York, 1923.

Arthur Train, *The Story of Everyday Things*, 428 pp., illus. by Chichi Lasley, New York, 1963.

R. Turner Wilcox, *Five Centuries of American Costume*, 200 pp., of which 107 consist of drawings, New York, 1963. (For comment, see above)

W. E. Woodward, *The Way Our People Lived*, 402 pp., New York, 1944.

EARLY AMERICAN PAINTING

Arts in the United States: *A Pictorial Survey*. Edited by William Pierson, Jr. and Martha Davidson. x-452 pp., including 4000 illustrations. New York, McGraw-Hill, 1960. A selected survey of architecture, sculpture, painting, costume and stage design, photography, and the graphic and decorative arts in America from the seventeenth century to the present. The illustrations are about one and one-half inches in height, and are useful only for identification purposes. Color slides can be rented or bought for all the plates shown, and this should prove of inestimable value for many of the plates reproduced in our "The History Of American Dress." The "Arts . . ." includes short essays by recognized authorities; the 6-page review of American costume is by Lucy Barton.

Virgil Barker, *American Painting: History and Interpretation*, 717 pp., 160 illus.

Waldron Phoenix Belknap, Jr., *American Colonial Painting: Materials for a History*. xxi-377 pp., profusely illus. (Cambridge, Mass., 1959). If consulted with caution, useful for advanced study of dress. American paintings and their European prototypes are frequently compared (many British mezzotints are reproduced), but this extremely valuable method can easily mislead those concerned only with styles of dress. The coverage of the New York area is thorough. Some assumptions with the plates must be weighed carefully with Belknap's main text, and also checked against other authorities.

Alan Burroughs, *Limners and Likenesses*, 246 pp., 191 illus., Cambridge, Mass., 1936.

Louisa Dresser (ed.), *Seventeenth Century Painting in New England, a Catalogue of an Exhibition*, 187 pp., 50 illus., Worcester, Mass., 1935. An interesting report which covers the problems very carefully.

William Dunlap, *A History of the Rise and Progress of the Arts of Design in the United States*, ed. by Bayley and Goodspeed (Boston, 1918) with a new selection of about 200 reproductions of early American art gathered by Alexander Wyckoff, and portions of the original 1832 edition reinstated. 3 vols., approximately 1200 pages plus illustrations, New York, Benjamin Blom, Inc., 1965. A source-book of incalculable value, but with many of the limitations, as well as advantages, of the on-the-spot report. It covers the period from about the later eighteenth century to 1830, and includes all the arts.

James Thomas Flexner, *American Painting: First Flower of Our Wilderness*, 368 pp., 163 illus., Boston, 1957. Covers the period to the Revolution.

Henry Wilder Foote, *Robert Feke, Colonial Portrait Painter*, 223 pp., 38 illus., Cambridge, Mass., 1930.

Henry Wilder Foote, *John Smibert, Painter: With a Descriptive Catalogue of Portraits, and Notes on the Work of Nathaniel Smibert*, 292 pp., 10 illus., Cambridge, Mass., 1950.

Oliver W. Larkin, *Art and Life in America*, 547 pp., 475 illus., New York, 1949.

Margaret Simons Middleton, *Jeremiah Theüs, Colonial Artist of Charles Town*, 218 pp., 51 illus., Columbia, S.C., 1953.

E. P. Richardson, *A Short History of Painting in America*, 318 pp., 151 illus., 4 color plates, New York, 1963. The most useful modern review.

Anna Wells Rutledge, *Artists In The Life of Charleston (Through Colony and State from Restoration to Reconstruction)*, 245 pp., 47 plates, Philadelphia, 1949.

ENGLISH SOCIAL HISTORY

Dorothy Marshall, *English People in the Eighteenth Century*, 288 pp., 57 illus., London, 1956.

Wallace Notestein, *The English People on the Eve of Colonization*, 302 pp., 23 illus., New York, 1954.

A. S. Turberville, *English Men and Manners in the Eighteenth Century*, 539 pp., Oxford, 1929.

A. S. Turberville (ed.), *Johnson's England*, 2 vols. (includes an essay on "Costume" by Talbot Hughes, and an essay on "Taste" by Osbert Sitwell & Margaret Barton), London, 1933.

E. N. Williams, *Life in Georgian England*, 175 pp., 135 illus., London & New York, 1962.

AMERICAN HISTORY

A. GENERAL

Charles M. Andrews, *Colonial Period of American History*, 4 vols., New York, 1934-38.

Daniel J. Boorstein, *The Americans, The Colonial Experience*, 434 pp., New York, 1958.

Alexander Brown, *The Genesis of the United States*, 2 vols., 100 illus., New York, 1964 (Reprint of the 1890 ed.).

Marshall B. Davidson, *Life in America*, two volumes, 573, 503 pp., and hundreds of illus. Boston, 1951 (For comment, see above).

L. H. Gipson, *The British Empire before the American Revolution*, 7 vols., New York, 1936-49.

Michael Krause, *The Atlantic Civilization: Eighteenth Century Origins*, 334 pp., Ithaca, N.Y., 1949.

Herbert L. Osgood, *American Colonies in the Seventeenth Century*, 3 vols., New York, 1904-07.

Herbert L. Osgood, *American Colonies in the Eighteenth Century*, 4 vols., New York, 1924.

Clinton Rossiter, *Seedtime of the Republic*, 538 pp., New York, 1953.

Arthur M. Schlesinger & Dixon Ryan Fox (eds.), *A History of American Life*, vols. I-III, New York, 1927-48.

Clarence Ver Steeg, *The Formative Years, 1607-1763*, 342 pp., New York, 1964.

B. SOCIAL

Carl Bridenbaugh, *Cities in the Wilderness, 1625-1742*, 500 pp., New York, 1957.

Carl Bridenbaugh, *Cities in Revolt, 1743-1776*, 434 pp., New York, 1957.

Carl Bridenbaugh, *Colonial Craftsman*, 213 pp., 17 illus. incl. several of weavers and tailors, New York & London, 1950.

Edwin H. Cady, *The Gentleman in America*, 232 pp., Syracuse, N.Y., 1949.

Willystine Goodsell, *A History of Marriage and the Family*, 590 pp., New York, 1939.

Howard Mumford Jones, *American and French Culture*, 615 pp. (esp. chaps. 7 & 8, "French Manners in America"), Chapel Hill, N.C., 1927.

Michael Krause, *Intercolonial Aspects of American Culture on the Eve of the Revolution*, 251 pp., New York, 1928.

Curtis P. Nettels, *The Roots of American Civilization: a history of American Colonial Life*, 748 pp., New York, 1938.

Russell Blaine Nye, *The Cultural Life of the New Nation, 1776-1830*, 324 pp., 37 illus., New York, 1960.

George R. Stewart, *American Ways of Life*, 310 pp., Garden City, N.Y., 1954.

Louis B. Wright, *The Cultural Life of the American Colonies: 1607-1763*, 292 pp., 30 illus., New York, 1957.

Anne Wharton, *Social Life in the Early Republic*, 346 pp., Philadelphia, 1902.

C. REGIONAL

the south

Carl Bridenbaugh, *Myths and Realities: Societies of the Colonial South*, 208 pp., Baton Rouge, La., 1952.

Philip A. Bruce, *Social Life of Virginia in the Seventeenth Century*, 302 pp., Richmond, Va., 1907.

Leslie F. Church, *Oglethorpe: A Study in Philanthropy in England and Georgia*, 335 pp., London, 1932.

E. Merton Coulter, *Georgia: A Short History*, 537 pp., Chapel Hill, N.C., 1960.

Wesley Frank Craven, *The Seventeenth Century South*, 451 pp., Baton Rouge, La., 1949.

Amos A. Ettinger, *James Edward Oglethorpe: Imperial Idealist*, 348 pp., Oxford, 1936.

Edmund Morgan, *Virginians at Home*, 99 pp., Williamsburg, Va., 1952.

Albert B. Sage, *New Viewpoints in Georgia History*, 256 pp., Athens, Ga., 1943.

Thomas Jefferson Wertenbaker, *The Shaping of Colonial Virginia*, 271 pp., New York, 1958.

Thomas Jefferson Wertenbaker, *Patrician and Plebian in Virginia*, 239 pp., Charlottesville, Va., 1910.

Thomas Jefferson Wertenbaker, *Planters of Colonial Virginia*, 260 pp., New York, 1959.

Maude H. Woodfin & Marion Tinling (eds). *Another Secret Diary of William Byrd of Westover, 1739-1741*, 490 pp., Richmond Va., 1942.

Louis B. Wright (ed.), *The Secret Diary of William Byrd of Westover*, 622 pp., Richmond, Va., 1941.

Louis B. Wright, *First Gentlemen of Virginia*, 373 pp., San Marino, Cal., 1940.

Louis B. Wright & Marion Tinling (eds.). *The London Diary of William Byrd, 1717-1772 and Other Writings*, 631 pp., New York, 1958.

new england

Brooks Adams, *The Emancipation of Massachusetts*, 382 pp., Boston, 1887.

James Truslow Adams, *Founding of New England* (vol. I of *The History of New England*), 482 pp., Boston, 1921.

George Francis Dow, *Arts and Crafts in New England, 1704-1775*, 326 pp., 39 illus., Topsfield, Mass., 1927.

George Francis Dow, *Everyday Life in the Massachusetts Bay Colony*, 293 pp., 106 illus., Boston, 1935.

Perry Miller, *Jonathan Edwards*, 348 pp., New York, 1949.

Perry Miller, *New England Mind: From Colony to Province*, 528 pp., Cambridge, Mass., 1954.

Perry Miller, *Orthodoxy in Massachusetts*, 353 pp., Cambridge, Mass., 1933.

Perry Miller & Thomas H. Johnson, *The Puritans*, 846 pp., New York, 1938.

Edmund Morgan, *The Puritan Dilemma: The Story of John Winthrop*, 224 pp., Boston, 1958.

Edmund Morgan, *The Puritan Family*, 118 pp., Boston, 1944.

Samuel Eliot Morrison, *Builders of the Bay Colony*, 365 pp., New York, 1930.

Samuel Eliot Morrison, *The Puritan Pronaos*, 281 pp., New York, 1936.

Kenneth B. Murdock, *Literature and Theology in Colonial New England*, 235 pp., Cambridge, Mass., 1949.

Clifford K. Shipton, *New England Life in the Eighteenth Century: Representative Biographies from "Sibley's Harvard Graduates,"* 622 pp., Cambridge, Mass., 1963.

Barnett Wendell, *Cotton Mather, The Puritan Priest*, 248 pp., New York, 1963.

the middle atlantic region

Rosalie Fellows Bailey, *Pre-Revolutionary Dutch Houses and Families*, 612 pp., 179 illus., New York, 1936.

Carl Bridenbaugh (ed.), *Gentleman's Progress: The Journal of Dr. Alexander Hamilton*, 267 pp., New York, 1948.

Carl & Jessica Bridenbaugh, *Rebels and Gentlemen in the Age of Franklin*, 393 pp., New York, 1942.

Rufus M. Jones, *Quakers in the American Colonies*, 603 pp., New York, 1962.

Arnold Lloyd, *Quaker Social History, 1669-1738*, 207 pp., London, 1950.

Frederick B. Tolles, *George Logan of Philadelphia*, 362 pp., New York, 1933.

Frederick B. Tolles, *Quakers and the Atlantic Culture*, 160 pp., New York, 1960.

Thomas Jefferson Wertenbaker, *The Founding of American Civilization: The Middle Colonies*, 364 pp., New York, 1949.

Thofe Leaves
They gather'd, broad as Amazonian Targe
And, with what fkill they had, together Sewd
To gird their Waift
Milton.

Index

SQUARE-TOED BOOTS, 78
SQUARE-TOED SHOES, 55, 70
Sronkova, 10
stables, 57
stadium blankets, 183
stagecoaches, 180
"Staircase Group," 288, Pl. 90A
"STAIRCASE," WIG, 164
Standish, Miles, 105
starch, 55, 134, 140
  colored, 55
  Dutch, the, 55
statute, 110
"STAYS," 174
  girls', 239
steamer rugs, 183
Steinkerque, 161
STEINKIRK CRAVAT (definition), 161
"Stenton," 165
STIRRUP HOSE, 76, 113, 169
stirrup, platform, 180
stockade, 50
STOCKINGS (see hose)
stock portraits, 17
stock (rifle), 265
STOCK (neckcloth), 115, 138, 161, 182, 215
  high, 249
  military black, 249
STOLE (cloak), 184
stolen garments, 181
STOMACHER, 88, 177, 178, 180, 192, 193, 219
  (definition), 174
  calico, 131
stools, 103
stoop, 128
storehouses, 128
STRAPS, 150
strap, wide leather, 138
"strapless-topless," 14
STRAW HATS, 192, 225, 239
"strip a woman to her smock," 115
Strong, Rev. Nehemiah, 289, Pl. 91C
Stuart, Gilbert, 217, 277, 288, 289, Pls. 76B, 87A, C, 90B, 91A, 92B
"Stuyvesant limner," 274
"style," 27
sugar, 57
SUIT, 116
SUIT, man's silk
  three-quartered, 65
sumac berries, 104
summer houses, 128
sumptuary laws, 109, 110, 116, 119, 132, 246
Sunday services, 85
"super-image," 19
SURTOUT, 159
  (definition), 136

surveying, 252
Susquehanna River, 200
"Susquehanoke" Indians, 282, Pl. 7B
swaddled (swaddling), 237, 248
swansdown, 141
Sweden, 39, 40, 199, 276
Sweden under Gustavus Adolphus, 40
Swedish, 30
  settlers of Penn., 199
Swiss of New Bern, 18
Swiss soldiers, 14
Switzerland, 276
sword
  belt, 49, 64, 66, 135
  canes, 218
  grip, 64
  guard, 64, 66
  hanger, 64, 66, 84
  hilt, 64, 84, 171
  pommel, 64
  quillon, 64
  sheath, 64
swords, 49, 57, 64, 66, 74, 84, 105, 116, 117, 135, 171, 218, 256
  miniature, 238

T

tablecloths, 129
tables, 103
  drawing, 129
TABS, 53, 70, 86, 100, 105, 112, 119, 133, (Fig. 9A)
TACE (armor, suspended plates or lames to protect upper thighs), 65, 66
TAFFETAS, 131
tailor, 47
tailoring, 24
tails, long, 246
tails of cows, 162
Tallmadge, Col. Benjamin and son, William, 289, Pl. 94G
Tallmadge, Mrs. Benjamin, her children, Henry and Maria, 289, Pl. 94B
tankards, 57, 103
tanneries, 101
tanners, 51
tape, red, 118
TAPUL (armor, ridge down front of breast-plate), 65
tar, 51
tassel cord, 83
tassels, 115
TASSETS (armor, suspended below the tace; at this period supplanting taces), 65, 66
  lobster-tailed, 117, (see page 280)
tavern, 102

ILLUSTRATIONS IN CHRONOLOGICAL ORDER

YEAR

1660–1670	PLATES: 4A, 4B, 7B, 8A, 8B, 9, 17A, 17B, 17C, 18, 20A, 3GB, 74A.

Fig. 15 p. 75   Fig. 16c p. 78   Fig. 17 p. 79   Fig 18 p. 79
Fig. 19 p. 80   Fig. 20 p. 83   Fig. 23 p. 87   Fig 28 p. 111
Fig. 29 p. 113   Fig. 30 p. 117   Fig. 31 p. 119   Fig 32 p. 120
Fig. 33 p. 121   Fig. 36 p. 133   Fig. 37 p. 133   Fig 41 p. 140
Fig. 48A p. 160   Fig. 48B p. 160   Fig. 94 p. 249   Print p. 82
Print p. 89

1670–1680   PLATES: 10, 13, 19, 74A.

Fig. 37 p. 133   Fig. 42 p. 150   Fig. 43 p. 151   Fig 44A p. 153
Fig. 48A p. 160   Fig. 48B p. 160   Fig. 54D p. 170   Fig 55A p. 173
Print p. 206   Print p. 232   Fig. 83E p. 236

1680–1690   PLATES: 11A, 74A, 74B.

Fig. 38 p. 133   Fig. 44A p. 153   Fig. 48c p. 160   Fig. 48D p. 160
Fig. 49 p. 163   Fig. 54D p. 170   Fig. 55 p. 173   Fig. 62A p. 185
Fig. 67 p. 205

1690–1700   PLATES: 23, 46A, 74A, 74B.

Fig. 44A p. 153   Fig. 48c p. 160   Fig. 48D p. 160   Fig. 49 p. 163
Fig. 54D p. 170   Fig. 55 p. 173   Fig. 62B p. 185   Fig. 64A p. 188
Fig. 64B p. 188   Fig. 64c p. 188   Fig. 68 p. 205

1700–1710   PLATES: 45, 49A, 71B, 71C, 71D, 74B, 94F, 95F.

Fig. 44A p. 153   Fig. 48c p. 160   Fig. 48D p. 160   Fig. 50 p. 163
Fig. 54B p. 170   Fig. 54c p. 170   Fig. 54D p. 170   Fig. 55 p. 173
Fig. 61 p. 183   Fig. 62c p. 185   Fig. 64 p. 188   Fig. 65B p. 190
Cuffs p. 155

1710–1720   PLATES: 24A, 42, 45, 49A, 58B, 69D, 71B, 71C, 71D.

Fig. 44B p. 153   Fig. 45A p. 154   Fig. 48E p. 160   Fig. 50 p. 163
Fig. 54A p. 170   Fig. 54c p. 170   Fig. 54D p. 170   Fig. 56 p. 176
Fig. 61 p. 183   Fig. 62TB p. 185   Fig. 64D p. 188   Print p. 141
Print p. 272   Cuffs p. 155   Shoes p. 259

1720–1730   PLATES: 24B, 26, 30A, 45, 46B, 47, 49A, 58B, 65A, 69D, 95J.

Fig. 48E p. 160   Fig. 50 p. 163   Fig. 51 p. 166   Fig. 52 p. 166
Fig. 54B p. 170   Fig. 54c p. 170   Fig. 57 p. 178   Fig. 61 p. 183
Fig. 83F p. 236   Cuffs p. 155

1730–1740   PLATES: 25, 41, 43B, 45, 54, 69c, 69D, 71A, 94A, 95D, 95E, 9GD.

Fig. 48F p. 160   Fig. 51B p. 166   Fig. 52 p. 166   Fig. 54B p. 170
Fig. 54c p. 170   Fig. 54D p. 170   Fig. 57 p. 178   Fig. 61 p. 183
Fig. 65D p. 190   Fig. 66A p. 191   Fig. 96 p. 249   Cuffs p. 155

1740–1750	PLATES: 22A, 22B, 30B, 30C, 30D, 34A, 39, 43A, 43B, 44, 51, 53B, 58A, 59, 61A, 65B, 68B, 69A, 69B, 69C, 69D, 71A, 78, 79A, 93A, 95G.

Fig. 39A p. 133	Fig. 47A p. 158	Fig. 52 p. 166	Fig. 53 p. 167
Fig. 54B p. 170	Fig. 54C p. 170	Fig. 54D p. 170	Fig. 54E p. 170
Fig. 57 p. 178	Fig. 58 p. 178	Fig. 61 p. 183	Fig. 84 p. 242
Pr. Left p. 175	Print p. 148	Cuffs p. 155	

1750–1760	PLATES: 16A, 27, 29, 31A, 31B, 37, 44, 49B, 49C, 51, 52A, 52B, 52C, 52D, 55, 56, 63, 67, 68A, 78, 79A, 80A, 80B, 80C, 93B, 95A.

Fig. 45 p. 154	Fig. 47A p. 158	Fig. 54B p. 170	Fig. 54C p. 170
Fig. 54D p. 170	Fig. 54E p. 170	Fig. 57 p. 178	Fig. 58 p. 178
Fig. 60A p. 182	Fig. 61 p. 183	Print p. 146	Print p. 146
Print p. 146	Print p. 146	Cuffs p. 155	

1760–1770	PLATES: 31C, 35A, 35B, 36, 38, 40A, 40B, 40C, 40D, 40E, 48A, 48B, 52A, 52B, 52C, 52D, 53A, 57, 60A, 60B, 62, 70A, 70B, 72A, 72B, 75B, 78, 80B, 80C, 82, 93C, 94D, 96B.

Fig. 46 p. 156	Fig. 47 p. 158	Fig. 54E p. 170	Fig. 57 p. 178
Fig. 58 p. 178	Fig. 60 p. 182	Fig. 61 p. 183	Fig. 90 p. 245
Fig. 92F p. 251	Fig. 97 p. 255	Print p. 168	Cuffs p. 155

1770–1780	PLATES: 28, 32A, 32B, 33, 50A, 50B, 66A, 66B, 70A, 70B, 75A, 75B, 79B, 80B, 80C, 81A, 81B, 81C, 82, 87B, 93E, 94C, 95B, 95C, 96A.

Fig. 39B p. 133	Fig. 47 p. 158	Fig. 59 p. 179	Fig. 60 p. 182
Fig. 61 p. 183	Fig. 62TL p. 185	Fig. 63A p. 188	Fig. 63B p. 188
Fig. 65A p. 190	Fig. 65C p. 190	Fig. 66B p. 191	Fig. 66C p. 191
Fig. 66D p. 191	Fig. 66E p. 191	Fig. 72A p. 218	Fig. 72C p. 218
Fig. 79A p. 226	Fig. 79B p. 226	Print p. 198	Print p. 216
Shoes p. 259	Cuffs p. 155		

1780–1790	PLATES: 16B, 16C, 61B, 64A, 64B, 73B, 75C, 77, 81A, 81B, 81C, 85B, 86A, 86B, 87A, 88, 89, 93D, 94H, 96C.

Fig. 62BT p. 185	Fig. 63B p. 188	Fig. 63C p. 188	Fig. 69 p. 214
Fig. 70 p. 215	Fig. 71 p. 217	Fig. 73 p. 210	Fig. 74 p. 221
Fig. 79 p. 226	Fig. 80D p. 226	Fig. 85 p. 243	Fig. 86 p. 243
Fig. 88 p. 254	Fig. 89 p. 244	Fig. 90 p. 245	Fig. 95 p. 248
Fig. 98 p. 252			

1790–1800	PLATES: 49D, 49E, 73A, 73B, 76A, 76B, 83, 84A, 84B, 84C, 85A, 85B, 87C, 90A, 90B, 91A, 91B, 91C, 92A, 92B, 94B, 94E, 94G, 95H.

Fig. 66BT p. 191	Fig. 72B p. 218	Fig. 75 p. 222	Fig. 76 p. 223
Fig. 77 p. 223	Fig. 78 p. 224	Fig. 80 p. 226	Pr-Rgt. p. 175
Print p. 210	Shoes p. 259